CROSWELL BOWEN

M O N T E I R O
& C O M P A N Y

BARBARA MONTEIRO

MONTEIRO & COMPANY, INC.
355 Lexington Avenue ◆ 8th floor ◆ New York, NY 10017
Tel: (212) 832-8183 ◆ Fax: (212) 832-9563
bam@monteiroandco.com ◆ www.monteiroandco.com
Facebook: Monteiro & Company

CROSWELL BOWEN
A Writer's Life, a Daughter's Portrait

BETSY CONNOR BOWEN

Potomac Books

AN IMPRINT OF THE UNIVERSITY OF NEBRASKA PRESS

All rights reserved. Potomac Books is an imprint of the
University of Nebraska Press.
Manufactured in the United States of America.

Library of Congress Cataloging-in-Publication Data
Bowen, Betsy Connor, 1944– author.
Croswell Bowen: a writer's life, a daughter's portrait /
Betsy Connor Bowen.
pages   cm
Includes bibliographical references.
ISBN 978-1-61234-558-1 (hardcover: alk. paper) 1. Bowen,
Croswell, 1905–1971. 2. Journalists—United States—
Biography. I. Title.
PN4874.B6298B69 2014
070.92—dc23
[B]
2014010151

Set in Lyon Text by Renni Johnson.

For Bob

Contents

Illustrations

Prologue

He's a young boy of twelve, and he stands at attention in front of an American flag. His eyes are serious, concerned, intent; his brow is furrowed, but the shock of brown hair is boyish, and the cheeks are still soft, his lips full. He has removed his cap and holds it smartly, waist-high; he lifts his right hand in salute. It's a proper salute. He has been taught well.

He salutes to show respect for the ideals he believes in: to honor God and country; to stand ready to be of service to others; to be brave, courteous, and kind. From a young age, he has been taught that there is a difference between right and wrong, trained to examine his life, to obey the Ten Commandments, to confess his sins and repent. He believes that conscience is the law of God written in the mind of man and that there is a life beyond death, for which his time on earth is but preparation.

The year then was 1917, when Woodrow Wilson had asked for a declaration of war to go to the aid of England and France, to make the world safe for democracy. But the young boy's dreams had been filled with men going over the tops of trenches and being tangled in barbed wire. In one that

Croswell Bowen, c. 1917.

often recurred, he has been assigned with ten other soldiers to shoot a spy or a traitor. In the dream he shoots at something near the man he is supposed to shoot at, but he never knows if his bullet hit him and he is worried about this as he wakes up.

This young boy became a writer, and was my father, Croswell Bowen. He saw a fairly decent success. He wrote first for newspapers and then for magazines, both as a freelancer and a staffer, among them the innovative New York newspaper *PM* in the late 1940s and *The New Yorker* of editor William Shawn in the 1950s. He was the author of several books, one a biography of the American playwright Eugene O'Neill.

As a person, he was a mass of contradictions I had no time to figure out, and a sometimes difficult man. When I was a child, he was often absent, but when he was home, I blossomed in his love. As a young adult, I distanced myself from him. Eventually, forgiving him for whatever faults he had was easy. Living my own life took over.

Then, several years ago, responding to the questions of a nephew, I edited a World War II memoir that had lain unpublished in a barn where he'd left it. What I saw there opened my eyes. I saw that war had impassioned my father as a writer. I began to see a pattern in the subjects he chose to write about that revealed what he was clearly striving for: journalism that served democracy. He sought out the help of men who could articulate the role of journalists in a democracy. Judge Billings Learned Hand had written, "The business of the press . . . is the promotion of truth regarding public matters by furnishing the basis for an understanding of them," and I recalled my father quoting that often. He had interviewed Supreme Court Justice Felix Frankfurter, and they corresponded. The Justice had advised that "fertile endeavor in a society means an unremitting process toward concentration on essentials by which the great body of people of good will can be united." My father pasted Frankfurter's words on his typewriter: "Mastery of a subject, sincerity, stout-hearted humanity: the public always responds to these qualities. If it were not true, there would be no basis for the democratic view."

Slowly, with increasing conviction, I came to think of my father as one among a certain breed of reporters, some of them men with bigger names like Walter Cronkite and Edward

R. Murrow and I. F. Stone, others with names history would easily forget. These were men who made up their own minds about what was right and what was wrong, who saw it as their calling to speak truth to power, who held to the highest ideals of reporting because they were essential to a democracy. I asked myself whether it had been the intense heat of World War II that had forged these ideals, for clearly these men saw democracy under threat in the world. Words were their weapons against tyranny.

Perhaps it was some inner urge toward wholeness that propelled me, now that I had lived most of my life, to want to relive his. I wanted to experience the great events of the twentieth century as he had, not knowing, as we do now, what would happen next. If I could see him as simply one human being poised on the moving edge of history, I might untangle the contradictions in his nature and know him more clearly, face-to-face.

But the questions I could have asked him in those rooms where he sat alone and typed, I could not ask now. He was gone. Most of the people who had known him were gone, too. What remained were only my memories, pages upon more pages of words and photographs. There were stashes of over a century's worth of family papers, more than I had suspected even existed. I traveled to find as much as I could, and read and reread what I found. In a forty-year career, he had written scores upon scores of newspaper and magazine articles, some of them available only in libraries, some newly online. He had written four books. There was the World War II memoir, and an autobiographical novel, unfinished and in fragments, that I'd found in his desk after he died. There were his correspondences, and what others had written about him.

As I pieced all this together, a new question emerged. How could the pampered eldest son and appointed heir of a Toledo, Ohio, real estate and insurance entrepreneur have become the man he had become? In the jumbled and disarrayed remains of his writer's life I glimpsed much at play: a certain kind of family, the big events of history, fortune good and bad. Toward the end of my work, as I weighed those forces, I asked myself if the deepest one, the one that underlay everything else, had not come from within. I came to see in the proud salute of that young boy the germ of an ideal self he would create, a truth-telling man of words, a man whose words could make the world a better place.

Was this ideal self the overarching theme of my father's life that would make the puzzle pieces fit together? Late in the work, I noticed something I had previously ignored, right there on a page in his novel, a character by the name of Stanley Lincoln. Here was my father's ideal self, the man he most admired, walking and talking, living in a hotel on Twenty-third Street and Seventh Avenue in New York City. Lincoln had worked with the fabled investigative reporters of the Progressive Era and was a man of complete integrity, absolutely fearless, who went from city to city exposing corruption in high places and social injustice wherever he found it.

But where in my father had this imagined ideal self come from? From another episode in the same autobiographical novel, I could tell that Stanley Lincoln had been born in him when, as a young man, he had felt the sting of exclusion from a social hierarchy he had sought to join. His anger at that, transformed over the years by empathy for the pain of others, had grown into an ideal self that endeavored to set things right. Stanley Lincoln had stood tallest in him in the years of his best political reporting, and remained with him in his last days as he turned inward to write about his own life.

My father's ideal journalist self did not help him become an outstanding family man. He had success as a writer, but at home things did not always go well. But now as I looked over what I had written, I could see that war had changed him in ways none of us back then understood. It may have fueled his writing, but it weakened his ability to withstand the stresses of the very thing he had wanted so much on his return—life as a husband and father. Flawed as he was, I always knew he loved us deeply, but in the end, our family scattered, each to our separate ways.

Yet with all this, there had emerged something I had not seen before: a certain risk-taking kind of moral integrity. There was always the next story, the next chance to find and tell the truth. And always there was the absolute certainty that finding the right stories and telling them with the right words could create a better world. He was a crusader, a tilter at windmills perhaps, but a man who never gave up—not on himself, on the people he loved, or on the power of words to make things better.

Just as my father did, today's reporters scramble against difficult odds to earn a living. The old institutions of news-gathering are crumbling; perhaps new ones are emerging. Change brings uncertainty. But men and women who do the hard work of earning our trust as witness-bearers help lead us through difficult times, and we must value them. We will always need them.

ONE

Skull and Bones, Paris, and the Crash of 1929

Tap Day in the spring of 1927, Cros's junior year at Yale, the elite college he had been sent east to attend, was the day when Skull and Bones, formed in 1892, chose the men who would replace its outgoing members. I see him alone in his rooms on the Timothy Dwight quadrangle, waiting but not seeming to wait, a book in his hands but not really reading. Things he had hoped for all his life might be fulfilled in one moment.

He had often walked past the Skull and Bones hall on High Street in New Haven. The grim, tomblike sandstone structure with padlocked iron doors had no windows. Everything about Bones was secret. That made it all the more powerful. There were rumors about strange rituals inside, but nothing was known for sure. It was said that if a conversation about the Society began, any Bonesman present would leave the room. Everyone knew Bonesmen had ability and character. Scroll and Keys men, the second best, had politeness and geniality. There were other societies, and there were the fraternities, but Bones was the top.

Surely he would be tapped. To make Bones, he had put himself where a man could let his abilities shine, where the sifting happened. Freshman year, he went out for the student paper, *The Record*, and played scrub football. In his sophomore year, he shone in a play put on by Playcrafters, the dramatic society. True, he could be rowdy. He was arrested for disturbing the peace outside the local Hyperion Theater, but the school did not view such things with alarm. The New Haven police liked to ride herd on Yale men, and still they went on to excel. In May, he took the lead in *Biddie Sweeps Out*, another Playcrafters performance.

Hadn't he hit it off with one Bonesman when he'd sung next to him in Glee Club, palled around with another in the Literary Society? He and another had sat next to each other on the milk train, coming back to New Haven after a weekend in New York. And then, when Father had come east, he'd invited several Bonesmen up to his rooms and entertained them lavishly, ordering ice and breaking out a hip flask for drinks all around. The Bonesmen had been charmed, although the college had not.

The Bonesman who tapped him would be one of the seniors, perhaps accompanied by an older member who'd stolen back into New Haven to lend his presence to the taps. The tap would come at eight o'clock. There would be a knock on the door. He would not rush to open it. But once he reached it, he would open it casually, as if he had something else on his mind.

Carrying a human skull, the Bonesman would ask, "Are we alone?"

"Yes." Cros would usher him into his rooms.

The man who came to his door would be of impeccable social standing, so sure in his ways, so confident in himself that just being around him made one feel better. His suits would look like they had been made only for him, even if they had come off the rack at Brooks Brothers. Their eyes would meet. On the Bonesman's face would be a smile of recognition, of acceptance, of approval. Cros's smile would be gracious and unsurprised, his gaze manly, eye-to-eye. He knew the man would have to hurry back to Bones to report his acceptance, so he would not offer him a chair. They would savor the moment.

"I offer you an election to the so-called Skull and Bones," the man would say. With those few words, Cros would become one of them. "Do you accept?"

"Yes."

And with that, his future would change. Bonesmen met in secret every summer, where they got introduced to each other, were instructed in each other's doings. They came to trust each other, rely on each other in their business and professional lives. If a Bonesman was in need, the others came to his aid. They attended each other's funerals. Being a Bonesman was for life.

For Cros, eight o'clock came and went. There was no tap. The one thing in the whole wide world he'd wanted, the one thing that would have made his happiness perfect, had not come his way. Waves of remorse washed over him. Should he have declared himself a "neutral," a man who would not join any of the societies, even if they asked him? Now that he would never be a Bonesman, he was the worst of all possible beings, one who had hoped to be tapped but was passed over. They called it being a "stone man." Anger welled up in his chest and closed his throat. He was the victim of a deep injustice. He could barely put words to his rage.

But this was final. It was the end. It had all been in vain. He had had it. He was out.

In the days that followed, a memory repeatedly came back to him of something that had happened one morning several months earlier on a very cold winter day, a memory that seemed to have something to tell him about what Bones was all about. About how it felt to be looked down upon for being the person you were.

On that day, he had heard the seven o'clock bells, turned over, and gone back to sleep. The porter would wake him in time to dress and take breakfast before Chapel. But the porter did not wake him. When he had finally come into his bedroom, Cros was angry. He scolded him for making him late.

"But, oh it's terrible, Mr. Bowen," the porter wailed. His face grew almost white; his expression was blind terror. "Mr. Stein done hung himself . . . when I went into his rooms to wake him this morning . . . there he was hanging in the doorway leading to his bedroom. He had an electric cord wrapped around his neck, his eyes staring at me. I ran and told the campus police. It's been awful. That's why I was late. I gotta go now and wake the others."

Self-loathing flooded Cros. He had cursed the poor porter before the man had had a chance to tell about his wretched experience. And Raoul Stein had been his friend. He was a sad figure, like a lost child. His face had an unmistakably Semitic look: deep, pleading eyes with heavy dark features. "My father went to Yale," Raoul had told him, "and was a Deke." Deke was the best junior fraternity, a path to Bones. "He was the first and only Jew ever taken into Deke," Raoul would often say. He had become a powerful Wall Street banker.

Before one of the big football games, Raoul had asked Cros to come up for a drink to meet his father. He looked like he had come out of old-world Vienna. He smoked a Turkish cigarette in a holder, and his clothes were beyond style and taste. There was an air of such patrician elegance about him that Cros felt inferior, like a farm boy.

He could see that Raoul did, too. The father seemed gracious, but he made no effort to put the two of them at ease. He was like an actor playing a role. Cros even sensed he was mildly contemptuous of him for being a friend of his son, that anyone who would be friends with his son must be a loser. Did this man think neither of them was going to make it at

Yale, that he was better than they were because he had made it despite the handicap of being a Jew?

But had Raoul Stein's father been right? That making it to the top should not be undertaken lightly? Knowing how vicious the game could really be, was he unsurprised to find his own son dead, hanging by a lamp cord?

But it was more than that. Cros felt he had been partly responsible for Raoul's suicide. The afternoon before, he had ordered a rented piano for his rooms and told Raoul he could practice whenever he liked, so long as his roommate was away. When he came in that evening, the roommate said, "That Stein guy was in here playing on your piano. I asked him what was going on. I didn't like the idea." From the scorn on his face he knew the encounter had been painful for Raoul. He had probably felt accepted and valued at one moment, and at the next, not.

Now that Bones had passed him over, huge chasms of self-loathing were opening up, the same huge chasms that had opened up for Raoul, and they could swallow you. Had he been too informal, that morning on the milk train with the Bones man? Should he have sat a few seats away from him rather than beside him? The memory of a slight pulling away when he lowered himself down came back, but he'd ignored it back then. And in Glee Club—did the Bonesmen think his antics there were amusing, or had they just pretended to? Did he talk too much? Did he try too hard? Was he a man who barged his way in, was too familiar, used things he wasn't welcome to? Someone who would never make it?

That evening Cros would have eaten alone at a restaurant in town and gotten back to his rooms after dark, his gait slow and his shoulders slumping. He could not fall asleep. The next day he stayed in bed late, didn't make it to Chapel on time, cut classes again, and instead wandered off campus and pondered the injustice that had befallen him. And the next day and the ones after that, too. His marks, just safely above the edge, dropped. Another demerit would mean he could not graduate.

The list of those who had made Bones began circulating. All white Anglo-Saxon Protestants from the East. How could he have thought he could break in? They were a closed circle and they intended to keep it that way.

That weekend he went into New York City, raised Cain, and did not come back on time for Monday Chapel. To hell with them all. He was leaving. He was out.

The full name of this young man was Badger Croswell Bowen. His family called him Cros. When she was annoyed with him, his mother called him Croswell. His classmates called him Dizzy or Diz. To them, he was a skittish kid out of the Buckeye state, tall and well-built, always rushing around like he was about to jump out of his skin, always wanting to get to know you better. He'd go out for track and then drop it, fall in love with a girl who barely knew him, cut class on a lark.

He was born in 1905, a firstborn son. His father was Badger Croswell Bowen, from Southern gentlefolk of Scots-Irish descent, who had brought his new bride, Anna Louise Connor, the beautiful, gently educated granddaughter of an Irish political émigré family, from Waxahachie, Texas, to the city of Toledo, Ohio. Their first home was a small rented house. Three years later, after the birth of a second son, William Dougherty Bowen, or Billy, the family moved to a larger, newly built house. Louise, who had by then dropped her girlhood name "Anna Lou," raised the two boys with the help of one housekeeper.

Toledo was a fast-growing city, but there were open fields where the boys played cowboys and Indians. On the western end of Lake Erie was a beach where they swam. For church and school, Louise dressed her sons in stiff-collared shirts, knickers, and knee socks until they reached a certain age; then in suits and ties.

Bowen was a dapper man with a goatee and a direct style, always impeccably if flamboyantly dressed, but enterprising and reliable. Men trusted him. Louise mingled easily with the wives of Bowen's business associates and at dinner with the family, relayed the gossip she had overheard at ladies' lunches. In Toledo, such a couple could make its way, and Bowen and Louise certainly did. The elite of the city accepted them as one of their own.

The Bowens had arrived in Toledo just as a spiral of prosperity was beginning, built on cars. At the 1904 St. Louis World's Fair, the Toledo windshield manufacturer Libby and Co. exhibited the largest piece of cut glass ever made, a punch bowl that could have filled a small room. By 1914, the assembly line process had become so streamlined it took only 1.5 instead of 12.5 hours to build a Model T Ford. In 1918, Toledo's Willys-Overland was the second largest automobile company in existence. Toledo's spark plugs and transmissions and windshields fed Ford's assembly lines, and by 1929 a new car was being produced every three minutes. Libby and Co. became Libby-Owens-Ford; Owens became Owens-Illinois. Toledo got its own radio station. The wages of industrial workers flowed into the banks as deposits. The banks lent the dollars out to businesses to keep them growing and to individuals to buy what businesses sold.

Bowen and his partner, William C. Welles, founded Welles-Bowen, a firm that sold insurance and developed real estate. Mornings, Bowen's step quickened as he left early for the office. At dinner, he spoke with glowing authority of the firm's more and more certain command of capital. He was participating in the birth of an alliance between government and private enterprise that made Toledo one of the crowning achievements of the Progressive movement. Toledoans like him reformed the patronage system that had corrupted local politics, brought in fairer elections, hired a city manager, and approved a development plan. Business leaders funded a university, an art museum, parks, city transportation, a zoo, and a minor league baseball team with its own stadium. The housing market boomed.

Toledo businessmen were self-assured and boisterous. They had fought and defeated the politicians who controlled Toledo's government through graft and favoritism. They had created a new establishment, a more civic-minded and better one, all on their own, and they were proud of it. With them, things were what they were, and you could say it out loud. Eastern politeness and reserve got you nowhere. They were builders and bankers and manufacturers, and they knew how to get things done. Toledo's growth proved it.

Bowen had a hand in Toledo's prosperity. Welles-Bowen's residential housing developments—Westmoreland, Parkside, Old Orchard, De Veaux, and Hampton Park—won him praise for his idealism, vision, and love of artistry. He helped found the Rotary Club, was active in the Chamber of Commerce and Community Chest, and was a leader in the city and county planning commissions. He was named a director of the Security Home Trust Company and sat on the boards of several other banks. He belonged to two country clubs.

In 1922, the family moved to 2048 Richmond Road in Westmoreland, one of the neighborhoods of fine mansions Bowen had designed. The receptions grew grander and grander. Bowen had been a prominent Progressive Party member and a Theodore Roosevelt supporter, so when Franklin Delano Roosevelt visited Toledo in 1927, he stayed with the Bowens in Westmoreland. Bowen installed an elevator to accommodate his by then wheelchair-bound guest.

That the Bowen family would "take its place" in Toledo, it fell to Louise to make happen. She converted her husband to Catholicism and together the Bowens attended their local parish church. She sent the two boys to good primary schools, and later to dancing school so they would be invited to the right parties where they would meet the right girls. She and Billy shared a vision, real though rarely discussed, that each of their sons would someday marry a Toledo girl and join their father at Welles-Bowen. The staff at the Toledo Club would always be willing to serve. The banks would always lend money. The boys would lead Welles-Bowen into the future, turn more and more acres of raw Toledo prairie into streets and houses. Toledo would be their whole world, and it would be good.

Still, to prepare their boys for the future, the Bowens looked to the East. Louise dutifully and carefully took them to be interviewed by the best New England prep schools, to the Catholic Newman School, and then Choate for Cros and Phillips Exeter for Billy, so that their admission to the best colleges would be assured—if they kept up their grades. They did. "I must keep up my grades so I can get into Yale," Cros wrote in his diary.

When Cros first arrived at Choate, the clothes his mother had shopped for in the Toledo department stores would have been not quite like the other boys' clothes. He would ask her to buy his clothes in the East, and she would. But then he had begun to feel even deeper differences—not just dress, but ethnicity and religion. It was hard not to, in the close quarters of a boarding school. He was a Catholic boy. Sunday Chapel was Episcopalian. Catholic boys went into town for Mass on Sunday while the Episcopal boys stayed on campus. Catholic boys gave their confessions. They fasted. A Catholic boy's confession was specific and anguished. "I wrote on my hand for the algebra exam." "I lied to the master about why I was late." He spoke the truth as he knew it. Heaven and Hell were real places. But even the most horrible sin could be forgiven if it was confessed and you promised not to do the same thing again, or at least tried very hard not to.

The Episcopal boys' confessions named only "various sins which we from time to time may have committed against Thee in thought, word, and deed." Was all that anguish for nothing? But still, Cros always felt better after confession. It was a puzzle.

Chapel was daily. To all the boys, Protestant and Catholic alike, most of them the sons of men who had made or inherited great fortunes, Choate's headmaster George St. John taught a theology flavored with the social gospel. For those who had great wealth, "giving back" to society was the right thing to do. Noblesse oblige. "Wealth brings responsibility," he would say, and his voice would grow stern. They were to start right now, right here. "Ask not what Choate can do for you," he would intone. "Ask what you can do for Choate." (Cros would, in later years, be heartened that a young John Fitzgerald Kennedy had heard them as well.)

But still, the WASP boys accused the Irish Catholic boys of hanging together.

The Irish Catholic boys said the WASP boys hung together.

The fights on the field were sometimes very nasty. St. John seemed to ignore it.

It was a knot too tangled to unravel.

Cros did well on the Yale admissions exams, impressed the interviewer as a well brought-up young man. He was admitted.

Nonetheless, the differences remained. The social hierarchy was quite clear. The rules were simple. Seemingly effortless adherence to a highly developed code of gentlemanly conduct was the first of the three elements required to reach the top. Choate and Yale taught it: certain manners of speech and tones of voice; customs, skills, tastes, and implicit attitudes toward self and others that would make him fit in, be one of them. Cros tried hard to master it. He felt he had succeeded.

The second was an independent income. Most of Eastern money was old money, and most of the old money was

WASP money. An income was necessary to be a gentleman, but working for it was, well, somehow ungentlemanly. He would not have to work for a living. His father had assured him of that.

The third element of a Bonesman was a long Yankee pedigree. Cros had ignored that. It had not been necessary for success in Toledo. Why should Bones not bend its rules for him?

He had been so very eager to try.

Back in Toledo, when the news of their son's break in the ascendancy toward taking his place reached Bowen and Louise, they struggled to grasp the meaning of their son's downfall. Louise was sick at heart, but rallied. When Cros came back, she let go of some of her social life and returned to mother duty again, would slip into his room at a mid-morning hour to raise her son's shades and stay for a quiet tête-à-tête. She simply surrounded him with love. It was all she knew how to do. Cros relaxed in her care. Soon, he glowed. He was her eldest son, her young Irish prince.

Bowen Sr. was determined that the family would prevail. He went to his office as he always had, handled his business affairs with equanimity, bolstered his wife with adoration. He did not discuss the situation with Cros, but he and Louise whispered together pillow to pillow.

A solution emerged. Bowen spoke with Yale. Something could be arranged. Over lunch at the Toledo Club, he told Cros what he had learned. Yale students who did not fully complete their junior year could attend graduation and reunions with their class. However, it would be a very good idea if he spent a successful year at an equivalent university.

Cros broke their gaze, tilted his head to one side. He did not want to go through again what he had been through this past year. He simply refused to encounter another entrenched hierarchy he could not penetrate.

"The Sorbonne is a possibility."

Cros leaned in. Paris! Where Hemingway and Gertrude Stein and Scott Fitzgerald had gone, discovering life on their own terms, making all things new again.

Paris!

As Bowen and his fine upstanding son left the club, their steps were in tandem. As different as their reasons were, they both believed that the Sorbonne was the answer. And such a consensus was the mark of a successful negotiation.

On October 15, 1928, an ambivalent, inwardly rebellious but outwardly obedient Cros and his mother departed from New York and headed for Paris via Le Havre on the French Line's *Rochambeau*, a smaller ship than the Cunard's new *Mauretania* and *Lusitania* but, with quadruple screws and a cruising speed of 15 knots, just as fast. In Paris, they stayed at a fashionable hotel, the Foyot. Louise loved the plentiful heat, the linen sheets, and the fat down comforters. Cros registered at the Sorbonne and looked up people he knew who were in Paris. Louise registered at the Alliance Française for French lessons. She joined the American Women's Club, writing to tell her husband that she hoped the social events there would keep their son from "the other life," meaning the "cafés, etc."

Cros did not spend much time at the Sorbonne. He cut his classes, though he passed his exams. He loafed.

Paris was everything Toledo was not. It was everything Yale was not. It was heaven for anyone who did not fit in and did not really want to. It was a place where the expression of all ideas, the adoption of all behaviors, of all values, was possible. Nobody told anybody what to think, how to act, or what to believe. One could be oneself there; one could be happy. Cros felt, at least for a while, that he belonged there.

After Christmas, Cros went to St. Moritz for the skiing and the society. Louise went to Rome, hoping for an audience with the Pope, for which she'd had a Parisian couturier make her a black dress (but the audience could not be arranged). Cros returned in January for classes at the Sorbonne while Louise traveled to Florence and shopped for the Toledo mansion.

Back in Paris, Cros finished at the Sorbonne. Then he and Louise returned to the United States.

The *Rochambeau* passed the Coast Guard lightship stationed at the head of Ambrose Channel that led into New York Harbor. At the pier, they disembarked and went to stand by their luggage in the Customs Hall. Louise would have first spotted Bowen in the crowd outside the Hall. Cros hired a porter to take their luggage to his father, and then the three were together. Louise and her husband embraced. Cros felt the warmth of his father's smile of innocent delight, the smile that had always showered all the love in the world on him.

Yes, he would take his place, just as they wanted him to. Love and duty had softened the sting of having been passed over by Bones. He would return to Yale and be with his class for graduation in the spring, and then he would marry a Toledo girl, the right kind of girl, the Stranahan girl, perhaps. She was beautiful, and a lot of fun, and her father, R. A. Stranahan, was the founder of Champion Sparkplugs and a good friend of Father's. They would honeymoon abroad. Then they would both come back to Toledo. He would join Welles-Bowen and make a career in real estate and finance.

He was home. He was safe.

There is an oil portrait of Cros by a Parisian artist done in that Sorbonne year, when he was a young man of twenty-three. He is handsome, well-dressed, and well-groomed. He wears a white shirt, a vest and a suit jacket, and a neatly tied tie. The tip of a folded handkerchief peeps up from his breast pocket. His lips are tender and full like a child's. His eyes are soft, but his head is turned away from the viewer and his eyes look past him, into the distance.

I look into them and wonder why. Perhaps he has seen something in the world that troubles him, something that has kept him from a life he still wanted, something he does not know how to set right?

June 1929. Back in New Haven, Cros's classmates baited him with jokes about lessons in love taught by beautiful French women. "Ooh la la!" I see them saying, throwing an arm across his shoulders. The ceremonies began. The band played "Gaudeamus Igitur." Bowen and Louise were in the crowd. Billy was there too—he would be a sophomore next year. Whereas Cros was boisterous, self-confident, unpredictable, and outgoing, Billy was quieter, more reliable, fastidious, and aloof. He looked to his older brother to see what his own future might hold, but he was not sure he wanted it to be like Cros's.

As Cros watched his classmates receive their diplomas, he only knew that his path at Yale had not been what he'd wanted. One day he would come back to New Haven and prove to them that he was as good as any Bonesman. He did not know how he would do it, but he would.

That summer, a "grand tour" of Europe was Cros's present from the family. He wanted to see Paris again; he was pleased. He steamed to Southampton and traveled to London. He would have visited his Irish relatives in Dublin, listened to tellers of tales beside peat fires in whitewashed Irish cottages, seen castles and cathedrals and museums.

But best of all, after that, he returned to Paris for several months, with plans to travel with Charlie Yost, a fellow American from upstate New York he had hit it off with. He would be back home in Toledo soon enough to take his place, but now he was content just to be soaking up the city.

I see Cros dropping himself down at an outdoor table at his favorite café, Les Deux Magots, a late morning sun spilling over the low roofs. There is excitement in the air. In the cafés of Montparnasse, there are Americans everywhere. Artists, composers, poets, and writers, all together, all inspired by their work. Tonight he might linger into the early hours at the Moulin Rouge, revel in the intoxicating mix of workers, intellectuals, and artists, and delight at the yelps of the cancan dancers lifting their skirts higher as their battements and *grands écarts* revealed more and more.

But no! He had to get back to the hotel and pack his bags. Tomorrow he and Charlie were leaving for Geneva, and then a three-week trip to Russia.

The waiter brought his breakfast, set it down next to an unopened *Paris Herald*. Cros put down a literary magazine he'd found in a bookstore, sipped his coffee, spread jam on the croissant, cut himself a piece of cheese, picked up the *Herald*, read the headline. He tensed, gripped the pages. He set down his coffee, bent closer.

"Brokers Believe Worst Is Over and Recommend Buying of Real Bargains," the headline read. The Dow Jones average had dropped by 25 percent from where it had been when he last saw it. The checks he was writing on his bank account got cashed because of the checks his father wrote to him on his stock account. That stock account was sending him to Europe. If that ended, everything would end.

He read further. He relaxed. Brokers were saying high-grade investment issues could be bought now without fear of a drastic decline. The worst was over. He had seen this before. The trend would be up. He would mention it in his letter to Father. He returned to sipping his coffee.

Although they did not see it, Cros, the Bowen family, all of the business elite of Toledo, and the entire Yale Class of 1929 were at the top of society at a time in America when the top was fast rocketing away from the bottom. It was easy to ignore. But the signs were there that they would emerge into a broken world. To support the First World War effort, government spending had grown far beyond tax collections. The huge investments made in manufacturing had gone toward mechanization. Mechanization gave rise to an explosion of individual worker productivity. Productivity gains created an excess of labor supply, and the power of organized labor declined. Mergers conglomerated small independent companies into larger ones that could extract greater efficiencies and economies of scale by incorporating the new technologies. The economic benefits of all this flowed toward the small fraction of the population at the top of the ladder. By the end of the decade, two hundred corporations controlled half of American industry. The bottom 80 percent of all income-earners had been removed from the tax rolls completely, though taxes on the rich also fell throughout the decade. In 1925, set loose by an expansion of credit, the stock market had begun a rise that was not supported by underlying growth in the economy.

But in Cros's world, nobody talked about that. They would not have mentioned it even if they had been concerned about it, which most of them were not.

Cros and Charlie Yost set off for Geneva and then Russia. Leningrad was dreary. The palaces and domes shone in the sunlight, wrote Charlie, in whose keen observations Cros might have sensed the career diplomat he would later become, but up close they had not been painted in years, were shabby, broken-windowed, and desolate. Communism was not just an economic system, Cros would later say; it was spreading across the liberal arts and the sciences and seeping into social life. Everybody was in a union, even musicians. Charlie and he went to a concert that never seemed to start, so Cros bounded up onto the stage and played the piano to great applause. At last, the tardy musician appeared.

Then the two took a train across a plain of fall fields, wrote Charlie, birch and poplar in gold and russet, traveling toward the Caucasus. Their compartment attracted a hodgepodge of visitors laden with hampers of food and drink that led to much talk in French, German, and Russian. At the train stations, they filled the tea kettles with water and bought freshly cooked chickens, ducks, eggs, and bread; milk, fruit, and nuts. They crossed the Caucasus, visited the bazaars of Tbilisi, and cruised the Black Sea to Odessa, where they saw a great refrigerating plant and room after room of pork, beef, mutton, fruit, and eggs for export to Germany and England while, a Soviet doctor told them, the people in town were severely underfed.

In Kiev they visited a church built in the eighteenth century, which, Charlie wrote, was "an appalling and overwhelming mass of gold and silver ornateness . . . preserved by the government as an object-lesson in the wanton extravagance of the old regime." They followed an ill-smelling monk with foot-long greasy hair and shifty eyes through the long, dark, catacomb-like corridors where, in niche after niche, lay the mummies of monks or saints covered with red cloth on which a gold or silver cross was stitched. Only the black bony hands were visible.

At last, they boarded a train to the Polish border. "I feel a sense of relief as if I have just escaped," wrote Charlie. Cros agreed.

They were back in Paris by November. By then the market had slid another 15 percent.

The crossing back was uneventful, but back in Toledo, Father seemed gloomy. The twinkle was gone from his eye. Mother stayed in her sitting room all day. At the Christmas parties, though, things seemed as they always had been. Swathed in white, the debutantes blushed and smiled nervously. The men were gallant in their white ties and tails. The candles flickered. The talk was gay, the dancing late, and the drinking heavy. But there were no Christmas parties in the homes of laid-off workers who had bought houses and were having a hard time paying for them. Henry Ford's assembly line jobs were shrinking, as was demand for the spark plugs and car windshields Toledo industry made.

But the stock market was recovering just a bit. There were times, late at night, spent with friends he had known since childhood, when the music still played and the dancing was slow, when it was possible to believe life would go on as it always had.

TWO

Several Reversals of Fortune, All in a Row

One summer Cros had worked in the Toledo office of a large brokerage business based in New York. Over champagne at a wedding, the man had offered him a job back east when he graduated. He wanted to get back to New York. It would be good training for Welles-Bowen. He decided to take the man up on it. They met at the Yale Club for lunch.

The other Toledoan was a Hoover, "The Crash is over, things are about to get better," man. "I've just finished reading Secretary Mellon's report on the year," I see him saying. "He's projecting profits will return to normal." He spread his napkin over his lap. "The Fed will stand by as the market works itself out. Liquidate labor, liquidate real estate— values will be adjusted, and enterprising people will pick up the wreckage from less competent people."

Cros agreed. The market will take care of it. Back in Toledo, he'd heard the Stranahan girl's father saying that.

But he wasn't sure he believed what else Stranahan was saying, that the enterprising would pick the wreckage up from less competent people. His father was not an incompetent person, and Mellon did not seem to understand the vastness of the human tragedy that was unfolding. Cros took a sip of water.

"People will learn to content themselves with slower growth." The man opened the menu.

"Yes. They will." Cros nodded.

"We're taking a hard look now at our staff. I've had to cut mine by fifty percent."

"Oh?" Cros put down his water glass, leaned forward.

"Protecting capital. It's prudent. Reducing the salaries of the remaining employees." The man leaned away, knitted his brow, looked aside.

"You're not hiring?" Cros looked for the man's eyes, shifted in his chair.

The man leaned forward, looked at Cros. "For your own sake, now is not the time to find a job on Wall Street."

"I understand."

They ordered lunch, finished quickly, and parted on a street corner. Cros headed uptown. He felt shaky, so he walked faster, then saw a streetcar and broke into a gallop. Out of breath but now smiling broadly, he bounded onto it. Reaching into his pocket for the fare, he felt a wave of relief. At last he could tell himself the plain truth—he had never wanted to be a Wall Street man anyhow.

Cros asked about job openings at the Yale Club's placement office. William Randolph Hearst's International News Service was hiring. Their reporters tracked down the stories that were sent over the wires to the teletype machines of the evening and morning dailies. He called for an interview. He wanted that job. The INS was a big steam engine of life idling at the platform. It might pull away at any minute, but in the dining car on a tablecloth was a place card with his name on it. It just had to be.

The INS's New York offices were in the World Building in Lower Manhattan's Park Row, a cluster of nineteenth-century skyscrapers near the old New York City Hall. The *Times* and the *Tribune* both had buildings there, but the World was the tallest because it had been the first one to have an elevator. Cros headed there. A rush came into his step. He walked around the World Building twice, taking everything in. His face took on a broad smile. This was going to be his new home. He could tell.

He rode the elevator up to the INS floor, rushed out, found the newsroom. I see him spotting the senior editor at the back, maybe a round-faced cigar-puffing type with a green eye shade and suspenders.

The man's phone rang. He answered it.

Between gaps in the conversation, the man glared up at him. "So you're a Yale man. Writing the great American novel?"

"Not at all, sir." He let himself smile, just a bit.

"What about the Pulitzer Prize? You won't get one here. No Pulitzers around here for you."

"Fine, sir. Anything you send me on, I'll go."

"Ever write for a paper before?" The man dropped the receiver back on its hook, took a puff on his cigar.

"*Toledo Blade.*" He'd had a job there one summer, through a friend of Father's.

The man looked up, assessed him again. "Figured you were a literary type. Maybe not. If the *Blade* says you've got the stuff, you're hired."

Cros called back to the *Blade*, said he was in New York looking for a job with the INS. "They'll take me if you recommend me."

"Good luck, Bowen. Newspapers are a young man's game. Try not to get ink in your veins. You'll never get out of this business if you do."

He got word that he was hired. When he called home, Father congratulated him and Mother cried.

His first day on the job, he was lost.

The INS newsroom was a cacophony of voices. Toledo seemed like a ladies' tea by comparison. Swaggering photographers, eager cubs, young men on their way up, old men on their way down. All on meager salaries. But as the days went by, it began to feel like home. Each newsman had a large solid wooden desk, and they were all arranged in rows, with the managing editor's desk at the back of the room. On every desk was a telephone, its bell-shaped mouthpiece mounted on a candlestick-like stand with a rotary dial at the bottom, earpiece hanging on a hook. And a tall black upright Underwood. The rewrite men picked up the phones and hunched over the typewriters, banging on the keys with two fingers, pounding out the stories the reporters phoned in. They demanded more details, checked with their other sources, hashed things out with each other and the editors.

"Copy!" the reporters all shouted as they handed their stuff to the managing editor at the back of the room. The newsroom was frenetic. The pressmen were compiling the paper right up to deadline, and there was no time for a reporter who hadn't finished his story to carry his own copy to the press room. A copyboy would pick it up and run it there for him. Soon Cros was shouting "Copy!" out with the rest of them. This was real training for a reporter. Editors would send him back to get more information, just to teach him to get it in the first place. "If your mother tells you she loves you, check it out," they'd say. Lore held that a reporter phoning in with details on the slaying of an infant had been asked, "What color were the dead baby's eyes?"

Pretty soon Cros had a byline. He was "Croswell Bowen, INS Staff Correspondent." He didn't have time for the elevator, so he'd clatter down the stairs with pencil and notebook in hand as if the World Building were on fire. He wore a fedora straight out of a film noir gangster movie, brim turned down in the front and press card stuck in the band. "I'm Bowen of the INS!" he'd shout, then wade in to get the story.

A few weeks on the job, and Cros was thriving. Back in Toledo, the *Blade* might follow a lost puppy for days on the front page. Highway accidents were big news. Plane crashes were better. But in New York there were gang shootings, fires, thefts, murders, one right after the other. City government was shot through with corruption. Police violence was uncontrolled. He was learning about that from the "outside men," the beat reporters who came back to their desks and hammered out their stories, and from the savvy regulars who wrote the columns. His assignments were filler pieces for small-town newspapers: "Americans Want Pretty Bathing Tubs," "Missionary to Use Plane in Alaska," or "Helen Keller Flies; Claims Able to Hear."

But Cros knew that in New York, the big story was police brutality. While, with one hand, Mayor Jimmy Walker allowed speakeasies to boom and took payoffs from bootleggers, with the other hand he had appointed Grover Whalen, a dapper mustachioed man who wore a bow tie and horn-rimmed glasses, as Police Commissioner. Whalen had been a private sector businessman, nonmachine though vehemently anti–"Red menace," and was as adept at burnishing the police force's public image. He built up morale by spiffing up their uniforms with spats while continuing a long tradition of using brute force to control the public. "There is plenty of law at the end of a nightstick," he observed, making it clear that with his "Whalen's Whackers" he was willing to bring police violence to whatever new level it took to combat the unlawful.

Chumley's was a speakeasy Cros frequented in the Village on the corner of Bedford and Barrow. The building was unmarked. You entered through a small anteroom hung with black curtains that concealed the patrons from raiding police long enough for them to exit through the back door into an alley. Lillian Hellman, the playwright, and Ralph Ingersoll, a publishing innovator, drank there.

"'Whalen's Whackers' raided sixty speakeasies last night," Cros would hear at Chumley's over drinks around the table with the other reporters who gathered there after work.

"The police gave him the third degree," he would hear from another. That meant the police had beaten a man in a closed inner room at a police station house. Or "they got caught in a dragnet," meaning that, under the pretext of looking for a felon, the police had rounded up everybody at a speakeasy and held them overnight on vagrancy charges before releasing them. Crooks and gangsters had no constitutional rights. "Any man with a previous record is public property," Whalen had opined. He had no sympathy for the Communists, either.

To Cros in the INS newsroom, it looked like things were heading for a showdown between the police and the Communists when the Communists announced an August 6 rally in Union Square. Ever since twenty-five thousand marchers had gathered in support of an eight-hour workday and a ban on child labor in 1882, Union Square had been the chosen battlefield of the working class. In later years it would become a place of office buildings and condominium towers, but in 1930, as business failures continued, joblessness grew, and the Communists were announcing the end of capitalism, it was white hot with social activism. All the labor institutions were there, including the first labor-owned bank and the Amalgamated Clothing and Textile Workers Union. There was a slew of progressive agencies and relief organizations, left-wing book shops, bargain stores, soap-box prophets, artists, loiterers, and anarchist agitators. The Communist Party and the *Daily Worker* were two blocks south on East Twelfth Street.

Cros probably heard about the Communists' rally from reporters calling it into the INS newsroom. Placard-waving demonstrators, in a crowd estimated at between thirty-five and sixty thousand, taunted the police, all anti-Tammany, anti-police, anti-war, anti-rich, wanting jobs. When the band struck up "The Internationale," almost no one knew the words except for the party members surrounding the speakers' platform. There were hours of speeches. Then two thousand singing Communists marched into Broadway, defied the restrictions of the police permit for the demonstration, and turned south toward City Hall.

Whalen ordered the police into action. From all sides, hundreds of them waded into the crowd using horses, fists, clubs, and fire hoses to clear the area. The clash was over in fifteen minutes.

Whalen minimized any police violence that had occurred. But in the same breath he asked film companies to suppress a newsreel showing brutal beatings, one by an officer holding down a youth while another beat him repeatedly with his nightstick.

Everyone around the table agreed there was more to come. The situation could explode. City officials were under pressure to protect the right to free assembly and free speech. The police had used violence. The Communists had their hands on a powerful new weapon, the moving picture camera. Public opinion could easily turn against the police and the government, or both.

Back in his apartment, Cros devoured accounts of the Union Square rally. The *Times* said, "Hundreds of policemen and detectives swinging nightsticks, blackjacks, and bare fists, rushed into the crowd, hitting out at all with whom they came in contact." This was a story Cros wanted to cover for the INS client newspapers, which numbered around two thousand dailies across the country, without counting the tabloids and weeklies.

The next day the *Daily News* story read, "A hydrant was opened, and firemen and street cleaners aided in turning streams of water toward the remaining thousands, many of whom were stymied and unable to progress in either direction." Maybe Whalen had gone too far this time. Turning fire hoses on citizens was a big story, Cros could just tell, and he wanted to be there. He'd cover the next rally, be in the thick of it.

The day of the next Union Square rally dawned clear. The temperature would climb into the nineties. Clutching his notebook, press card stuck in the band of his fedora, Cros clattered down the stairs of the World Building and headed straight for the powder keg of history that was Union Square.

Clumps of men and women pressed together, carrying signs. He waded in. Some of the men were wearing suits; some had their jackets off, ties loose; many were tattered and unwashed. There were families, children being pulled along by the hand. Over the tops of people's heads he saw a large crowd gathering around a bandstand with a podium on it. He made his way through to the front just as the band struck up. When "The Internationale" ended, he looked back over the square and saw speakers mounting a half-dozen platforms, crowds gathering around them. All were antiwar, antirich, anticapitalism.

As the speeches wound down and the crowd thinned, Cros followed it out of the square and south to the *Daily Worker.* From ahead, he heard booing and jeering. He moved out into the middle of the street. The crowd ahead was blocking traffic. Then, further down, he saw a scuffle break out between a police officer and some of the people in the crowd. More officers joined in, jostling and hitting people. As Cros began running toward the melee, he heard a blast of police whistles. Then a whole slew of policemen came out from one of the buildings and began attacking the crowd with their clubs.

Cros saw a young girl in the crowd being trampled and began running in her direction. Then two men in the crowd picked her up and carried her off, screaming. He felt a blow to the top of his head from behind. He put his hand to his head and felt warm, sticky blood streaming from his scalp, but he did not stop running. He saw the men carry the girl into the offices of the *Daily Worker*.

Then it was all over. The screaming crowd ran away from the police. As if by some silent command, the police retreated back into the building they had come out of. Cros found a phone booth and called in what he had seen to his INS rewrite man. The pages of his notebook were wet with blood, and there was blood on the telephone dial. His shirt began to get cold around his neck. "You better get yourself to a hospital," the rewrite man said.

So he did. Somehow the *New York Times* found out about it, because the next day the *Times* headlines read: "Police Battle Reds in Union Square Riot" and "Injured Reporter Leaves Hospital." According to the *Times*, Bowen of the INS had suffered a "concussion of the brain," was "said to have been hit over the head with a policeman's nightstick" at the Friday night rally, and advised to remain in the hospital for several days more. The INS called Cros's parents to assure them that their son was not seriously hurt. To Bowen and Louise, Cros cabled, "There is nothing to worry about. I thought I would wire because the papers are sure to exaggerate to make a good story." But the *Times* reported that although the Beekman Street Hospital had wanted him to stay for observation, he had left immediately, insisting he "felt fine." So to his anxious parents, he softened the news, cabling that "the doctor said I had a slight concussion and put me to bed with an ice bag on my head. Will be out late Saturday."

"Bowen got hit with a nightstick in Union Square," they would have said at Chumley's as he came in through the door.

"A lump in my head and a bloody shirt," he'd have said with a grin. "My brain's just fine."

But the story wasn't over yet. Roger Baldwin of the American Civil Liberties Union (ACLU), founded in 1920 to defend the civil liberties stated in the Bill of Rights, was demanding a police hearing. Cros and two other reporters were called to testify. "Mulrooney Lays Riot to Red Attack," the *Times* said. "But Liberties Union Demands He Lift Charges Police Used Clubs Without Provocation."

The police inquiry took place in the West Sixty-eighth Street Station. The presiding officer was Deputy Chief Inspector James S. Bolan, a short, plump man who sat at a wooden desk facing the attorneys. The witnesses supporting the police were to one side of him and those opposed to the other. Next to Inspector Bolan's desk was a single chair for the witness being questioned.

Roger Baldwin presented the case against the police. Baldwin was the ACLU's head, a professorial, Harvard-educated type who viewed the class struggle as "the central conflict of the world." He was trying to balance the ACLU on a thin ridge between a corrupt city government, a police force prone to using violence against civilians, and the idealistic and impassioned Communists. Unfortunately, now, by frequently lining up with Communists, Baldwin risked the ACLU being charged with becoming a Communist front, weakening its credibility to challenge government. Nonetheless, on this matter of police violence, he was going to take that risk.

Inspector Bolan was a Tammany man who had risen up through the ranks, getting his first promotion in 1901 when he jumped from a ferryboat into Hell Gate channel and rescued two drowning men. He spent his off hours surrounding himself with Jazz Age gangsters. Sherman Billingsley had, in the midst of Prohibition, created the Stork Club, "New York's New Yorkiest place." Bolan was on Sherman Billingsley's payroll, tasked with tipping him off before police raids, for which he thanked him with a private Stork Club room where the drinks were free.

At the inquiry, Bolan presided at the desk with a gavel in front of him and a worried air. The hearing time was set for two p.m., but two p.m. came and went and he was still conferring in whispers with uniformed policemen, crossing and uncrossing his arms and glancing quickly across the room. Around three p.m. he gaveled the proceedings open and closed the hearing room.

First to testify were those supporting the police. Two police inspectors, three police captains, a burlesque actor, and an insurance agent successively took the stand. Inspector Bolan directed the police attorney to question each one, and then Baldwin of the ACLU to cross-examine. All claimed that the melee had broken out when the police saw a fellow policeman, Lieutenant Woods, being beaten with a lead pipe.

The opposing witnesses were a Communist doctor, an alleged assault victim, and the three newspapermen at the demonstration, Cros among them.

The Communist doctor described the wounds received by the girl who was brought into *The Daily Worker*.

The second witness, the alleged assault victim, described being hit with a billy club.

Charles Yale Harrison, a copyreader for the *New York American*, took the witness chair, and then Lester Blummer, a reporter for the *New York Telegram*.

Then Baldwin put Cros in the witness chair. The police had attacked the crowd, Cros answered, and he knew, because he also had been hit with a billy club.

The next day's *Times* headline read, "Red Riot Versions at Inquiry Disagree. Police Deny Brutal Tactics at Union Square, but Newspaper Men Back Accusations."

The Communist press called Baldwin a sanctimonious petty-bourgeois liberal and an agent of the police and denounced the hearing as a whitewash. They appointed their own "labor jury" where working class witnesses would recount their side of the story, to be printed up in a party pamphlet distributed around the country. The ACLU expressed satisfaction with the hearing's fairness and called again for the cessation of police violence.

Whalen was out: Mayor Walker called a press conference to accept his resignation. Walker was charming. He joked that his only requirement for Whalen's successor was a man who would "shun publicity" and not upstage him.

It might be one thing for the Communists to charge police brutality, but it was something else for respectable members of the working press to do the very same thing. Cros was beginning to really like this job.

Toward the end of 1930, the country was getting worse. The stock market had stayed in the dumps. President Hoover vetoed a World War I veterans' relief bill because it would require a rise in taxes. In Europe, Germany was turning Nazi. Back in Toledo, even more of the unsecured loans the banks had made on wildly inflated real estate holdings became worthless. The real estate market kept on collapsing, and the Hoovervilles along the Maumee were still growing. The country was looking for a way out, but it was also looking for somebody who could explain all of this.

Suddenly, Sinclair Lewis was that man. He had just won the Nobel Prize in Literature for his novel *Babbitt*, satirizing American commercial culture in the fictional Midwestern town of Zenith, Winnemac, where his central character, George F. Babbitt, lived.

Bowen of the INS had read *Babbitt*. Zenith, Winnemac, was a lot like Toledo, Ohio. On December 10, 1930, Sinclair Lewis arrived in New York. His publisher invited the news media to a press conference.

Lewis sat behind a desk in a small room facing reporters

seated on folding chairs. Cros ignored the assembled reporters, hitched his chair up close to the distinguished Nobel laureate, parked himself to the side of Lewis's desk with his back to the other reporters, and fixed Lewis with a glare.

"Listen," Cros said, leaning even closer to Lewis. "What're you gonna expose next?"

Lewis glanced appealingly over the room. The reporters sat in amused silence.

"What do you mean, what am I gonna expose next?"

"I mean what're you gonna expose next?"

"What have I exposed already?"

"Babbitt," snapped Cros. "You exposed Babbitt and all the others, and now I wanna know what's next on the list."

Sinclair Lewis simply sat quietly and looked at Bowen of the INS. The reporters were stone-faced. Then Lewis got up from his chair, walked around the desk, and silently appealed to them for help. One of them went over and gently drew Cros aside. Lewis returned to his seat behind the desk. The other reporters took over. The questions became more sedate, giving Lewis, by then visibly relaxed, the chance to say what his publishers wanted him to say.

"It was pretty dull, too, after Bowen dropped out," would have been the general opinion at Chumley's.

After the Sinclair Lewis encounter the INS must have wanted either to rough up Washington or tone down Cros, because in short time he got transferred to the capital, where the style was more gentlemanly. Reporters carried walking sticks, left calling cards, and never rushed. Rarely did they even use the telephone. That would have seemed disrespectful. They visited their sources in person.

On his first day on the job, the Washington INS newsroom editor told Cros the government had just released the name of the Unknown Soldier. Cros began crashing into offices for confirmation, being turned away but always going a step higher, until he got to the top of the chain of command, Secretary of State Henry L. Stimson's office. He created such a ruckus in the anteroom that Secretary Stimson had him thrown out. He would have started all over at War but a suspicion dawned on him. He called back to his office.

"Before I do it all over again, is this a joke?"

The chuckle from his rewrite man gave him his answer. It seemed this was the Washington INS's way of seeing what their new reporters were made of.

Cros made the cut. Nobody else had ever gotten as far as Stimson's office. Cros was assigned to the State Department. Because of the ruckus he'd raised, though, Stimson ordered a background check on him. When the results were laid before him, he glanced at them and said, "Well, he's a Yale man. I guess he's all right." Stimson had been Skull and Bones at Yale.

The year 1931 saw terrible dust storms. Prairies turned into deserts. Farmers abandoned their land. People made do with less, many went on relief, and the lines of shambling, sad-eyed men waiting for food got longer and longer. Whole families took to the road looking for work, riding the rails, sleeping in their cars and trucks, huddling together in shantytowns outside of cities. Some just gave up and died. Fear fed on itself like the wind-driven tumbleweeds that massed up against fences all over those dusty deserts.

For Cros, things dragged on in Washington. He wrote his INS stories the way the INS bosses wanted him to, but he was edgy. The *Washington Post* reported that at a debutante party for the daughter of a rich businessman, two orchestras, a popular singing quartet, and a well-known radio star provided the entertainment for a thousand guests who ate their way through a full dinner, a five-course midnight supper, and breakfast at four a.m., while just steps away, a long line of the unemployed waited in a breadline.

In Toledo, with a nation far less able to buy cars, Willys-Overland was laying off more workers. State and city revenues could not provide the public assistance the unemployed needed because the incomes of the few people earning enough to pay taxes were shrinking.

The *Toledo Blade* offered a prize for the person who knitted the most sweaters and socks for the unemployed. Louise got busy; she loved to knit. But Bowen was having heart pains. The doctors found nothing serious and assured him that he could easily live for another twenty years. But he just got more and more worried. Building contractors were not waiting until the market for houses came back—they wanted to be paid immediately. The banks didn't want to wait, either. It seemed like people who had admired him before, people he had counted on, were not standing by him. They turned against Welles-Bowen. Louise could tell his heart was broken. A trip to their Southern relatives cheered him up enough so that, once back in Toledo, he seemed ready to enter the game again.

Then, in Washington DC, Cros got a call from home. Louise asked him to come back to Toledo for his two weeks of vacation from the INS. She and Father wanted both boys to be back with them; there might not be many more times when they could all be together again.

In New York, on his way to Toledo, Cros would have gone down to the Village to see Elizabeth Boutelle, a girl he had met in New York and become very fond of, who was living on the second floor of a small town house on Christopher Street. They had been writing and phoning each other, seeing each other when they could. The flame was still there, even though Cros's job kept them apart. I see them putting a record on the Victrola and dancing together, watching the lights of the city come on, glad just to be alone in the same room. The deep, slow wails of Village blues trombone solos came back to him as they danced, and with them the memories of how she was always deliberate where he was opinionated, reliable when he was unsure, calm if he was agitated.

They sat together on the couch. Light came in from the window that opened out onto the street. Her face was fresh and her eyes bright. Cros was steamed up about Washington. His fist punctured the air.

"Oulahan is the worst." Dick Oulahan of the *New York Times* was the dean of Washington reporters, all two hundred of them, men from newspapers across the country, towns large and small. "The joke on Oulahan is he got the scoop on the burning of the Capitol by the British; he's been there so long."

Hoover was trying to control the press, blaming them for his problems, asking reporters to submit questions to him in writing. Oulahan let him get away with it. Hoover's press secretary suggested reporters would do well not to use the terms "financial crisis" or "unemployment" in their stories. The press charged censorship and the White House backed down, but the number of press conferences declined and the number of written statements increased.

Stimson controlled what went on at State Department press conferences. "But I've kept on Stimson's good side." He hadn't been fired. "So far," he added, tilting his head to one side and shrugging his shoulders.

Elizabeth's eyes twinkled. Cros quieted down.

In Toledo, Louise was waiting for Cros in the sitting room. She put her face up to him for a kiss on the cheek. Billy had already arrived home. He had decided on a future in the military. In a few days he would have to report to reserve officers' training at Fort Ethan Allen in Vermont.

The three sat together. Louise told the boys about their father's heart problems. "It's never been as bad as this," she said. "He's very brave. We go for drives and it seems to help."

When Father came home, the talk at dinner would be of their friends, the Spitzers and the Rheinfranks and the Stranahans. The de Vilbisses had had a reception on their new yacht. But Father didn't talk about the city plans or the new houses he had in mind. Louise seemed to guard him, to fill in for him.

After dinner Bowen would have taken the two boys into his study. I see him dropping into his easy chair and his body collapsing, his shoulders crumpling. They could see he was very tired. He spoke slowly.

"Welles-Bowen is on the edge."

Cros and Billy looked down at their shoes, then up at each other, then at him.

"I will have to refinance in New York."

So for days the three sat together quietly, all day long, Father sad all the time, the boys just wanting to be with him, hoping being there might comfort him.

One evening Cros, Billy, and Louise went to dinner at the home of friends. Bowen had said he would meet them there after work, but then he called to say he would be staying late at work downtown. Back at home they found him sitting alone by the fireplace, ashen.

"The bank will not open tomorrow." The day was June 16, 1931.

On the next day, the Security Home Trust Company, of which Bowen was a director, failed. For days the talk, when it came, was of nothing but the bank. Security Home's closing meant Welles-Bowen's loans would be called in. He would have to negotiate new loans to pay off the old ones, because all his money was tied up in the land and houses that he was developing. He would go to the home office in New York. If the banks would not lend to him and he could find no one else, he would have to sell the firm to pay off the loans, and there would not be many bidders.

Then came the evening before Bowen was to leave for New York and Billy for military training in Vermont. I imagine the three—the father and his two sons—in Bowen's study, the window open and the light growing dimmer as a breeze came in. In a letter to Louise that lay in a drawer of his desk, "To Be Opened in the Event of My Death," he had written that if anything should happen to him, Louise would control the family money until the boys showed sufficient business sagacity to take over. But he would not have told them about the letter. It might have alarmed them. The whole family went to Union Station to see him off. Then Billy left for Vermont.

"Father called home," Louise told Cros the next evening. He had gotten the loans. He would take the train for Toledo tomorrow and arrive at nine. Everything would be fine.

But things were not fine. The call came from Mr. Lehman, the vice president at Welles-Bowen. Lehman's voice was careful, hesitant, and gentle.

Cros knew, with his first word, what had happened. Lehman said that the office in New York had informed them that early in the day Bowen had been taken to the hospital with heart pains and died there of a heart attack at 5:30 p.m. He was fifty-five years old.

"The first one struck as he was coming out of the subway. He rested in the office. Then another one. They took him to the hospital."

Cros felt everything go very still and he stayed for a long while by himself, resting his head on the gentle wood surface of his father's desk, breathing in the smells of his father's pipe tobacco.

Cros told Louise. He stayed with her as she wept. Then he helped her to her room. He went to Father's study to call Elizabeth. He would leave for New York the following day to bring his father's body back home.

In New York, Cros made the arrangements for his father's coffin to be put on the train to Toledo. Sleepless, he watched the morning sun rise over the Midwestern prairie.

At home, they placed the coffin in the front reception room and opened it. Louise bent to give her husband a last kiss. "He looks so well and at peace," she would write in her diary, and spent the rest of the afternoon next to him.

The next morning the house began filling with flowers and the guests came. They received them all, and then sat quietly together when they were finally alone.

Elizabeth had gone to the hospital where Bowen had died and spoken with the people who were with him at the end. Cros brought her note to Louise. "I know what it must mean to you not to have been with Mr. Bowen through all this," she had written. "So I feel that I must tell you again that the doctor assured me that he was in no distress either physically or in spirit throughout the whole thing."

He read her Elizabeth's last sentence: "He was in bed and comfortable when the sudden final attack came and that was over almost before it began."

Bowen's death changed everything. Louise opened the letter he had left her. At parts, she would have silently cried. "No man in the world could have received more from a wife than I have from you," it read. He wanted her to feel free to remarry if she chose, but if she did, two-thirds of the estate would be set aside for their sons.

"I'll send you whatever I can," she told the boys. She would write them a small check against the monthly life insurance check, but until things got better, there would not be much more.

In mid-July, Cros left for Washington. "I have never seen anyone so affected as he stood beside his father's grave to say good-bye," Louise wrote in her diary.

At Welles-Bowen, Lehman took Bowen's place at the firm. That fall, Billy did not go back to Yale for his senior year. Louise wanted him with her in Toledo. He took a job as an assistant manager at Welles-Bowen. He was a comfort to Louise, but he stayed at home and became withdrawn. That winter around Christmastime, he was in an automobile accident that almost killed him. Louise resolved not to depend on him for comfort and to keep her grief to herself. That spring Billy resigned his position at the firm and went to California to try his hand at writing radio scripts.

Cros knew he was lucky to have his INS job. In Washington hundreds of reporters were lining up for every vacancy. He had top assignments, covering Stimson's press conferences at State. He took notes on the prepared questions the reporters asked and the prepared answers Stimson gave. He filed his stories and kept quiet.

But as Hoover's prepared releases dragged on, unemployment was worsening. There was drought in the South, dust storms and crop failures; famine was spreading among small farmers. On the street corners of New York, well-dressed men sold pencils to keep alive, but Hoover said that taking care of people was not a government function. Government should lend for the purpose of keeping business going. The Red Cross would take care of the hungry.

Then came Mukden. Halfway around the world, Japan and China had been trading insults and aggressions for at least a decade, but relations were tenser than ever. The Japanese seized the Manchurian city of Mukden on the pretext that an explosion on its railway had been caused by Chinese Nationals. In fact, the explosion had been staged by the Japanese. Acting in what it called self-defense, the Japanese Army began occupying Manchurian cities and towns along the railway.

At the next Stimson press conference, Cros sat in the front row. Stimson had been suggesting that the whole incident had never happened at all. Cros had had enough. With a hard glint in his eye, he leaned forward, stared at Stimson, and asked, "What about Japan?"

Afterward, the INS bosses called him into a room and

closed the door. "Washington has its rules. They were here before you got here, and they'll be here after you leave," they'd have said.

Four months later, when Stimson announced it was the policy of the U.S. federal government not to recognize international territorial changes executed by force such as the Japanese action in Manchuria, Cros was not there to cover it.

He'd been fired.

THREE

Greenwich Village Years

Cros's father had died. His fortune was gone. And now he'd lost a good job because he'd offended the higher-ups. He was angry.

He went back to New York and found an apartment in Greenwich Village, in the same building as Elizabeth's, one floor below. He found a job on the *New York World-Telegram*. It was not steady work. He could pay his rent, but there wasn't much left over. He ate well when his old friends invited him uptown to the silk stocking district for dinner, where there were no breadlines, no apple sellers. His trust fund suits from New Haven were wearing thin. The style was to be light and charming. The poor were simply not mentioned socially. There were times he was angry he didn't still have a trust fund. But mostly he wanted to talk about what he was seeing happening to people—in the Village, in Union Square, the soup kitchens in Times Square, the Hoovervilles in Central Park and along Riverside Drive.

But what he said would fall on deaf ears. People just didn't want to hear about it. The rich ignored the poor until they suspected there might be a revolution, and then they were afraid of them. The middle class looked at unemployed men and saw lazy people who didn't do anything. The poor looked for relief, and if it was not there, some of them looked to communism.

The talk dragged on about the same old things—life back in college, what had happened to their friends. They all seemed very interested, though, when Cros talked about what R. A. Stranahan, the family friend from back in Toledo, was saying. The Depression was nothing more than a thunderstorm that would soon be over. Now all they saw was the damage, but things would get better soon. It was a time of opportunity.

Cros was searching for a subject to write about, so on a trip back to Toledo he interviewed his friend R. A. Stranahan. Stranahan was a businessman, as his father had been, but he seemed to be taking the Depression in stride. Maybe a piece on his outlook could help others see a way forward. Maybe it could help him do the same.

"I will quote at random some of the things R. A. Stranahan said to me," he wrote to Hugh Leamey, an editor at the *American Magazine*, where he tried to sell the piece. "The Depression, so-called, does not exist for me. In the first place, the Depression ended around February and March of this year, 1932. In the second place, we have passed through a Depression before and will pass through them again and again, unfortunately. The reason the Depression seems to go on and get worse is because a depression is like a severe storm. There is a great deal of thunder and lightning and darkness and everything is obscure and in confusion. Then, when the storm is over, the wrecks are washed ashore and the havoc wrought is visible to the eye. We forget, for the moment, that the storm is over."

"Be sure and tell me when the *American Magazine* publishes your article," Louise wrote.

But Hugh Leamey wrote back, "I am not sure that Stranahan should be a major article."

When he read the response, Cros's pulse raced. He clenched his jaw.

"Frankly, I question seriously whether without a great study of the magazine and a great deal of effort, you would be able to produce a satisfactory major article about him. Of course, we would not deny you the right to try, but I wonder if you fully realize the many obstacles that arise and the difficulties you would have to overcome."

It seemed Leamey thought Cros couldn't write the way the *American Magazine* wanted. Cros forced himself to finish the letter. "On the other hand, if you do not have the time to carry this farther we would be glad to turn your letter over to a staff writer who is going Toledo way shortly and let him do the necessary investigating and if it promises well, go ahead with the story."

For that, they would pay him $50.00.

Did this man think him a fool? The idea was good. They just wanted their own writer to do it. He needed the fifty dollars, but he did not reply. He kept on looking for work, and when he found it, he tried very hard to keep it.

At 144 West Twelfth Street in the Village was the home of Carl and Betty Carmer. Carl Carmer was known as the greatest host in town, his wife the greatest hostess, and their house the most welcoming and lively of any. Cros became a frequent guest. They had two floors of a brownstone. On the third floor lived the theater critic Joseph Wood Krutch.

Carl and Betty's dining room on the parlor floor had an enormous table. Around it after work, as many as a dozen young writers and editors would drop by for drinks and conversation. Betty, seated at the table in a soft-colored flowing hostess gown modeled on an early American portrait, served tea from a silver service. Carl stood in front of the marble fireplace and poured his guests real scotch, not bootleg, made on the Isle of Skye by an ancestor. The rooms were sparsely furnished with furniture and portraits evoking the American past in which Carmer was immersed.

Carl was a decade older than Cros, but struggling like everyone else. He was tall, taciturn, a grave, gracious, congenial man with roots in upstate New York, educated at Hamilton and Harvard. Betty Black Carmer, herself an artist, was from New Orleans, a diminutive, chipper, quick-moving woman of French Creole heritage blessed with unfailing Southern hospitality. Both of them loved people. When they had first come to the city, Carmer had a job but then lost it. For a while, Betty had supported them on a receptionist's salary.

Carl was at work on a book he'd begun as a young academic transplanted to Tuscaloosa, Alabama, where he taught for six years at the university and became fascinated by the local folklore and culture. Now, while working as an assistant editor at *Vanity Fair*, he was writing up the notes he'd taken back then into stories about his experiences there. Like the painter Thomas Hart Benton, known as a "regionalist" since the 1920s, when he had been painting a series of murals called "America Today," Carmer wanted to document everyday life across the United States, to bring the flavor and facts of regional culture to the reader.

In one of Benton's state-commissioned Indiana Murals, he had portrayed a Ku Klux Klan gathering, a fact of Indiana life the state did not want publicized. Carmer, too, put the Ku Klux Klan into his work, in words, but he weighted his portraits toward a celebration of the democratic values of diversity and tolerance. He called himself an "upstate New York Republican." He believed democracy could set itself aright.

The Communists did not.

Cros agreed with Carl that democratic values could prevail, but he also wanted to find out more about the Communists. So he went to some of their meetings. Attendees were given a secret name to conceal their identities.

John Reed Clubs were springing up in cities across America. John Reed was a journalist who had gone to Russia to cover the Russian Revolution, written *Ten Days That Shook the*

World, become a Communist, and died in a Russian prison, a hero back home.

The John Reed Club of New York met in the Village on Wednesday nights at 8:30 p.m. Two or three hundred Reed Club Communists from Greenwich Village, Chelsea, the Lower East Side, and some from the Bronx and Brooklyn, children in tow, crowded into the second story of a loft building on Sixth Avenue. The main room was up a long flight of stairs, its high walls painted green, with hot yellow lights, noise, excitement. Men and women in work clothes stood arguing with each other or reading *The New Masses*. Clutter was everywhere.

The New Masses aimed to create "proletarian literature." Its pages were filled with workers, farmers, strikers, dishwashers, linemen, miners, construction workers, pneumatic drill workers. It was proud not to be afraid of slang, radio, vaudeville, strikes, machinery, or any other raw American facts. It would turn the realities of proletarian life into art. If it was crude, that was the expression of something young and vital, groping and undeveloped. It spoke to the lowbrow, the tenant farmer, the failure, the rebel—to the men and women at the bottom. The motto was "Art Is a Class Weapon" or "Down with 'Art for Art's Sake.'" Art should have no special inner nature or form. "Marx says culture is always class culture."

Cros would have gulped at the biographical sketches of contributors with their working-class backgrounds—textile worker, dishwasher, bakery worker, and house painter. What would he describe himself as? The impoverished son of a Toledo banker and businessman with a fancy Eastern education who wanted to be a writer? To them, wasn't he just a wealthy do-gooder like the ridiculous socialite in the cartoon who congratulated herself on her charity work? The caption read, "Ladies, it gives me great pleasure to announce that we have saved five thousand starving children in the past year. And we hope there will be more next year." Regionalists like

Thomas Hart Benton were "vague liberals," perhaps sympathetic with workers but not really one of them. Was he, too, a "vague liberal"?

Verbal battles raged on the floor of the John Reed Club, and surely Cros got into some. Hadn't he been fired, too? He was a worker who worked with words. He banged a typewriter. There were no jobs. Thomas Hart Benton was creating proletarian art. Carl Carmer was, too.

"Go back to Yale," might have shouted a man in grease-blackened work pants, unshaven, rowdy.

"John Reed went to Harvard. What's wrong with Yale?" I see Cros tossing out.

"Who are you, putting yourself in the same bucket with Reed? Reed proved himself. You haven't."

Cros looked down at his hands. He had never held a hammer, turned a screwdriver, sawed wood. The guy in greasy work pants had hands that were thick, callused; his fingertips were too big to hit just one typewriter key.

He didn't belong here. They were who they were and he was who he was. He left and never went back.

Cros loved to throw parties in his Village apartment. Prohibition was still in force. He would offer a guest a choice of scotch, bourbon, vodka, or gin. Then he would pour a splash of bootleg clear grain alcohol, add a dose of the right food coloring to suit the request, throw in a few ice cubes, give the thing a stir, and the evening would begin.

At parties like that, people spoke freely about what they had heard about or read in the papers—business failures, foreclosed houses, repossessed automobiles, men committing suicide by jumping out of windows or shooting themselves through the head with revolvers. Class war was brewing right over in Union Square, where the Communists ran a free people's restaurant, and the hungry lined up for it and talked of proletarian revolution. All around, dazed, sallow-faced, shambling men waited in bread lines, resting against walls. They had all seen it. But what could be done about it? The opinions were lively, contentious, hearty. The subjects were communism, art, and the new psychoanalysis.

In many ways, Greenwich Village was as close as anything could come to Paris. You could feel freer there. Many expatriates of the 1920s had arrived back in the Village— Malcolm Cowley, Matthew Josephson, Slater Brown—the older generation that had gone to Europe after World War I. Malcolm Cowley had written *Exile's Return* about them, about the artists who had known each other in Paris after World War I—Hemingway, Fitzgerald, Gertrude Stein. Stein had called them all the "Lost Generation" because they had cut themselves loose from America, gone to Europe looking for a richer culture, and found it. But now they were back. They were the older generation.

There was a younger generation that had come to the Village. Cros was among them. There were poet and journalist Charles Norman and his good friend, poet e. e. cummings, both neighbors in tiny Patchin Place, a renovated stable walled off from the rest of the Village. Charles Norman was only a year younger than Cros but had come to the Village many years before, then gone to sea and made that the subject of his earliest poems. He would become a close friend, always around. There were Bill McCleary, playwright and editor, and "Scottie" James Reston, future *New York Times* columnist, both from the Midwest.

In the arts, Modernism was in the air. In dance, there was Isadora Duncan. In painting, Hans Hofmann, Abstract Expressionist artist and teacher, who had a school at 52 West Ninth Street. After classes, the art students all headed for the Cedar Tavern. Joe Gould, sometimes homeless, sleeping in doorways, supported by an unknown benefactor, was at work on the "longest book ever written," an *Oral History of Our Time*, which turned out not to exist except in fragments.

Some of the old Provincetown Players were still around and remembered the playwright Eugene O'Neill when he had been starting out.

Cros and Elizabeth became inseparable. She shared his struggles and listened to his troubles. She encouraged his writing and his thinking. She knew his enthusiasms and she lifted him up during his depressions. He did not have to explain himself to her. When he used his last dollar to pay his monthly rent and his lunch was tomato soup at Horn & Hardart made from hot water from the Automat's spigot and free ketchup from the tables, she would have cooked dinner for him. People who knew them said they could not have loved each other more. Billy wrote Louise that they each took care of the other when one of them was sick and that they could have taught married people how to treat each other. Cros wanted to be with her for the rest of his life. Writing was all he wanted to do, but he wasn't earning enough money to support a family. So he waited.

At the Carmers', the talk was of the 1932 presidential election. It presented stark choices. The Republicans said, "The people themselves, by their own courage, their own patient and resolute effort in the readjustments of their own affairs can and will work out the cure. It is our task to assist that recovery by leadership and policy." The Democrats said, "Drastic change in governmental policies that brought about the situation is the only hope. Encouraging monopolies, expanding and contracting credit, and isolationism are at fault. This has to be changed." Roosevelt was their candidate.

The country was still spiraling downward. In Washington DC, angry, hungry World War I veterans, called Bonus Marchers, came from all across the country to demand their pensions. They camped on the White House lawn until Hoover ordered Army Chief of Staff General Douglas MacArthur to drive them away. A Red Cross administrator in Arkansas told a starving group of farmers his supply of forms had run out. The farmers marched on the town's grocery stores with guns drawn. The merchants distributed $900 worth of free food. No shots were fired. The Communists applauded the farmers' conduct as "direct action."

Even Hoover had begun to act. The Federal Reserve Board made its first major expansion of the money supply since February 1930. Congress created the Reconstruction Finance Corporation and passed the Federal Home Loan Bank Act and the first Glass-Steagall Act. The top tax rate was raised from 25 to 63 percent.

They might not agree on the whether direct action or democratic process was the way to correct it, but the Socialists and the Communists did agree on one thing: the capitalist system was unjust. "Unemployment and poverty are the inevitable products of the capitalist system. The few own the industries. The many do the work," the Socialists said. Norman Thomas was their candidate. "Starvation in the midst of plenty," the Communists added, and then they proposed their solution: the violent overthrow of government and the institution of a system like the Soviet Union's. In the Carmer circle, Stephen Vincent Benét, who had just won the Pulitzer Prize for his Civil War epic *John Brown's Body*, was a Socialist. John dos Passos, Malcolm Cowley, and Matthew Josephson had declared themselves Communists.

Roosevelt squared solidly off against the Communists. "This campaign is more than a contest between two men. It is more than a contest between two parties. It is a contest between two philosophies of government." Violent overthrow of the government was not the right path. What the country needed was "[t]he right kind, the only kind of revolution this country can stand for—a revolution at the ballot box."

Cros was solidly for Roosevelt. He had watched him in action in New York as governor, striking powerful blows against Tammany Hall, a system of graft and political corruption that pervaded New York City government. When he called on the nation to reform the capitalist system to save itself as a democracy, Cros was 100 percent sure that was the path to take and that Roosevelt could do the job.

So he was very happy when Roosevelt defeated Hoover in the fall election. A new coalition of urban workers and Negroes had joined the still traditionally solid white South, and a landslide resulted. Democrats won control of Congress. The Communist *Daily Worker* said the New Deal would only prolong the death throes of the capitalist system, but to the rest of the country the election meant both constitutional government and free enterprise had triumphed.

In his acceptance speech Roosevelt gave his word. "I pledge you, I pledge myself, to a new deal for the American people."

Then, almost immediately, in March of 1933, there was a third banking panic. That year the market hit its very bottom, down to 40 from a high of 350. Ten thousand banks went out of business, and over two billion dollars in deposits evaporated. One quarter of the nation was out of work. The United States went off the gold standard to make way for the government spending Roosevelt believed would save capitalism.

Meanwhile, Cros still struggled to find a subject to write about. All through the passage of the Works Progress Administration, the National Labor Relations Board, the Rural Electrification Administration, the Banking Act of 1935, the Emergency Relief Appropriation Act, the National Labor Relations Act, and the Social Security Act, he took his notebooks to a Washington Square park bench and thought. Who was he? What did he have to say?

Malcolm Cowley's *Exile's Return*, published in 1934, had been a new way of looking at literary history. Cowley traced the influence of the writers he had known in 1920s Paris on each other. They were a generation, and, he claimed, they had appeared in a cluster, surrounded by empty years. They had a common fund of memories, a shared feeling for life. They read each other's work. They compared themselves to each other.

Could Cros speak for his generation? He was a rich man's son who had lost his fortune. He was not alone. Others of his same age and circumstances had found themselves scrambling for the rent. But it had made them wake up to a bigger world than they'd known before. People of all classes mixed together in ways they had not before. That was the way a democracy should work.

Perhaps he could. He had an idea for an essay. "I am a member of the lost battalion of ex-wealthy men's sons," he wrote. "You can catalog me as one of those young men who have had advantages—a refined upbringing by a good family, an expensive education, numerous charge accounts, a checking account, extensive travel, and frequent invitations to wear a white tie and tails and associate with nice girls. In general, you might say that I possess an excellent background. But that's about all I possess."

He described problems he had heard about from friends who faced being "overqualified." One had gotten a job selling life insurance at $35 a week. But the sales manager wanted his friend to write a letter to all his classmates asking for their business, so he quit. Another had a job in a big corporation but lost it when it became known he had gotten it through a friend of his father's. He wrote about how his values had changed. Money was no longer to be taken for granted, a nuisance necessary to a gentleman. "To think that I used to spend $50 or $75 on a single weekend in New York or Boston. Today I find difficulty scraping up my $30 a month room rent."

He and his friends had been affected as a class by the Depression, just as the generation of fifteen years ago had been affected by the World War. "Whereas its members were shell-shocked, we have been depression-shocked. Where their subsequent reactions to catastrophe were heavy drinking and the flaunting of sexual freedom, we have reacted to the economic upheaval with despair, loss of faith in our economic organization, and generally chaotic thinking."

Out of it all had come a facing up to reality. "There is a sharp slump in snobbishness. Silly prejudices against college people engaging in certain types of work are passing. The man is raising the level of the job rather than the reverse. There is no guarantee of a job. Family influence can hold us back."

He sent the essay into *The Forum* magazine, where his friend Charles Norman was sending poems. "It is my sincere hope that the voices of other men and women of my generation will be heard more and more," he wrote.

One day Cros opened a letter from George F. Havell of *The Forum*. "I Was a Rich Man's Son" had been accepted: "Please let us know if you wish us to notify any of your friends of your contribution to the January *Forum* magazine."

He'd have rushed to tell Elizabeth. They had been having difficult times, finding trivial reasons to argue, moving apart and then back together. She had begun seeing someone else, a man in Boston, but she kept coming back to him, even though they both knew, just as Louise had said, that he did not earn enough money to support a family.

At last, he had done a good piece of writing about something important, and it was getting recognition. But he was about to lose the woman he loved, the first woman who had really believed in him. One evening, before they were to see a movie together, she told him she was planning to get married.

Then she left.

Cros went to the movie alone. He came back to his apartment, didn't fall asleep until late, and then woke up in the middle of the night with a pain around his heart. "This sounds kind of romantic—but it was there as definitely as anything I have ever had happen to my body," he wrote to her. "I thought of the pain that Father used to speak of around his heart.

And for some cockeyed reason, I prayed to God to let me live. Why, when I am not sure I believe in God? I don't know.

"I want to live," he wrote to her. "I want to live long enough to write some worthwhile things before I die. I will never go through again what I went through last night. I value you. And all that we know now that we can mean to each other. But I value life too. Perhaps I value life more. All of which does not mean that I no longer love you and want you for always and forever. It simply means that I have had my share of Hell on this earth. And it is now up to me to walk out of it and lock the door behind me."

Cros recovered and kept on writing. Billy studied acting, working in a theater nearby on Twelfth Street, took up painting, and got a job as a New Deal administrator with the New York City Emergency Relief program.

Uptown, Cros's friends grew more outraged in opposition to Roosevelt. People who had money hated him because he wanted to give money to the poor, money that came out of their pockets. A group of millionaire businessmen, led by the Du Pont and J. P. Morgan empires, planned to overthrow Roosevelt with a military coup and install a fascist government. The businessmen tried to recruit General Smedley Butler, promising him an army of five hundred thousand, unlimited financial backing, and generous media spin control. The plot was foiled when Butler reported it to Congress.

In July 1935, Roosevelt decided to change strategy. He launched a second wave of New Deal legislation. This time, he would put people to work. Relief was not enough; people needed pride. A centerpiece of the program was the Works Progress Administration (WPA). Federal One, under the WPA, was for workers in all the arts—music, literature, and visual arts—divided administratively by each specialty and headed by professionals in the field. The Federal Writers' Project aimed to harness the talents of unemployed writers, indeed of anyone whose trade made use of the written word—editors, research workers, lawyers, teachers, librarians—in better ways than giving them blue-collar jobs on construction projects. The only requirement to get a job in Federal One was being on the unemployment rolls.

The Federal One Writers' Project aimed to compile a comprehensive portrait of America, a broad documentary of rural and urban life. There would be accounts of ethnic group traditions and customs regarding planting, cooking, marriage, death, celebrations, recreation. There would be songs, essays, stories. There would be life histories, called "life sketches." The project arranged for thousands of interviews with ordinary Americans living ordinary lives, blue-collar workers, small farmers, people of all trades, all ranks of society, black and white, all ethnic groups and callings. Some of it ended up in the *American Guides* series, which packed the folklore, culture, history, geology, and ecology of all forty-eight states into separate volumes, each with photographs, maps, and drawings, and some with tours.

Cros's friends who met at the Carmers' felt the pull of Federal One. The project could be seen as upholding an ideal of what American democracy was about. Cultural pluralism and diversity were a new ideal, from which to build a national identity. Like Walt Whitman's poem "I Hear America Singing," regionalism could celebrate harmony. America could not espouse democracy while ignoring differences. The country had to earn the right to call itself a democracy. Out of this would come a usable past for America, a documentation of what it was, who it was, and where it was going and why.

Cros soaked up these ideas because they were fresh and modern. He liked Carl Carmer because he was a good friend, but also because he could learn from him. He respected what Carmer did, and tried to master it, and just by being around him, he learned about being a writer.

He was lucky.

FOUR

Bowen's New Deal

Yes, Cros Bowen was a lucky man. He had been fired from a plum job into the worst years of the depression, but he had survived. He'd gotten and then lost the *World-Telegram* job, but found another one as a humble copywriter in the classified promotion department of the *New York American*. He could pay his rent. And the worst of the Depression was over. The 1936 election landslide had delivered victory to Roosevelt. The economy was growing and unemployment falling. The stock market was trending upward.

In Toledo the Civil Works Administration was pouring millions of dollars into the city. Now there was a roadway where once had been an old canal bed, a new public library, a hospital and tuberculosis sanitarium, a bridge over the Maumee, a university, a cathedral, public housing, and an expanded art museum. Willys-Overland had come out of bankruptcy and was reorganizing itself as Willys-Overland Motors. The real estate market was picking up. Louise had, with advice, returned money to the Security Home bank that her husband had withdrawn from as it was failing, so even though Welles-Bowen told Louise it would be able to resume paying a dividend on her shares of the company's stock, most of the family money was still gone. She began planning to sell the Westmoreland house.

But abroad, Europe was moving toward war. In February of 1936 Hitler placed the Gestapo above the law, and in March he occupied the Rhineland. In May Mussolini seized Ethiopia. His plan to encircle the Mediterranean and re-create the Roman Empire was underway.

Cros and Billy talked about whether the United States would enter the war. Billy was sure they would and he was sure he would be called up. Both of them hoped they could find a way not to bear arms. Billy had trained for the Army, and he hoped he could use his experience writing radio scripts to get a communications job behind the lines.

Cros was moving in a different direction. He was building a darkroom in his apartment. He wanted to train himself to be a photo reporter. The modern reporter, he decided, should equip himself with both the camera and notebook, "the oldest and newest of the means of recording impressions." The camera could change news gathering. It had captured police violence on film back in the days when he'd been working for Hearst, covering that Communist rally in Union Square. Pictures could tell the truth in ways words could not.

Cros had heard around the Village that Berenice Abbott, well known in Paris as a photographer and a returned expatriate from the Lost Generation, would be teaching a course in documentary photography at the New School. Sponsored by the Photo League, a group of photographers who, beginning in 1930, had been promoting social activism through depictions of the lives of American workers, the course had two evening sessions, fall and spring, and met once a week for fifteen weeks. Cros enrolled.

When Berenice Abbott stood before her first class that fall, Cros saw a petite woman with short-cropped hair, a pointed chin, and almond eyes, not so many years older than himself. She was passionate about photography. She began with an explanation of the elements of a great photograph—composition, light, focus, subject, emotion, balance. She talked about the importance of perfecting the hands-on work of getting the image onto paper after the shutter clicked. She told them that there would be a study of lenses, cameras, and exposure. There would be practical workshop experience in printing, developing, enlarging, and finishing.

She talked about the debate going on over whether photography was art. Some thought it was a mechanical process that anybody could master, with no room for shaping by the artist. But others thought it could be an art like painting or drawing if you played with the image using techniques such as "soft focus." Abbott disagreed. She refused to call what she did "art," calling it "documentation" instead, and insisted on sharp focus.

She told her students that there were two kinds of photographers—those for whom the hands-on process of turning a raw negative into a print was enjoyable and fascinating, and those for whom it was not. She had a scientific, quantitative bent and enjoyed the precision of the chemical process that made a photograph. To become photographers, the ones who did not enjoy the process would simply have to buckle down and learn.

Cros was one of those who had to buckle down. And he did. He bought a thirty-by-seventy-two-inch sheet of three-quarter-inch plywood. He rested one end of the plywood on the sink in the bathroom of his apartment and nailed the other end to two one-by-two-inch posts that supported it over the bathtub. He bought a developer and trays and laid them out along the table, sealed off the window with another sheet of plywood, and put a red bulb in the light fixture. He bought a Rolleiflex, the latest model, with a hand-cranked film advance and a pop-up focus finder.

He did not use the large-format camera Abbott did. She

wanted its added detail and control, but she had to use a tripod and duck her head beneath a focusing cloth to see the exact image. What she saw was full size but upside down. She didn't even use an enlarger; she contact-printed her eight-by-ten negatives to get maximum detail.

Cros liked the speed and flexibility of the small camera. It meant he could work quickly without drawing attention to himself. He began shooting pictures around the Village. He paid attention when Abbott said the purpose of a picture was to present reality unadorned so that the viewer immediately recognized "this is the way the world really looks." He used natural light and tried to catch people being spontaneous instead of posing them. He learned to achieve composition by framing a shot rather than manipulating the subject. Documentary photography done right, Abbott said, could be history.

Cros filled notebooks with what he learned in her classes. "The Aesthetic of Realism," "Equipment," "Developing your Pictures." He took notes on tripods, filters, the exposure meter, film.

Bowen's 1936 was about photography. What Berenice Abbott taught the thirty-one-year-old Cros changed his life. "Selection makes the photographer a true historian," Abbott would say. "As no two people are alike, or no two epochs, or no two leaves in nature, neither are two cities alike."

She taught Cros courage. She did not worry about recognition. She believed a photographer should find a subject he was passionate about and throw himself into it regardless of the world's reaction. The rewards would not come immediately. They might come eventually.

He wrote, "I began to see all the world as a location for my photographs and all the people in it as models. Farmers' freshly plowed fields were not rows of promised fertility, but possibilities for pattern shots to be photographed, preferably from a high tower or an airplane. The enjoyment most men experience in staring at a pretty girl was always somewhat spoiled for me because I was apt to look at her face in terms of eye socket shadows, distortions, highlights, skin texture, all the things that tend to make a woman take or not take a good picture."

The skill of capturing what he saw on film became as important to him as writing. He had a new credo. "I believe that a modern reporter should handle a camera as he handles a notebook and typewriter so that he can return from his assignment, whatever it may be, and say: This is what I heard and this is what I saw."

He began looking for work as a photographer. He learned tricks of the trade that would make his photographs stand out from the other ones piled on an editor's desk, certain knacks like choosing carefully what he photographed, getting angles, making people do things, getting them to look unposed, "all the things that, if they go wrong, spoil pictures. A photographer's skill in using cameras, light meters, films, color filters must be as much taken for granted as that a reporter can take notes and pick news leads."

He learned the difference between an ordinary photograph and a good documentary shot. "A good documentary photographer tries to illustrate an idea, not just take nice pictures. If the picture also happens to be an artistic composition, he's in the money. Such a print can serve as a key picture, around which an entire story can be built. . . .

"Like an artist or writer or composer, the photographer must make his way over one of two roads," Cros wrote. "He can do hack work, girls undressing, or people making fools of themselves, or faked up advertising shots. Then he will eat occasionally. Or he can take pictures with a degree of integrity that satisfies some creative drive in him. Then he is assured to starve. And it's virtually impossible to do both."

A photographer, Cros wrote, "must love life and people with violent enthusiasm. He must see everything as new and exciting as if he'd never seen any of it before. Especially, he must love his work, because the financial rewards are very slim indeed."

And he did.

Cros's New Deal was about photography. It was also about finding a place in the country. He began spending weekends scouting out farms outside the city, in the country to the north. With the Westmoreland house about to be sold, if he presented it in a businesslike way, Louise might help, especially if she thought she could store her things from the Toledo house there. "All the financial experts on Wall Street are saying you ought to have part of your money in a farm," he wrote, hoping his reports would demonstrate the "unusual business sagacity" that Father's letter had said he would require before he could handle money from the estate.

Billy, who had come back to New York from Hollywood after his try at writing screenplays there, was in favor of the idea. He wrote Louise that Cros had "thoroughly researched this." They would give up the West Eleventh Street apartment they were renting together and "take cheap rooms to live in during the week."

"Perhaps you understand my need for the country, for a place I can escape to from the city on weekends," Cros wrote Louise. "I believe the sight of hills, growing things, and the doing of menial tasks such as cutting down weeds and fixing up things around the house are vitally important to my spiritual welfare as they are to my mental welfare."

At first Louise agreed. Then she stiffened and suggested that Cros should borrow part of the money from a bank. She had no intention of storing her things in a place that was unheated and vacant in the winter. He wrote back that if she did not like the idea, he would drop it entirely, but "I honestly think if I do not have this farm I will die." After much back-

and-forth, she acceded, and in 1937, for $3,000, he bought twenty-five acres of a run-down sheep farm with a house and a barn, two chicken houses, and a shed on the side of a hill on a rocky road in the town of Sherman, Connecticut.

A lot of the people Cros knew from the Village were moving to the country, several of them to places near Sherman. They were artists and intellectuals, young, poor, and happy, partying together and, in their own ways, helping each other out. They lived in the country to get away from the corruption and oppression of the business culture, from the despair of the city, the hard concrete pavements with no open spaces, no fields where crops grew, and no forests where animals could live. Living was cheaper, closer to the land. Prohibition was gone. You could drink liquor now, not just hard cider, play jazz on the gramophone, and wake up hung over. Your neighbors had been living the rural life for generations and knew how to survive. They might have looked on you as odd, but when you needed them, they would help you out.

Many of Cowley's Lost Generation had already clustered together in Sherman, others close to it. Historian Matthew Josephson and poet Hart Crane had settled there; Arshile Gorky had painted there. Malcolm Cowley bought land and an old barn in Sherman in 1936. The Tates; Slater Brown and his wife, Susan Jenkins of the Provincetown Players; Peter Blume the painter—all lived nearby, as did Henry Christman and the book designer Robert Josephy, whose second wife had been the first wife of Bill McCleary, one of the regulars around the Carmers' dining table. There was a dark side to this paradise. Arshile Gorky had hung himself from a barn rafter, and Hart Crane had jumped off a ship returning from South America and drowned.

Cros and Billy gave up the West Eleventh Street apartment they had been sharing and rented the basement apartment of the Carmers' brownstone at 144 West Twelfth Street. They would take the train to Brewster NY, and then drive the rest of the way to Sherman in an old Ford they kept in a lot near the railroad station.

The farm had been in the same family for generations, but the last owner's father had died. She had moved to town where life was not so difficult and was desperate to sell. There was a lot of work to be done. The sheds were in such bad shape they had to be torn down. The barn needed reroofing. There was a hand-dug spring-fed well behind the farmhouse, but no plumbing and no electricity. The windows leaked. The plaster was falling down, and the whole place needed paint.

The house was built on a hillside, so half of the dirt cellar was granite ledge. In the spring a brook ran through the cellar, turning it to mud. The back porch looked out over a patch of rocky field into woods that had once been pasture, with stone walls running through it. The field behind the house was too rocky to mow, so Cros found an old scythe in the barn and attacked the tall mid-summer grass. He installed plumbing and a hot water heater. In the spring he primed the pump and got the water going. The gaskets would usually dry out over the winter and were shrunken and leaky. Getting the prime to hold took many trips to the well for more water to pour into the pipes, but after several hours of vociferous castigation of the whole damn system—and if that didn't work, driving to the hardware store for new gaskets—water gushed from the faucets like magic.

He called the place Hidden Hollow. He could live there cheaply. He would go into nearby Danbury and buy up day-old bread, add sugar, eggs, and milk, and bake up a bread pudding. He lit the place with oil lamps and heated with wood. He made friends with Dan and Marion Gerow, Quaker farmers down the hill, and stopped by whenever he could. Billy planted a vegetable garden.

For Cros, 1938 was a new beginning. The Knopf editor Constance Lindsay Skinner had asked Carl Carmer to write the

Hudson River volume for her Great Rivers of America series. Carmer was busy with the administration of the MacDowell Colony, an artists' colony founded in 1907 in Peterborough, New Hampshire, and only had time for library work. He hired Cros to do the "leg work." Using Hidden Hollow as a base, Cros spent the next two years traveling the river by boat, airplane, train, automobile, and foot. While he combed the Hudson Valley for stories for Carmer, he took pictures for a prose-photography book he planned to do on his own. He traveled both sides of the valley and typed reports to Carmer in the evening. He described the people he'd talked to and what they said, and arranged for Carmer to meet the best of them.

Constance Lindsay Skinner was a new kind of historian with a new idea about writing history. She believed that the land, particularly rivers and their valleys, engaged people in a "practical and physical struggle with their environment" that gave rise to regional cultures that were alive, ever-changing, yet rooted in history, and certainly worthy of being written about. Her style was to combine history and fiction into a narrative that conveyed a place's unique magic. Depression audiences loved her books. They had been economically and culturally demoralized by the Depression and wanted to regain their faith in America. Each book was packed with local folk culture, strange customs and stories, accounts of livelihoods wrested from the land by the accumulated know-how of generations. Each revealed an undiscovered country, but one that modernity might swallow whole, so there was urgency about documenting it.

Just as Carmer had found Alabama rich with strange history, simmering conflict, and curious folklore, the banks of the Hudson yielded up the same. Cros sought out people of all kinds—German tar makers, Anti-Renters, Irish brick-yarders, landed gentry—and mailed reports to Carmer. One of the first reports he did was about a visit to the Armstrong family estate. On a future trip he would search out Hudson River people at the very bottom of the social scale, about whom there were no books written, just legends. They lived upriver in the hills and believed in witches. The Armstrongs, though, were at the very top, Hudson River aristocrats with roots deep in American history.

On May 11, 1938, looking for Roseton, the Armstrong place, Cros parked in front of the Newburgh Public Library and went in to see if he could find out more about the family. Armstrong ancestors had fought in the Revolution. They were large landowners who had made their fortune manufacturing bricks. Eventually they sold off most of their land and got out of the brick business. Now they lived very quietly, keeping vineyards on the land that remained.

The librarian was a bird-like lady wearing a blue serge skirt that hung down to the tops of her high-buttoned shoes. She motioned Cros to a sit at a library table, brought out a stack of books, set them before him, and went back to her desk. He was absorbed in leafing through them when he felt her presence behind him. Furtively, like a daring schoolgirl, she sat herself across from him, drew her chair closer, and made him promise not to tell anyone what they might talk about.

"I wouldn't think of it," he said.

There were several books about the Armstrongs, but there were also legends. Soon the librarian was whispering to Cros of the strange murder of a young and beautiful girl. Just off the old Post Road, around 1848, they found her, stone dead, near a boulder somewhere between the Armstrong place and the Walsh place. Her body was carried to Newburgh. The librarian knew it was so because Miss Walsh, who lived near the Armstrong place, had been a parlor maid in the Armstrong house and had lived with them in New York for a while. With her very lips she had told her who the murderer was—one of the Armstrong sons.

"Of course," she said, "the Armstrongs hushed it up. You

know the truth is never printed. They were a rich and powerful family, and they could get away with a thing like that."

A gang of Irish workers led by a Catholic priest, angry that Negro labor was being brought North to do heavy work for less money, swore that a Negro had done the foul deed. They searched the wharves and under the hatches of schooners. Down around a dock on the Hudson they found a Negro in hiding. They dragged him through Water Street and hung him from the limb of a tree in front of the old Court House until the sheriff cut him down. The townspeople said he was buried in the Court House yard.

The librarian whispered on. Shortly after this, she said, the Armstrong son disappeared. The family claimed he had gone to Europe to study. But neighbors told of a horribly contorted face peering from behind the grilled window above the door of the Armstrong mansion. They said he had gone insane and the family kept him locked up. "Their daughters and sons go to the country club and fine schools, but just look into the past of these fine-feathered folks and see what you find," the librarian hissed.

That night Cros wrote to Carmer, "I am a lousy researcher because I become too affected by my material and it almost sends me to pieces. . . . The revolt of the fifty-year-old old maid, the lower Hudson River classes forever striking out against the landowners. . . . I just can't take this stuff calmly like you can. It gets me. It's too damn unreal or like being thrust into the midst of a Eugene O'Neill play. She works twelve hours a day in the library and feels library workers ought to unionize."

The next day, driving to Roseton, Cros picked up a Negro who had been collecting junk from a junk heap. He said he wished he was back down South because a man had "more show" down there, and there wasn't much work up here. He had worked for the Armstrongs back over twenty-five years ago. He led Cros off the Post Road for a mile or so to the Armstrong place. It was a farmhouse on 250 acres, covered with vines, painted red, on top of a high bluff overlooking the Hudson. Just beyond it was Danskammer, a point that stuck out into the river. The Armstrongs had once owned it until they sold it around 1875 to a wealthy sugar planter who had fled Spain.

Noel Armstrong was charming. He spoke with a slight British accent and was not well. In his old clothes, he looked as if he had just discarded colonial costume. He had the air of a retired British army officer mingled with that of a country gentleman. His wife was from the publishing house of Harper's and had great vitality. Their house was full of old family photographs, but they led a secluded life. Their two children had gone away to school and were said to have greatly improved by associating with children their own age.

Armstrong's great-grandfather had been a colonel in the British Army and fought against the Colonies. Armstrong claimed to have the Burr-Hamilton dueling pistols. Cros wrote to Carmer, "Colonel Popham . . . was a great friend of Colonel William Armstrong. He borrowed the pistols. . . . I personally believe they are authentic. They are beautiful and I photographed them."

Cros hinted to Armstrong about the tragedy of the beautiful girl. After a long pause, Armstrong spoke. Yes, there had been an uncle who was sent to an insane asylum in Philadelphia. He hadn't known the uncle existed until he was sent to dispose of his belongings; he was never spoken of in the family. There was another uncle whom Armstrong called "Uncle Henry, the wild one." He had spoken once of a "dirty old abortionist" in Newburgh. When the girl was found murdered, the "abortionist" doctor accused Uncle Henry of having murdered her. Old Captain Armstrong, Uncle Henry's father, went to Newburgh and told the doctor he'd better keep quiet about that. Armstrong said that before he died, Uncle Henry showed people a clipping of a man in California who had confessed to killing the girl.

Cros typed up his notes for Carl that evening. He knew he was doing important work. There were stories to be had all along the river, and he was finding them. Carmer had said antiques dealers made the best sources because they knew the stories about the old homes. "So far I have made arrangements for the antique guy I told you about to go with us on Tuesday," he wrote. "But Noel Armstrong would be good for you to meet," although he was hoping they'd "go easy on his two poor old uncles." He couldn't help but like the doddering old aristocrat who had with such dignity confessed his family's long-guarded secrets.

Cros's next report to Carl was on people who believed in witches. They lived in the Traps, a section of wild country on the Minnewaska Trail. Cros blew into Kerhonkson at about eight o'clock and saw a sign that said "Minnewaska." A gas station attendant said the Traps were just about eight miles away. Cros had learned from people who had grown up on stories about the people of the Traps that they were "kind of bogey men." In the surrounding country anyone who lost a horse or pig knew where it had gone. The inhabitants of the Traps swooped down by night and raided the countryside, but before dawn they were back in their mountain hideouts. The sheriffs were afraid to go up there—men from the Traps were known for being good shots.

He wrote to Carl, "The Traps are an amazing section and the wildness of the scenery and the strange rock formations could perhaps turn people into anything. They must have been terribly remote from the world. The road runs right up into the heavens. That trail must've been an engineering feat. It's an amazing drive. Part of the scenery takes your breath away, but the rest of the way, almost tropical growth seems to be closing in on the road."

Cros drove over bridges and under a bridge and along a precipice and around a hairpin turn, but no "Traps." The houses, most of them early American, were generally abandoned. Then he saw a light in a house. He pulled into a dooryard and a woman came out who told him practically the only old timer around was old man Burger, who had a gas station down the road.

He drove up to the gas station and asked if he could get a Coca-Cola. Inside was an old man with a big white moustache. That was Burger. Did he know any witches? Their talk wandered and wandered on the subject of what could be done to increase business in the gas station. Finally, old man Burger started to talk.

"There was Pol Withy. She was a witch. I suppose you know witches can't die until they sell out. I mean until they sell their witchcraft." Burger looked straight at Cros and lifted his eyebrows. "Charlie Bill was a city guy, come up here years ago, and we used to call him 'Mayor of the Traps' for fun. So Pol says to him, 'I can make you folly me around, Charlie Bill,' and he laughed and said she couldn't make him do no such thing. But she had her witchcraft and sure enough, she was soon makin' him folly her around every where she went."

A city guy himself and therefore wary of the same fate as Charlie Bill, Cros took his leave.

A short while later, he was onto the story of another people who believed in witches known as Bushwackers, Pondshiners, or Hill Billies. Many of them had been wiped out by the influenza epidemic in 1919, but there were several dozen of them left. Just as he was entering the mountains, he saw a boy walking alongside the road looking for work. The boy guided Cros to the top of the mountain where the Bushwackers lived on land they had squatters' rights to, and introduced him to George Proper. Proper lived in a revolutionary era-type frame house, poorly built. Proper was fairly well poised and very talkative, lean and wiry, and his face rather intelligent. He had a ferocious dog with a bad case of worms who threatened Cros and his guide. Proper was against liquor, seemed to have a trace of religion in him, and lived entirely alone. "Always been a bachelor," he said.

George Proper told Cros that Fran Ingals was said to be a witch and that she lived all alone in a little house not so far from him. But he didn't think she was a witch. She was a relative of his, an aunt. He sometimes visited her, bringing in wood and water and something to eat. She might talk to him, though.

So Cros and the boy made their way through thick underbrush, over little rivulets, through sumac confines and berry bushes, through ravines along an old footpath to the house of Fran Ingals, the witch. "The witch was wizened and had a wrinkled face and her hair was cut short so that it hung straight around her neck," Cros wrote. "Her back was slightly hunched, and she hobbled about her room and didn't like it at all that she was being accused of being a witch. She apologized about the appearance of her room, the bed being unmade and the dishes not entirely clean, but it was rather neat all in all."

Their next visit was with Bertha Sigler, who was said to know for sure Fran Ingals was a witch. She was fussing over her stove when Cros went in, her husband fixing beeswax frames inside a big box. She began talking immediately.

"I say it's the devil's contest," she said right off. "I wish that Fran Ingals would dry up and blow away. She's a real devil's serpent."

"How do you know she's causing trouble?"

"Why," she said, "when this fortune-telling fellow came to Hudson named Al Herrin, I had him read my fortune gazing into a crystal, and he said that Fran was doing me harm. He said that she was spreading evil spirits all over the place."

"Did you believe him?"

"Why yes. He's pretty good, he is."

"You think so?"

"Why yes, they even published his picture in the Hudson paper."

These travels among the people on the banks of the Hudson made Cros think new thoughts. The backwoods country folk were insular and sometimes inbred. The aristocracy was enfeebled. Inbreeding hadn't done it, but generations of inherited money had. In the middle were the working people. They struggled to earn enough money to live, and when they couldn't, tried to do without. They made things happen. He liked old Armstrong, but the man's world was narrow and stultifying. He was becoming a writer, and he could spend his life chasing stories and maybe even get paid for it. He was very glad not to be a Wall Street man.

Just after Carmer's *The Hudson* came out in 1939, Cros wrote to him, "I do want you to know, Carl, that I have never forgotten or that I will ever forget all that you have done for me and meant to me, both you and Betty. Sometimes I shudder when I think what might have happened to me if you had not called me back from Hidden Hollow. Then as I floundered trying to get adjusted, you always seemed to know the direction in which I was to move next." He was sick with a toothache, and couldn't think straight, and the letter wasn't really saying what he hoped it would say, but he wrote, "I don't think I need to tell you I am grateful. It's more than that. There is not much I can do to repay you. Things like that cannot be repaid. But I want you to know that I am fully aware of everything you have both done for me."

His camera, his reporter's notebooks, and his search for stories opened up Cros's world. To get stories, he had to make people at ease with him and be at ease with them. He had to listen. Because he listened, they talked. Most of them didn't know what Yale was and had never heard of Skull and Bones. They were from many walks of life, many social classes, many ethnicities. He would never have been able to get those stories if he had kept his trust fund and not had to work for a living. He was lucky.

Doing the Hudson River book with Carl was a leg up. Cros could go after top assignments now. When *Life* asked its star staff photographer Margaret Bourke-White to do an article on the Hudson, Cros and Carmer spent six weeks with her, Cros assisting, pointing out places where he had gotten his best shots, generally making things easier. They went up in an airplane and Cros took his first aerial shot. She was famous, brilliant, and beautiful, and Cros was proud to be working with her.

When *Town & Country* sent Carl Carmer to do a story on a Mississippi river boat, Cros went along as a photographer and Betty for the fun of it. At the fancy dress ball at the end of the trip, Carl and Betty appeared dressed as a riverboat gambler and his lady. Cros slung his camera around his neck and came as a photographer. There was hackwork, too, pictures of fabulously expensive interiors and shots of beautiful women. But to his *Yale Alumni Magazine*, Cros wrote, "It was a lucky month for Bowen in his career as a photo reporter. He had a four-page article with pictures on a river packet on the Ohio and Mississippi in *Town & Country*; a color page of Vassar girls digging Indian relics in the *American Magazine*; three pictures of Mt. Tremblant in Canada in *Harper's Bazaar*; and a picture of a theater in a traveling trailer in a Junior League magazine in May."

There was more, too. The publisher Hastings House was interested in the prose-photography book he had been working on. He was calling it *The Hudson: Great River of the Mountains*.

Photo reporting had put Cros on the cutting edge of a revolution in photography. Americans were beginning to like getting stories through pictures. Photojournalism was breaking into the magazine world. The *American Magazine* had published F. Scott Fitzgerald, Sherwood Anderson, and Dashiell Hammett. But it hadn't changed much since 1906 and was looking like it might not survive the competition from Henry Luce's *Time, Life,* and *Fortune,* which were telling stories in full-color, beautifully produced photographs. Photography extended beyond magazine journalism's traditional subjects to a new focus on art and social justice. A generation of great photographers was emerging: Margaret Bourke-White, Alfred Eisenstaedt, Henri Cartier-Bresson, Carl Mydans, Walker Evans, Dorothea Lange, and Ansel Adams.

So far newspaper photography had not been keeping pace. Then a new newspaper, *PM,* came along. Ralph Ingersoll had been a Henry Luce disciple at *Fortune,* then developed the "Reporter at Large" style at *The New Yorker* with its first editor, Harold Ross. This was the "new journalism," in which the reporter does not purport the objectivity of the "who, what, where, when" style of reporting but takes the reader with him as he uncovers the story. Now, with financing from Marshall Field, the wealthy Chicago department store heir, Ingersoll was implementing his ideas at *PM.* He would bring the top-quality photojournalism of Luce's magazine empire to a newspaper. Reporters should be free to express their own opinions, not bound by loyalty to advertisers; hence the paper would accept no advertising.

PM hit the stands in 1940. It was a tabloid, printed on heavy stock with good layout and glossy ink that didn't rub off, and stapled for easy handling. It used sharp color photographs by top-rate photographers. It cost more than its competitors on the newsstand, five cents a copy, but it promised more.

PM's politics were liberal. In New York, a town where the other newspapers were conservative, it embraced the New Deal from the beginning. It stated its editorial philosophy on the very first page of its first issue. Cros saved his.

PM is against people who push other people around.

PM accepts no advertising.

PM belongs to no political party.

PM is absolutely free and uncensored.

PM's sole source of income is its readers—to whom it alone is responsible.

PM is one newspaper that can and dares to tell the truth.

PM's opinions, Ingersoll proclaimed, would be pro-FDR, pro-intervention, pro-labor, and anti-fascism. Roosevelt had written Ingersoll personally to welcome *PM*. Of the eight daily newspapers in New York, all avidly read, only one had endorsed FDR in the 1940 election. All of them hoped *PM* would fail. They did not even allow it space on their delivery trucks. The paper had to devise its own delivery system. To *PM*-ers, that was only more proof they were doing something important. But so far the paper still needed Marshall Field's money to keep going. Nobody knew how long that could continue.

Cros knew that writing for *PM* meant you were the best. Ralph Ingersoll was known to fire writers. He said that it was impossible for him to put the paper out "on the competence standard by which any Hearst or Scripps Howard man could hold down a job." The Newspaper Guild said Ingersoll seemed to think that the country was full of talent, and all he had to do was keep employing people and letting them go until he found the genius he was seeking. He was a writer himself and hated to fire writers, but he had toughened up. Once when he fired a group of writers and the union objected, he asked them to send in their ten best stories. He replied with specific comments on each one's work. "In my opinion he is an undistinguished, hackneyed writer." "He has difficulty making himself clear." "I thought his stories were wordy; their construction was tortuous, and they were not therefore up to my standards." "I have kept him on because he was identified with the leftist political position and dropping people of that persuasion is often misunderstood as red-baiting, and so he has been here because of his politics. I am not going to do any of that anymore." And then Ingersoll set a deadline after which he would not print a word in *PM* of a writer whose work he did not like.

An idealistic New Deal liberal photo reporter like Cros Bowen felt himself made for *PM* and *PM* made for him.

Very quickly, though, Cros's attention shifted from New York to Europe. Hitler had invaded Poland. Britain and France declared war on Germany. Then Hitler invaded France. Billy decided to join the Army "ahead of the draft," and in October of 1940 he left for Fort Dix. Cros was busy readying his Hudson River photographs for Hastings House, writing a "word track" text to go with the pictures. Carl Carmer was writing an introduction.

Great River came out in 1941. Reviewers compared it to James Agee and Walker Evans's *Let Us Now Praise Famous Men* and Erskine Caldwell and Margaret Bourke-White's *You Have Seen Their Faces*, even though it was only in part about the rural poor, but also about the Hudson River region's landscape, social history, and folklore.

But war fever was all around. The economy was booming from all the borrowing and spending needed to build an armed force. In Toledo, Willys-Overland contracted with the government to make military vehicles for the war. Jeeps began rolling off the assembly lines headed straight for the front.

Cros wanted to go to the front—not to fight, but as a war photographer. He applied to the American Field Service (AFS), formed in 1914 by "Gentlemen Volunteers," mostly men on their "Grand Tours" who found themselves in France at the outbreak of WWI, who wanted to aid the wounded. Now the AFS was about to send its first unit of ambulance drivers to serve alongside the British Eighth Army fighting against the Axis powers in North Africa. Cros said he had no money but would like to go along and take pictures of the work of the Field Service. They looked him over, checked on him, and said he could.

Then he went to see Charles Colebaugh, managing editor of *Collier's*. "I am going to the Middle East to take pictures, but I need money." Colebaugh assigned Bill Chessman, the art editor, to look over the peacetime picture stories Cros had done. In a week they agreed to advance him a sum of money and an expense account as well as full credentials as a representative of *Collier's*. It was more than enough to purchase his uniforms, kit, and a large supply of photographic materials and equipment.

In only a few weeks he found himself in Grand Central Station boarding a train that would take his American Field Service ambulance unit to Nova Scotia and then to the Middle East.

It was another change in fortune, and it had happened very easily. He was still a lucky man.

FIVE

Bowen's Short War

Cros was on top of the world.

It was the dream of anyone who had ever worked as a newspaper reporter, covering a war representing one of the most powerful magazines in America. Besides, Cros was curious. He wanted to see North Africa and the Middle East, to walk the Holy Land where Jesus walked, explore crusader castles and the Sphinx and the pyramids. See the lands of Lawrence of Arabia, his boyhood hero. And to be a glamorous war correspondent, to astound the people back home in Toledo.

Red Cross brassard displayed on his uniform and American Field Service identification card tucked safely in his breast pocket, Cros stood in the drizzling rain in Halifax Harbor waiting to board the *Warwick Castle*. From his shoulder hung the sturdy leather case that protected his cameras. Around him were the hundred other members of the first unit of the AFS to enter the war. Like him, they had signed on as volunteers, paid $200 of their own money for their uniforms and kit, and on November 6, 1941, boarded a train headed north out of New York. Their departure was a military secret.

Ever since he'd shepherded the whole lot through Boston, Cros's luggage had been a problem. Now, among a pile stacked somewhere on the dock waiting to be loaded were his duffel bag and sleeping bag, two large suitcases, a small one, two cases of 144 flash bulbs, two heavy boxes of photographic chemicals and films, and a canvas bag of toilet articles, pajamas, and a clean shirt.

The *Warwick Castle* was big and gray, almost in complete darkness, and alive with troops slowly moving across two gangplanks, each soldier carrying a duffel bag, a canvas-covered helmet, a Bren gun, or an officer's suitcase or trunk. At the same time, into it were being loaded all the miscellaneous paraphernalia an army carries: boxes of medical supplies, metal boxes of money, hymn books, dominoes, phonograph machines, typewriters, band instruments, order blanks, extra uniforms, blankets, rifles, guns, camouflage netting, bicycles, and portable kitchens.

Cros heard the crisp call of a command. A group of soldiers came to attention and began to file off the ship, but in the rain they seemed less like human beings and more like grotesque gnomes and giants doing strange things in the darkness. Then, from the *Warwick Castle*'s afterdeck, came the clear and gentle sound of Tommies' voices in song. The slow and simple melody rang out in the night. The lyrics told of a soldier's joy upon returning to civilian life.

Around him, his AFS unit raised its voice in reply. He joined in: "Sewanee River," "East Side, West Side," "Let Me Call You Sweetheart," and "Down by the Old Mill Stream," until the activity on the troop transport slowed and the singing got softer and less frequent, like an old clock running down. Lone Tommies began returning to the ship to fetch heavy boxes of ammunition and machine guns and antiaircraft guns encased in wooden boxes. The drizzling rain stopped and the black sky became gray before the rising moon.

At last, just before dawn, came the order for the American Field Service men to go aboard. Cros filed up the gangway and a soldier handed him a ticket with a cabin number marked on it.

"Who says America is not in it?" he said to himself as he passed the American naval officer flanked by several MPs at attention at the end of the gangplank. He was now aboard an American troop transport commanded by the U.S. Navy taking British soldiers to war.

Cros's unit reached the AFS Mobilization (MOB) Center in the desert near Cairo in early 1942. After a week of British Army organization and desert warfare instruction, they convoyed northeast to Lebanon and Syria to await orders for the front, Cros all along taking pictures for his *Collier's* assignment. By May, they were back at MOB Center, with orders to proceed to Libya in the Western Desert. But complaints had reached Cros's commanding officer Jimmy King that the pictures he was taking for *Collier's* violated his photographic pass. He got leave to go into Cairo to report to the British and develop his negatives.

Cros checked in at the reception desk of Shepheard's Hotel with all his supplies and most of his personal kit. The following day he would straighten things out with Colonel Philip Astley, head of public relations, the British Army Public Relations Office at General Headquarters of the Middle East Forces. It was good to have his first bed in seven months and the longest hot bath he'd ever taken in his life. Then he got out his best uniform and groomed himself to impeccability.

The front porch of Shepheard's Hotel was filled with officers and pretty girls sitting at tables and drinking scotch and soda. Their talk was flirtatious and light, but on the subject of the coming "flap" it turned to excited elation. The "flap" was Rommel's expected attack, as inconsequential as the wind blowing open a desert tent. The British were masters of understatement. A soldier who had had his arm blown off would say he'd gotten "a bit of a packet." The talk moved on, but anxiety floated in the air.

Cros found his fellow war correspondents gathered at one of the terrace tables. Ben Robertson of *PM* was the most pleasant, from the red hills of South Carolina where so many of his father's Southern relatives had come from. Cros and he took an instant liking to each other. Cros loved it that Robertson insisted on wearing civilian clothes—he said a uniform made him feel uneasy. Joseph Levy of the *New York Times* was the most serious and earnest. He was upset because his Palestine dispatches were criticized by both Arabs and Jews and he was having trouble with his health. George Lait of the International News Service was the most philosophical and easygoing; he was still recovering from malaria, having spent several weeks in the hospital. Harry Zinder of *Time* and *Life* was the hardest working and had the most contacts. Frank Kennedy, bureau chief at the Associated Press, looked continually worried. The British showed him more respect than other American correspondents because they thought the AP was a kind of unofficial U.S. government news agency like their own Reuters. Harry Crockett of the AP had just arrived in town to replace Larry Allen, who was now a prisoner of war.

Cros turned the talk to his upcoming meeting with Astley. The lowdown on him was that he was the son of a wealthy and powerful family in England, married and divorced from screen actress Madeleine Carroll, with whom he had lived for a time in Hollywood. It seems the brass hats at Whitehall reasoned that since he had lived in Hollywood, he would be able to deal most successfully with American newspapermen. But he'd succeeded in antagonizing an awful lot of both American and Fleet Street war correspondents, who told him they'd been able to circumvent him by using their previous connections at the War Office in London.

Much of the correspondents' talk concerned trouble with the censors. When a censor was inept and not sure of the "stops"—matters not to be mentioned—he was apt to cut most everything out. A good censor tried to leave in everything he could and still obey the rules and conform to the "stops." The censors were very touchy about stories of the high life among the British officers.

"The best way to begin a piece from the front," said George Lait, "is to say, 'As I write this dispatch on my typewriter, enemy machine guns are beating a devil's tattoo on my tin helmet.'" They all chuckled.

Cros found Astley sitting in a canvas camp chair behind a table covered with a blanket. Astley greeted him with restrained cordiality and then, in a sweeping arc, carried a cigarette in a long ivory holder slowly to his sensitive mouth.

Cros explained that he didn't like going up to the front with his pass reading as it did. Please, would he change it? He was a simple American just hoping to help.

"Quite impossible," Astley said without moving a muscle of his face.

"But," Cros said, "I came here to put my cameras to work for the British. After all, I believe in what you are doing. I want to tell your story in photographs. I only want to help."

"But, my dear fellow," Astley said, suppressing a yawn, "everybody wants to help. We have rules here and both you and ourselves must abide by them. *Collier's* can get all the pictures they want from us through the Ministry of Information in New York. Frankly, I think *Collier's* is trying to use you and the American Field Service as a subterfuge to get exclusive pictures at the front."

That round was Astley's.

But the next one wasn't. Immediately Cros hotfooted it over to Douglas Williams at the British Embassy, to whom Charles Colebaugh at *Collier's* had sent a letter introducing him. "Take it easy and have a drink," Williams had said. "I'll give you a tip based on years of dealing with government bureaus. First of all don't make an issue of anything. You've got your uniform, you've got your photographic pass, you're going up to the front. Let well enough alone. Take what pictures you like and I doubt very much if you'll have any trouble."

That was good advice. He would take it. And to pacify the censors, he would do a quick piece on the eternality of the British Empire and send it through them. Later, he would do another piece, "Tobruk Was a Final Lesson," on what he really thought—that the arrogant overconfidence of the British military class made it vulnerable to defeat—and would try to publish it. But first, there was the girl question. The Gezira Sporting Club, which was virtually in the center of Cairo on an island in the Nile, promised several acres of cricket fields, tennis courts, and a racetrack around a large swimming pool with a big canvas-covered terrace beside which you could have tea and whiskey sodas in between plunges. To call a waiter, you clapped your hands together and called out, "Pasha." A seven-foot-tall Sudanese in a sweeping gold-embroidered robe bowed before taking your order.

But this was wartime. The men splashing around were officers who had had their bodies drained of water over months in the desert. The women, Cros noticed, were mainly nursing sisters from the hospitals at Alexandria, Cairo, and Tobruk, the rest of them transport drivers or clerical workers.

"Britain got her Empire just the way Germany is trying to get hers," Bowen overheard a girlish voice with an Irish lilt waft across the terrace from one of the tables. He introduced himself. She was Ann Matthews, now with the Women's Auxiliary Air Force (WAAF), who was from near Dublin.

Soon Cros and Ann were spending most afternoons at the club and nights at dinner, a movie, or a dance. On Sunday they went to Catholic Church together. She was very attractive in her tropical-weight khaki uniform, always freshly laundered. Soon, Cairo was romantic and gay and magical, full of beautiful Greek refugees, ravishing Italian spies, seductive

Egyptian courtesans, sensitive boyish British officers, Arab dancing girls, and dashing war correspondents, like himself.

But all too soon, it was their last evening together, in the darkened lobby of Shepheard's where a young British lieutenant played Gershwin softly and longingly. "Maybe it's my superstitious Irish blood, but I feel something coming," Cros told Ann. "It's a fear of not living some more, to the end of the war and the days of peace that will follow, not living until I've had a son and a home of my own and a wife who believes in me and loves me."

Very slowly, Ann said, "You are not going to die. You are not the type that dies. In England I worked in the GHQ in an RAF station. I watched the boys come and go when they went on bombing raids over Germany. I realized there was a certain type that died. I actually got so I could look at a young fair-haired RAF pilot and say, 'He's going to die.'

"But you'll be comin' back, you with that Irish talk you picked up in America. Very soon you'll come stridin' into Shepheard's Hotel and I'll be sittin' on the terrace having a drink, waitin' for you."

There was a suffused gray desert light in the MOB Center tent when Cros awoke. For a moment or two he struggled to understand why he was not in a bed with clean sheets. The AFS men were making last-minute preparations on their ambulances, weaving gray tape into the big fishnet camouflage covers of their vehicles. The camouflage nets spread out in front of the ambulances made nice pattern photographs. He got shots of men making mechanical repairs, refueling, changing tires.

At dusk Cros went to the Catholic Canteen, where Father Wickham-George had his study. He was a sensitive Oxford man, very hardworking and gracious. He received Cros cordially. Without saying anything, the Father put his halter around his neck, sat behind a prie-dieu, and motioned for him to kneel and begin his confession.

"Bless me, Father, for I have sinned. I have not been to confession for two years. I have missed Mass. How many times? I don't know, Father; I only went every few months."

"All right, my son."

"I have taken the name of God in vain I don't know how many times. I do it all the time every day. I have made love to girls. No, father, none of them were married. I have not written to Mother frequently. I have hated. I hated the public relations officer in Cairo. For these and all the other sins I cannot remember I ask forgiveness."

As penance Cros got nine Our Fathers and nine Hail Marys.

There were three Americans and two British Tommies at Benediction. Cros joined in the words of "Tantum Ergo" and "O Sarutoris." Then he took Holy Communion with the others, and with it came the strange cleansed feeling he had always gotten ever since he'd had his first Communion as a little boy.

Tucked in his bedding roll, back in his tent, something Father Wickham-George had given him resonated with the confessions of his childhood, and he was no longer afraid. He fell asleep.

The day started like any other. The dinner rations were as dreary as ever, bully beef stew made with dehydrated potatoes. The tea tasted salty. Something was wrong with the Tobruk water distillery. The dessert was two slices of canned peaches but the cook had added canned milk and the resulting mess had curdled.

Cros brought his broken cot frame over to the metal shop where Syd Aft, the Liverpool tinsmith of the workshop crew who said he would fix it, was just finishing his supper and lighting his pipe. As he was drilling holes for the wood screws, they heard a faint buzzing sound. Moving across the ridge were airplanes, droning steadily.

"Going home," said Syd, looking up for a moment and continuing the drilling. "The old RAF going back for their tea. Good blokes, the RAF lads, they won the Battle of Britain."

The blacksmith, his foot moving the bellows of the forge, looked up from heating a red hot piece of metal and muttered, "Famous last words in the Western Desert, 'It's all right, they're RAF planes.'"

Syd chuckled. Then, in the distance they heard the interrupted buzz-a-buzz, buzz-a-buzz, the identifying sound of Eyetie or Gerry planes.

"Oh ho," said Syd. "Something's up. Watch for 'em coming out of the sun. They like to come at you out of the sun."

Sure enough, out of the sun they came, like a great flock of birds. You felt danger, you smelled danger, you heard danger. It was thick in the air. It was like the sound of a locomotive gaining speed. The time had come, the time had come. This was it, this was it. Then there was terror.

"What do we do?"

"Take cover," Syd said, pausing to take a quick pull on his pipe, then dragging Cros by the arm to a nearby dugout. Cros couldn't resist glancing upward. One of the birds dropped out of the formation and dove straight for him. The sound roared into his spine like the grinding gears of creation.

Dust churned up inside the little six-by-six cradle in the earth where Cross huddled with five other men, trembling, his sun helmet grasped in his hands. The sides of the dugout shook. Boom! This is serious. They want to kill us all. Boom! Don't they know we don't mean any harm? Boom! Why, they can't do this to me. Boom! But they are.

One of the men was groaning. Dust was getting in Cros's hair. Yesterday morning, at the hospital, an orderly let him have a basin of fresh clean water. He'd washed his hair and felt clean for the first time since he'd come into the desert. Now his sun helmet was off and the churning dust was grinding into his scalp. He was getting dirty again.

Boom! Would there be any pain if one of the bombs

dropped into the dugout? Then there was silence. Such a long silence.

"Stay in here, Jim," Syd called out. "You bloody fool."

"It's the blacksmith," a voice at the mouth of the dugout yelled out. "'Es been hit. 'Es lying there and I'm . . ." The voice trailed off. The Tommy had gone out to help his comrade.

They all filed out of the dugout. Billowing dust from the explosions was still settling to earth and they couldn't see more than a few feet ahead.

The blacksmith was being led to the South African Field Hospital, his whole arm covered with blood.

All during the night, Gerry kept up his bombing. The sounds of Gerry motors, the thud of bombs, the continual explosions, were becoming pains in Cros's body. He wanted to get out of this mess. He wanted to live and take more pictures and do another book and have a wife and babies, be buried in the New England hills or in Toledo next to Father's grave, under green sod, where the seasons changed and snow and spring came and went overhead.

Cros went over to Mort Belshaw's dugout. Mort had been a newspaper photographer before the war, and he and several other Americans were sitting up talking. But Cros couldn't seem to enter in. He kept visualizing those pilots overhead with their goggles on, pulling at levers that might at any moment send a bomb right on top of him. He cursed his goddamned imagination.

He went to another dugout and another but the men there were all just talking, saying anything that would keep their minds off the danger of death. Just as a Gerry flare dropped on the camp he ducked into a dugout with two Tommies sitting on their cots, their heads buried in their hands. One of them said nothing, just looked up at him, but in his eyes was a terror that Cros remembered having seen on the face of a child whose mother was striking him in a violent fit of temper. The other Tommy was grumbling half to himself. Here were two human beings as terrorized and bewildered as he. He could speak his thoughts if he liked. Here he would stay.

The bombing became more distant. After a while, Cros went back to his dugout and fell quietly asleep. Only occasionally did he awaken when there was an especially loud explosion. If he was going to get it, he was going to get it. The thought seemed to comfort him.

For four days, Gerry kept up his attack. At night the bombers came and in the day, artillery popped, and in the distance, great geysers of dust went up in the air. Cros knew that a man with a rifle, crouching in the foreground, with the explosion in the center of the picture, was a natural for publication. But somehow it seemed pointless to expose himself to danger for an explosion picture that still did not say much of anything except that dust and stones were being hurled into the air at a terrific rate of propulsion. And if a man was crouching in the foreground, he shouldn't be. He should be deep in a slit trench or flat on his belly. There were plenty of soldiers perfectly willing to pose for him with their bayonets drawn, crouching behind mounds or pointing their guns over the edges of slit trenches. But they'd all be faked pictures and they'd not even be characteristic of this kind of warfare. His sense of values seemed to be shifting. Getting the picture wasn't the most important thing. The first struggle was to exist, to keep from being killed, to survive. Then, too, it seemed crass to be merely here to take photographs, when all around him men were fighting and dying.

On his way back to camp Cros tried to collect his jumbled thoughts. It all seemed so unreal, like a big game. He did not feel any strong emotion, neither zeal nor hatred nor exhilaration. Then, walking past a wrecked troop carrier, Cros saw a glove. It was a single glove. Inside the glove was a hand, blown loose from the arm at the wrist.

He felt something now. Cros threw up.

All week long the attack continued. From reports and rumors and the BBC news announcements and official communiqués that came over the battery radio, the unit got a very confused picture. They couldn't figure out which side was winning.

Jimmy King suggested that he go out with the convoy of ambulances that tomorrow was going to evacuate the wounded from Tobruk Hospital to the *Londonhovery Castle*, the hospital ship that had just come into the harbor to clear the sick and wounded out of Tobruk. There might be some good shots at the pier.

The next day he photographed the operation. Those pictures turned out to be the best studies of wounded men he had done. He had a bad fall on one of the invasion barges and badly scraped his leg, but his Rolleiflex was not touched.

Back at camp, Cros went over to the hospital to get the scrape on his leg painted. There was a danger of desert sores, as there was from any cut in the Western Desert. That night he photographed with time exposures the Tobruk antiaircraft barrage. The tracer bullets made nice streaks of light on the negative; the bombs made semicircle flares.

His leg kept getting weaker and weaker, and there were terrible pains. He went to the South African MO at the field dressing station. He was worried that the pains in his leg were getting much worse, and they seemed to have little to do with the scrape. He was sleepy all the time and very irritable.

All week the pains came and went. It was worst at night. They kept him awake. This whole thing was becoming pointless. He simply could not fathom what adult world would produce this. He hobbled over to see the South African MO, who looked Cros's leg over casually.

"What you need," the MO said, "is to go back to Cairo and stay drunk a while and have a woman. I guess it would do us all good." He marked Cros's sick report ticket "bomb neurosis," the new term for "shell shock." Everything, it seemed, not marked GSW (gun shot wound) at the front was marked "bomb neurosis."

Cros tried to take a few pictures around the camp, but to get pictures he would have had to get around freely and he couldn't. Besides, he seemed to have lost his zest for taking pictures. The whole show kept looking sillier and sillier. Then Jimmy King told him the time had come for him to take leave to go back to Cairo with his negatives. Maybe after a soak in a hot bath at Shepheard's for two or three days, the pains would go away and the seemingly dead nerves would come to life.

That afternoon Cros packed his kit and make arrangements to go to Cairo. Jimmy King wrote out a note to the South African MO that he was to go back with the AFS truck and he should be given his medical papers so that he could report to an MO in Cairo.

The MO read the notice and said, "I want you to go back to Cairo hospitalized and under our supervision. You are sick and need care."

"Thank you, Sir," Cros said, "but I prefer to go back with the AFS truck."

"This," he said, "is an order. And if you don't go back with the medical corps, I'll have you placed under arrest and sent back."

Cros knew he was licked. But he got a feeling of relief. He hobbled back to Jimmy, who said to go back and get his negatives developed and get them off to America, and he was sure they'd be fine pictures. He said he'd see him again in Cairo shortly and to take it easy.

The Seventeenth South African Field Hospital was a concrete dugout about twenty feet in the ground. Cros's duffel bag, bedding roll, and photographic supplies had been checked on through the medical corps baggage detail, but he kept his leather bag of cameras under his head as a pillow. It seemed to give him a feeling of security.

His stretcher was put on the floor of the hospital receiving room with about twenty sick and wounded South African and Imperial soldiers. The MO for the ward and the sister were making the evening rounds. The MO was an older man, a colonel, and his bedside manner was a witty seriousness. He looked at Cros's chart and saw "bomb neurosis." Then he pulled back the blanket and tested the reflex in his knee and then his ankle. Neither responded. Then he pricked both his legs all the way up and down with a pin. The pricks in both legs felt the same, which is what he wanted to know.

"Put down," he told the sister in a low voice, "that the knee and ankle jerk are missing. No sensory loss. Obviously . . . but, hold on, I'd better cover myself. Say, 'does not appear to be functional.'"

When he had gone Cros realized what he had suspected all along. There was something going wrong with his body and it didn't have anything to do with his brain. If this thing was not in his head, what was it? It might be something very serious, and something permanent.

At Mersa Matruh, where the rail line to Cairo began, hospital tents rose out of the sand dunes. A few palms bent to and fro with the wind. It was good to be taken inside the hospital tent and away from the sun and wind-driven sand. The floor of the tent was covered with canvas. Sandbags around the entrances kept the sand from coming inside. The men were lying in two rows of stretchers, all still in uniform.

In the afternoon the wind increased, fluttering the tent flap and beating against the canvas walls. Orderlies stepped inside to brush the sand out of their hair and eyebrows. Somebody said it was a bloody *khamsin*, the dry, hot wind that carried sand and dust from the desert and could create an electrical disturbance that rendered compasses useless. Even in the tent the air was filled with a fine dust. It was no use trying to get the dust off your face or out of your hair. It became part of your skin. It coated faces and uniforms and gave a ghostlike appearance to all the men. Everybody was miserable, but nobody complained. This was much less of a hell than the terror at the front.

That night the pains in Cros's legs were more intense than they'd ever been. He asked the orderly for a narcotic, and he got a tiny glass with a white powder dissolved in it. But the pain did not go away and he knew it was just plain aspirin. Toward midnight he couldn't stand it and told the orderly, who offered to give him more aspirin but no narcotics. The MOs were all off duty, except for emergencies, and only an MO could give out a narcotic. Cros stuck it out a while longer, and then got up and hobbled out of the tent into the open.

The moon was shining brightly, and the wind had stilled. Everything looked magical, like some garden of paradise. His mind was crystal clear. He knew things that never were clear to him before. He suddenly understood time. He even saw pages of books he'd read, as if they'd been photographed on his brain.

He stumbled in the sand. It felt soft on his hands as he tried to break the fall. Then in the distance he heard the drone of airplane motors. He began seeing things that were not there. Troops were marching over there by those trucks. Something was very wrong. Time had the years mixed up. They were not this force's troops. They were Alexander the Great's troops, carrying water in big clay jugs. There were some more soldiers going by in another kind of uniform. Yes, they were the Persian troops of King Cambyses, more than fifty thousand, and they would go into the desert and never be heard of again. Perhaps some British desert patrol would come across evidence of where they had perished, or perhaps a bomb crater would turn up bits of their armor.

He heard someone behind him. It was the orderly.

"Dat is not goot, my boy, that you should be out here. You are sick. You have been talking to yourself. Come back and I will give you something to make you sleep."

"You talk like a Dutchman. Who are you?"

"I am a Boer, and I speak Afrikaans."

"Then what are you doing here? You are on the other side. You're fighting the British."

"Come with me, boy. First, pull yourself together. Everything will be all right."

He was gentle and he was good. He put his arm around Cros, and led him back into the tent. And he got a glass with something bitter in it and Cros swallowed it. He sat by his stretcher and talked quietly. Cros did not understand the meaning of his words, but they were soothing words and Cros knew he was his friend. Now he was happy because the pain was gone and he was falling asleep at last.

A hospital train had been made up at Mersa Matruh. Toward noon it started up, but Cros was scarcely aware of being on it because an amiable MO had given him a pill of morphine. He said Cros could have all he wanted on the train ride. It was wonderful to feel no pains in his leg, and to wander back and forth in a dreamy, misty world on soft clouds. He could make things happen so easily in this dreaming world. He was dancing, or making love, or eating a wonderful meal. He was lying on the grass at his farm in Connecticut. He was swimming in the lake. There was nothing wrong with his leg. The war was over. Everybody was happy.

At Number Six General Hospital at El Tahag, Father Wickham-George came and sat on the side of his bed. The strain of seeing so many of his boys coming down from the desert "shot up" was telling on him. His eyes revealed how deeply troubled he was.

Just before he left, he heard Cros's confession. Cros had

little to tell him, except that he had cursed and used foul language. But he was worried about his faith.

"Many times," Cros said, "since I have come out of the desert, I have doubted that there is a God. I have had many moments when my faith left me. I can't stop my mind from wondering how any just good God could permit all the pain and suffering I have seen."

"Your faith," the Father said, "will always come back to you. There are moments of darkness for all men. War and all its evils are not the ways of God. It is man's work, and he must pay for it, for he has visited these things upon himself."

A new stillness seemed to take hold of him. They talked quietly for quite a while and then the Father left.

The next day after, the MO sent for Cros. He hobbled the hundred yards to his tent with the help of a stick and sat down in front of his desk.

"There is nothing wrong with you," the MO said, "except what is in your mind. You Americans are incredibly naïve. None of your unit was trained for the front. Our men are trained, prepared. No wonder you went to pieces and this happened to your leg. Throw that cane away. Go ahead and walk. Get it out of your mind that anything is the matter with you. You're safe now, and you don't have to worry. Colonel Lister wants to have a look at you, however. He'll be around in a day or two."

On his way back to his ward Cros tried to walk without a stick. He fell on his face twice. It was inconceivable that this could happen to him. But was he sick in his body or sick in his head? Because if this thing was in his mind, he could lick it.

Two days later, Colonel Lister came to his bedside. He was short and thin, with a shy, sensitive face. He opened up his little bag and began using his rubber mallet on Cros's leg, striking his knee and ankle many times. He brushed his skin with a metal brush, and asked Cros if he felt it. During the examination, Cros asked him if he was any relation to Lord Lister, the pioneer of antiseptic surgery. He was.

"The family are still operating the old pharmaceutical house," he said.

Colonel Lister's hands moving over his legs were like the hands of a pianist moving over a keyboard. When he was all done, he smiled and tapped his temple with his finger. "Nothing wrong with you up here. I've got several ideas as to what is wrong with your leg, but I want to think about it for a while. Also, I want Brigadier McAlpine to have a look at you."

Brigadier McAlpine, the orderlies said, was a famous Harley Street specialist, and in civilian life it would cost hundreds of pounds for him to even cock his eye at you. The great day finally came. It was late afternoon, and as the brigadier and his staff of about a dozen colonels, majors, and captains entered the ward, there was a hush. They were resplendent in their uniforms. The least imposing of the lot was the brigadier.

"An American, eh, veddy glad to see you," he said as he shook Cros's hand. He performed virtually the same hocus-pocus on his leg that Colonel Lister did. After the examination, the staff assembled at the other end of the ward and held a conference. Finally, the brigadier came over to Cros.

"Your leg is not the result of anything upstairs, you know. Cheerio. I'll look in on you in Cairo."

That night Cros took a look at his chart. The final verdict was poliomyelitis . . . infantile paralysis . . . crippled for life.

The Fifteenth Scottish General Hospital in Cairo was the best hospital in the Middle East. Cros's bed was on a balcony looking out over the Nile with a road running parallel to it. All day he watched the armored columns whizzing past the hospital. They were pulling stuff out of Syria and Palestine and shoving it up into Libya to try and stop Gerry. Many of the trucks were loaded with Aussie infantry. Bare to the waist and unshaven, they yelled like cowboys as they passed by.

The orderlies bringing tea also brought news of the battle. It was not good news. Knightsbridge had fallen, and nothing seemed to stop Gerry. Everybody agreed that he couldn't possibly get past Hellfire Pass. But each morning the feeling of insecurity increased.

For two weeks, ambulance convoys had been coming up just below Cros's balcony all during the night and day to drop their loads. The drivers brought news, all bad news. One day he learned that Tobruk had fallen. Surely, the grapevine telegraph had gone haywire this time. The next day, Rome Radio said, according to Cairo newspapers, that Tobruk had fallen. Then, the next day, the War Office admitted that Tobruk had fallen. Cros was sick at heart. Tobruk would never fall. Had men died to hold that forlorn desert for nothing?

Then, as the days went by, the names of the places Gerry was taking got closer and closer: Devil's Cauldron, Knightsbridge, Acroma, Sidi Rezegh, El Duda, Gambut, Bardia, Fort Capuzzo, Salum, Hellfire Pass, Buqbug, Sidi Barrani. What's the use? The Gazala Line was smashed to hell, but Bir Hakeim, one of the strong points, seemed to be sticking it.

As the days ticked by, Cairo was less and less safe. The Mersa line had not stopped Gerry and he was at El Alamein. Some of his stuff was fifty miles from Alex. Some said he could drive a division into Cairo within twenty-four hours. The hospital was told that if the Germans entered Cairo, they were not to worry. Everything would remain the same, the same orderlies, and some of the same MOs. The only difference would be that the OC hospital would be German.

The American Embassy was burning documents. The GHQ of the Middle East forces was also burning documents and making preparations to move up into Palestine. It was reported in the papers that Egyptian troops would join the British at El Alamein in the defense of the Nile Valley. The next day the Prime Minister, Zahaa Pasha, denied it. All the soldiers said Generals Ritchie and Auchinleck would get a bowler hat for this, get the sack, or, in American, get fired.

Some of the war correspondents were clearing out by plane. A boatload of women and children had already been evacuated. An order had been issued that all sick personnel who would not recover in five weeks were to be evacuated to South Africa.

Captain John Ogden of New York City, attached to the AFS GHQ in Cairo, turned up and gave Cros news of his unit. They got out of Tobruk just before the coast road was cut off. They stayed a while at Mersa, camping on the beach. At the moment, they were at El Alamein. Mort Belshaw had been captured by the Gerries with a brand-new Leica on him. Captain Ogden took Cros's undeveloped films to get them processed and cleared by the censors.

Then a U.S. Army Intelligence officer attached to the Fourth African Military Mission, a major who was from Baltimore, arrived at Cros's bedside and said a British defense security officer wanted to look over his photographs. The major said he didn't know what the score was, but he had to play ball. All Cros could tell him was to find Captain Ogden, but it looked as though his photographs would become hopelessly embroiled in red tape.

That afternoon, Ann Matthews turned up. Cros had told an RAF patient he'd like to see her, and he managed to get word to her that he was here. When she arrived, Cros was wrestling in his bed with a washcloth and a piece of soap, trying to take a sponge bath. There was a screen around his bed that was supposed to hide him. Cros called out to Ann that he wouldn't be a minute. In his haste he spilled some of the dirty water out of the basin onto the bed. Then a gust of wind blew the screen over, revealing him sitting up in bed washing his armpits, his plaster leg propped up at the foot of the bed.

An orderly replaced the screen, he finished washing, and

finally, he was ready to receive Ann. She sat in a chair beside his bed. She wasn't in her uniform—it was her day off from the RAF. "I knew you'd be comin' back," she said. "But I'm sorry you had to come back like this." She was looking at him with pity. She probably thought he had been in some kind of screaming cauldron up there in the desert, fire and noise and smoke, and some vague kind of hell.

But she knew nothing of war. He hadn't, either, but now he did. It was a lot of things all added together, day in and day out. It was living in the ground like animals, being dirty and eating out of a filthy mess tin a dog wouldn't eat out of. It was terror, yes, but it was boredom, too. How could he make her understand? He didn't even try. Because she was far, far away, and they had lost each other.

"I should love to see America after the war," Ann was saying. "It must be simply a fantastic country. I suppose it's because I've seen so many Hollywood movies."

Cros looked away. Below his balcony, the walking patients coming back from an afternoon visit were checking in at the entrance. Some were minus a leg, some an arm. A lot had their arms in slings, or had bandages on their heads. He and Ann were the intelligent and the strong. They would do all right. But what about the others?

"Isn't there something I can bring you?" Ann was saying. "I do wish I could tell you some of the things that are going on that I've found out from decoding RAF signals. It's terribly exciting. I'll try and get up to see you in a day or two."

After she was gone, Chico, who worked in the operating room and had gotten to be a friend of his on the convoy out, came to tip him off to something. "The day after tomorrow they're going to ship a couple hundred patients out of the hospital down to Suez. A hospital ship is waiting there and it's bound for Durban. Your name is on the list."

For Cros the war was over. He felt a sharp, quick pang of nostalgia at the thought of leaving Libya, Egypt, Palestine,

Syria. But mainly he was glad, really, for he would be going home.

The U.S. Army Air Corps major brought Cros his films from the defense security officer. Captain Ogden came to say goodbye on behalf of the Field Service. General Auchinleck had ordered European civilians out of the city and five thousand women and children had been evacuated by boat.

At three in the morning, Cros was awakened by Jim, the best orderly, as far as he was concerned, in the entire British Army Medical Corps. He gave him a heroin powder and took his arm. "You'll be leaving in a half hour, lad. Have you everything ready?"

As he rode the hospital train from Cairo to Suez, Cros knew his life was being cut in half. Time had stopped to give him the lesson of what lay in war's outhouse. He had gone backstage with war and found out that Glory and Honor, the glamorous leading ladies, were second-rate whores. He had learned that in war the little guy's life and health came very cheap.

His train did not go directly to Suez. It first went to Alexandria. There it picked up what the hospitals had and then along the Suez Canal at all the RAF stations picked up what they had. Through the window Cros watched them being brought aboard. And then to El Tahag to take what Number Six General had to offer. Above his bunk they'd put a man who couldn't control his bowels. Orderlies came occasionally and wiped up the mess.

Rat-tat-tat-tat-tat. The steel wheels clicked sharply like the staccato of a machine gun. The men cursed and growled. The windows of the train were kept tightly closed because a *khamsin* was blowing up. The orderlies were so rushed they couldn't answer all the calls for "the bottle." Some of the men couldn't hold their urine any longer and let go in the blankets. The stench of festering wounds and the smells of men's bodies filled the car. The MO sauntered through and

Cros talked him into a couple of codeine pills. All morning, all afternoon, and into the night they picked up the useless, the sick, and the wounded from all over Egypt.

It was ten thirty at night when the trains arrived at Suez. Ambulances took them to hospital barracks much like those at El Tahag. They were handed basins of water to wash with, then fed, and given little glasses of liquid narcotics.

There was news there. The orderlies tipped them off that the Queen Elizabeth had just landed with a couple of fresh divisions from England. American tanks and guns had also just come in. There was a good chance of holding Gerry off. As he fell asleep Cros heard a U.S. Army bugle call taps. A gladness warmed him. Nothing could ever happen to his country and he'd be taken care of.

The Suez harbor was filled with ships flying the flags of many nations. The air was damp and salty. From the docks came the smell of ships' food supplies—meats, vegetables, bananas, oranges, eggs—being hoisted aboard. Cros's ward was just above the waterline. The bunk ahead of him was a bad spine case: a shell fragment had ripped away the lower vertebrae. To his right was a bomb neurosis case who kept getting out of bed and walked like a monkey. When the ship engines began to throb and she started to move out of the harbor, Cros fell asleep like an exhausted child.

Going through the Gulf of Aden, it was so hot that the nurses and orderlies fought their way through the heat in the ward. The patients lay in their bunks entirely stripped except for a pajama leg thrown across their loins. That morning the matron made the rounds with a nursing sister and told the men they must keep their pajamas on.

"It doesn't look well, really," she said.

After the inspection was over, the sister returned to the ward and told the men they could keep their pajamas off, but they should put them on during the matron's inspection.

Off the Seven Brothers islands, the MO decided it would be good for Cros's leg for him to get into a tub of hot water every morning. An orderly had carried some of the other patients into the bathroom in his arms. Cros wouldn't let that happen to him and told the orderly to get him some crutches and he would somehow get to the bathroom on his own.

When the orderly told Cros the bath was ready but he'd better hurry because someone else was waiting for him to get through, Cros threw back the sheet and took off his pajamas and put his legs over the side of the bed. For a moment he was dizzy. He looked down at his leg. It had shriveled into a horrible little toothpick and reminded him of the way the Kaiser's arm dangled from the shoulder. His ankle could not hold up his foot. His shin and ankle made a straight line. He loathed the sight of his leg. His body had always been a good machine incapable of being harmed by anything. It was inconceivable for him to be a cripple, to be pushed around, to be pitied, to be helped.

Why did he have to get crippled at this time in his life? Things were just beginning to look good. He was acquiring a nice skill, photography, getting to where he could walk into an editor's office and say, "Here are my pictures. It's a good story and you can take it or leave it." He got his best pictures because he could move around fast on his feet, climb up any hill, crawl along the ground. He supposed he could maybe still do studio work, take pictures of fashion models flaunting their wax limbs under artificial light or take portraits of people who were only interested in a flattering likeness. What a way to end up.

At dawn the ship dropped anchor just outside the harbor at Durban. Toward noon they moored alongside the docks. The orderly in charge of baggage told Cros that all his kit and boxes of photographic supplies were still intact.

At Addington Hospital, it was past ten o'clock by the time

his ward was put to bed. In the middle of the night, everyone woke up suddenly. There was a frightful roaring outside. The men groaned as they awoke.

"God damn those planes," one said. "Why can't they do this somewhere else . . . out of our hearing." Another man mumbled a string of curses. "There's no end to it," a tank commander near Cros's bed said. "They keep on and on."

Almost objectively, Cros noted that his distress at the noise of the dive bombing took the form of definite pains in his back. It was exactly at the lower third of his spine. It should be impossible, he reasoned, for noise to produce a pain in one's body. Yet it was there. Probably it was the association of ideas. He had had pains at Tobruk when the Stukas came over and it was the real thing. Now he associated the noise with the old terror he knew before he was evacuated.

Wendy, one of the day nurses, became a good friend of his. She was engaged to an RAF flier up in the Western Desert. On her afternoons and evenings off, she liked to go out with some of the soldiers who were passing through Durban by boat or plane.

Cros was getting to like hospital life too much. As he went on thinking about how easy it would be to die in a hospital and yet go on living, a Red Cross lady came by. There was a twinkle in her eye that told him it was all right to ask her what was the best bar in town.

"The Seaside," she said. "I'm driving by there in a little while in my car. Would you like me to drop you off?"

All Cros had to wear was a trench coat, his forage cap, and his slippers, although he only needed one slipper. He put the trench coat on over his pajamas, took his crutches, and started off with the Red Cross lady. This was his first venture into the outside world. He was supposed to have a pass to leave the hospital, but he and the Red Cross lady just walked out the main entrance as if it were the most usual thing in the world.

The Red Cross lady brought her car to the curb and drove Cros to the Seaside Hotel. She declined his offer to come in and have a drink. Her children were at home waiting for their supper.

Wendy, the nurse from Addington, was in the bar. She had on a red print dress.

"Would you like to meet two of your countrymen?" she asked. They were an Army captain from New Orleans and a purser in the Army Transport Service from the Bronx. Cros drank three bottles of ale and was gloriously happy.

"Did you know we were gonna take you home?" the Captain said, grinning at him over his highball. "All you need to get well is to be back in the good old USA. We've got a big empty transport and we're gonna put you in the colonel's suite."

"That's a very nice thought," Cros said, "but from my experience with the British Army it's going to take about six months of red tape before I move again. They understand what to do with English personnel, or Australian personnel, or South African personnel. But I'm American personnel and they haven't gotten around to that one yet."

"Then we'll shanghai you," said the purser.

The commanding officer of the hospital's military wing was a portly South African with a big black mustache. It was immediately apparent that he'd had too much lunch and too many highballs. Cros explained that he had a ship to take him home and please could he be discharged from the hospital to the ship. The officer made one phone call and another, no answer on either, so he gave up.

"You have a ship," he said with a great sigh of relief, "and we see no reason why you shouldn't get on it. Of course, we ought to check with Troop Movement Control, but we'll let well enough alone."

Early the next morning an ambulance took Cros and his array of luggage to the docks. The ship that was to take him home was gray and dirty-looking and not very big, but from her mast fluttered the American flag. A U.S. Army Military Police soldier rushed down the gangplank. He had a big black automatic strapped to his belt and carried a heavy nightstick.

"May I help you, sir?" he said, picking up some of Cros's kit.

Cros felt like crying.

The ship out of Durban for New York was an empty troopship with a capacity of about two thousand soldiers. It was built for the Delta Line to be used in the Caribbean run. Most of the fine furnishings of the first and second classes had been ripped out and replaced with steel tiers of bunks, just like at West Point. Cros's cabin was fore to the starboard just off the promenade deck and was reserved for the highest-ranking officer. His roommate for the trip was sitting on his bunk sorting out some important-looking papers. He was George Ross, from Racine, Wisconsin.

Ross and Cros went down to have lunch in the first-class dining room, used by officers of the Army, Navy and Merchant Marine. The food was wonderful: American coffee, steak, French fried potatoes, real butter, ice cream. After lunch, they went up on deck to take their last look at the receding shores of South Africa. All at once Cros realized that he was thoroughly weakened. Ross took him back to their cabin and helped him undress and remove his steel brace.

He slept the rest of the afternoon.

Thud! Crash! Cros was back in the desert. Gerry was dropping his stuff again. No use worrying. If it got you, it got you. The pain in his back, the buzz . . . buzz-a-buzz. No, the pain was in his leg. But this was not the desert. Perhaps the ship had been hit by a torpedo. That wireless operator today had kept telling them about warning messages. A German sub, based off Morocco, was within a radius of eighteen miles. If they were hit, Ross could still help him to a lifeboat. And even if he did drown, it wouldn't matter much. It would be better than being a cripple the rest of his life.

No. It was just a wave smashing the cargoless ship. Ross was snoring. Cros took two codeine tablets and the pain in his leg receded. He was going home. He was going home.

It was getting light as the ship neared New York Harbor. They seemed to be just coasting along. The waves rocked them ever so gently. Lightship *Ambrose* passed them to the port side. Cros's hunch that something else was yet to befall him had been wrong. They had made it. As they stopped in the Narrows and took on officers from the Immigration and Health cutter, Cros remembered the days when, a young reporter with a pass in his hatband, he had sped down the Bay in a cutter. How nimbly he had climbed up the rope ladder and scrambled to interview newly arrived celebrities. How fresh and eager and a little arrogant he had been. That was a long time ago. He was a different person now. War had done something to him, damaged him, though he was not sure yet just how.

Two screeching tugs helped the ship nose its way alongside a Staten Island pier just as the sun burst forth from behind the clouds. He was home and everything looked just the same. He boarded the Staten Island Ferry. Whirring wheels loosened the clanking chains that turned the ship free of its moorings. Standing on the prow, he gazed at his gleaming magic city. As the ferry passed the Statue of Liberty, small and blurry in the morning mist, he could see that living in these other countries and knowing their peoples had given him a new faith in America. Her conceptions of freedom and her deep-rooted respect for the dignity of man were part of the contribution she was ready to make. Now she might have an opportunity to give those things to the world. But that giving would have to be done with great understanding and tact and love.

They were approaching the ferry slip at the Battery. Water traffic was heavier than Cros had ever seen it. An army truck was waiting. He boarded it and they rolled off the lip of the ferry boat and clattered down the wooden planks of the old dock. Hurrying through the Battery, Cros smelled the familiar smells of roasting coffee and fried fish. They drove too far up the Westside ramp and slowed down as they searched the big gray-painted ships hugging the docks for the burnt hull of the once proud *Normandy* lying on her side in pathetic humility, sabotage suspected.

The army driver helped Cros get his stuff out of the truck and helped him up the stoop of his old apartment on Twelfth Street. Then Joe Andretsky, who used to do his laundry, came up the street. He stopped and looked at Cros, puzzled.

"Been away, haven't you?" he said. "Where was you?"

"I've been to war," Cros said proudly.

"Yeah?" he said. "Which war . . . you mean you was in this one?"

SIX

The Long War on the Home Front

Cros pushed against the doorbell, heart pounding, hand trembling, pushing again. Quick steps—Betty's. He knew it. There she was, eyes meeting his, searching his face for pride, sadness, fear, whatever war had put there. His crooked smile, two words, "I'm home," and she could tell that all he wanted was to share a good meal with people who loved him and sleep between sheets for a very long time. And not be bombed.

Carl lumbered out from his study, Cros steadying himself on his brace and crutches. Betty, on tiptoe, brushed his chin with her fingertip. Cros's heart surged. The war had lamed him, true, and it had changed him in other ways he did not yet understand. But he was alive and home. Carl picked up his bags and his cameras, put an arm around him, and they walked together toward the old dining table.

The century-old piano, the comfortable furniture—all was just as he had left it. Betty settled him on the couch, propped him up with cushions, fussed over him, chirped about how thin he was. He leaned back and squeezed his eyes closed for a moment, and then opened them. Stern American portrait faces looked down from Carl's walls, forthright, honest, frozen in time. Silent in their gilt frames, they reminded him that he was the only one who knew the meaning of what he had seen. His was the only voice that could speak it.

But this was a celebration. Carl got out his Isle of Skye scotch with poems on the labels, and they all drank to the end of the war.

"Let's have steak!" Carl said.

"Just pass it under the flame," Cros said.

"Just walk it around the stove," Carl said.

Betty laughed and their steak was rare, with avocado dressed in vinegar and oil, and Betty's biscuits. For dessert they had ice cream.

They sat and talked quietly for a while, but Cros was tired. Carl and Betty helped him downstairs to his rooms. Betty piled his cameras in one corner, helped him put things away, and made his bed.

He lay quietly for a while and then he fell asleep.

Boom! Cros's whole body cringed. He startled awake. Boom! They're coming at me. They can't be. Boom! They are.

He raised his head and looked across the room. Light filtered through the front window onto his desk and his telephone. There was a rattling of metal garbage cans and an engine whine. Out on the street two men shouted at each other. A truck pulled away. He looked down at his legs. He was in a real bed. Over there by the door were his duffel and cameras. There were no sand fleas, no desert grit blown in through the cracks of the windows. He was in New York City and those were not bombs. Just men emptying metal trash cans into the city truck. This was his old West Twelfth Street apartment.

Images from his dreams flooded back. He was in a desert. Something was burning, maybe a truck or an airplane. A man was trying to speak, but no sounds would come out. He tried again and again, reeling all the time, holding his head and then his stomach and then his knees, groaning like an animal.

There were faces, too. Faces of men whose stories he began to remember. The boyish face of the mad dispatch rider who had been given a message to deliver to a tank corps commander. The face of the orderly on a British hospital ship who saw his entire ward enveloped in smoke and flames, who kept quoting lines from the Bible having to do with the Lord leading a man through smoke and flames to salvation.

Cros lay there until those images receded. Was this what he had come home to? To a knowledge of war's underbelly that would not let him go? Was this the truth he had to bear witness to, the truth he had to tell, to cure his soul? The nuns had taught that God's love for mankind stretched everywhere, but maybe God had just not been at Tobruk. Maybe there was a special circle around the Middle East that made it Hell. "War is man's doing and he must pay for it," Father Wickham-George at MOB center had said. War was fallen mankind's own sinful insult to human dignity, even worse because it was mostly borne by the weakest, by the little guy. It didn't make sense, the waste of life he had seen.

Betty, bringing breakfast, knocked on his door. They talked as he ate, and then she helped him arrange his desk. She put a stack of paper beside his typewriter. He spent the next several days lying on his bed, reading through his notebooks, and sorting out his negatives.

One morning as Cros shook himself awake, he felt well enough to go out into the city to deliver his pictures to the AFS. He soaked in his bath and rested until the bath water turned tepid, and then with the strength left in his arms he lifted himself out. The effort exhausted him. He rested again, and then dressed. He strapped on his leg brace and struggled up onto his crutches. He rang up Director Stephen Galati. "It's Bowen, and I'm back with Tobruk pictures."

Galati wanted to use the pictures in the program for a benefit art exhibit at the Whitney Museum. "Bowen," he said, "one more thing. We're sending you to Neurological Institute. We want them to check you out."

The Neurological Institute put him in bed for a week. The doctors looked over his British Army medical reports and took more blood and punctured his spine and pricked him with pins and dull instruments. They changed the diagnosis from "poliomyelitis" to "myelitis" and said he might have caught it on the troopship over, during an outbreak of dysentery. Now he knew less than when he came in.

"What's myelitis? Another diagnosis?"

"It just means they don't know what caused it," the young intern said.

Cros bristled. "First it's bomb neurosis, then it's polio, and now it's myelitis. What's really wrong with me?"

"Don't worry about it, fella. None of us knows anything much about these paralysis cases. The best the experts can do is to write down a name." Myelitis meant a virus had damaged his nerves. The pains in his legs had been the nerves dying and the muscles going into spasm. The cast and brace had made it so he could walk with crutches, but that caused atrophy and inflexibility. "You've been in bed for a long time. You need massage. You need exercise. You need moist heat." Those were the new methods being used on polio out in Minneapolis that might help.

He had no money to go to Minneapolis. He had joined the volunteer AFS and it was up to him to get himself cured. He went back to his apartment, soaked in his bathtub again, rubbed his calf muscles and his ankles, and wondered if he would ever really walk right again.

He had a lot of work to do. He sat at his desk, typing out an outline for his war book. Much of what he had thought was important at the time was not. A lot of what he remembered now was.

He would write as long as he could, and then he would doze, but in his dreams the faces always came back. Another face, and then another. The man who saw his pal in the truck ahead of him, the truck on fire, being asphyxiated and burned inside the cab. He had started for the pal but the flames kept him away. The paint halo was peeling on the truck, and the man knew that the spare tins of petrol would soon go off. He stood and watched, dazed, watching his pal burning to death.

Night after night, trying to fall asleep, more memories came back. There was the young German soldier Otto, in the rubber rack next to him on the ambulance out of Bardia toward Mersa Matruh, blood seeping from his open wound, cringing as the ambulance veered and swayed. He'd listened as Otto learned from a Tommie's boastful chatter that Cologne had been fire bombed and his mother, who lived there, might have been killed. There was the train from Cairo to Suez, when they stuffed injured bodies into cars like baggage, anesthetized him with morphine and left him to rot in stinking filth, a discard of the battlefield, not knowing whether he would live or die.

The New York Cros came back to was a port city in a country at war. Cargo vessels and tankers lined up on the Hudson and East Rivers stocked with camouflage gear and artillery, awaiting the formation of convoys. The nightclubs were full. Broadway was packed with servicemen looking for one last fling on the town before shipping out. The whole theater industry was providing soldiers with free entertainment every evening of the week. A GI could dance at the Stage Door Canteen with a skinny hopeful named Lauren Bacall or catch the Rockettes at Radio City Music Hall. Dimouts were just a chance to dance in the streets. The glow of the city's lights could have aided enemy U-boats lurking out at sea, but nobody worried much.

Cros began getting around the city, but his crutch would hit a slick spot or a loose paper on the pavement and slip out from underneath him, or he would place his braced leg unevenly and fall. People always crowded around, trying to help, clambering to pull him up, and that made it harder. Once, a black man pushed his way into the throng and ordered everyone to back off. "Let him get himself up," the man said.

"He knows," Cros thought. "He's had to get himself up, too." Here was a man who knew nothing of the code of conduct they'd taught at Choate and Yale, but a true gentleman, a man whose conduct came straight from his soul. There was hope for democracy in men like that. In that moment, he decided he would write for the cause of the ordinary guy.

Then Cros heard the new methods for treating polio had come to New York. He called around to editors, trying to sell his Tobruk battlefield shots. *Look* took the nighttime exposure of Tobruk and the *Londonhovery Castle* evacuation, and Carl at *Town & Country* wanted his shot of the Angel of Tobruk, a plaster statue of the Virgin Mary left standing in a bombed-out church that the besieged soldiers believed brought them luck. None paid well, but *Esquire* was interested in his interview with an Australian sapper engineer who had explained to him how to rig land mines and booby traps to lure soldiers into touching them.

He wrote the piece from his notes. In his mind's eye, he could see the Australian field engineer driving him in a truck up a ridge behind Tobruk before the bombs had come, the wind blowing the dust into their faces like a sandblasting machine. The sapper said, "Troops are supposed to let the engineers look over the buildings in a captured enemy town before they go inside. Sometimes just a little jolt can bring down a building that looks all right. Then, of course, there's tricks to making the building come down. For example, you take up a board in the floor of a house. Say it's supported by three beams. You make the center beam a little higher so the board seesaws. Then a bloke steps on the middle of one and nothing happens. This is where the delayed action part comes in."

The sapper was steering the truck with one hand, gesturing with the other. "You have a battery and some contact points and a nice big charge. You attach contact points to the beam and to the short end of the floorboard. Two wires lead off to the battery and the charge. Maybe this board is over in the corner. It's a nice room and the staff of the General Headquarters is there. An officer sets foot on the wrong end of the board and bang . . . up goes the lot of 'em."

An MP had halted them and let them pass. "As I was saying," the sapper went on, "this delayed-action stuff is the best. Maybe there is a drainage pool or rain barrel in connection with a very lovely house, suitable for a nice GHQ full of officers. You run a mat wire into the water. Then you put a piece of metal two inches above the water and attach wire to that. Buried down in the basement, maybe, is a nice big charge of TNT and a couple of dry cell batteries. Maybe while the officers are messing a lot of water goes down the drain. The more water that goes down the drain, the quicker the house goes up."

The sapper had enjoyed telling about setting land mines and booby traps. He had found a useful niche for his special talents—practical jokes for death.

"Practical Jokes for Death" would be his title for the *Esquire* piece.

One night he woke suddenly from deep in his dreams again. A memory had come back to him that he could not sleep through. A mine had gone off, hurling a sapper into the air. His feet and shoes had been blown off at the ankles. For an endless moment or two, he stumbled on his bloody stubs and fell gracefully like a ballet dancer.

He could not find a way to put the footless sapper's dance into the piece. He knew they would cut it if he did. He struggled with himself and finally left it out. He kept "Practical Jokes for Death" as the title. "Curiosity is the best bait for booby traps," it began.

Esquire liked the piece, but they did not want to seem to disapprove of land mines. His title was too dark. They called it "Soldiers Learn the Hard Way."

He cashed the check, but the piece did not heal the wound in his soul. The footless sapper's graceful dance haunted him. He had not told the truth about what he had seen.

But he did make an appointment at a clinic and the physical therapy treatments worked. Cros's arm and shoulder muscles had become very strong from getting around on crutches. At the clinic he held on to two parallel bars and walked back and forth between them, at first bracing himself tightly and then needing them less and less, training what leg muscles he had left to hold him up. After a while he could get around without the brace, then replaced the crutches with a cane.

When he had gotten well enough, Cros got a desk job with NBC, monitoring the foreign news as it came in over the air and writing news scripts for broadcast. He also signed up with the Victory Speakers Bureau to give speeches. The Office of Civilian Defense was asking people who had been "in it" to explain the war's issues to citizens and arouse them to help. "America's participation in the war will be more effective if speakers help to keep the public well informed and in a fighting mood." He registered with the draft board, which classified him as 2-B, occupied in a war industry, so he would not get called up again. Now, if he was in a hurry, he would lope, hopping twice on his good leg, planting his bad one, and pushing himself along. He took up table-hopping in the nightclub circuit. Walter Winchell and Leonard Lyons began reporting bits of his conversation—one, how a British officer who'd just blown up an escarpment outside Tobruk had told him that reading Hemingway was much more interesting than war.

He spent a lot of time at the Overseas Press Club on West Forty-fifth Street, founded in 1939 by a group of foreign correspondents for members of the international press. Men—mostly men, for women were allowed only as guests, not as members—clustered around the tables, talked, smoked, and drank. There were great newsmen there. There was S. Miles Bouton, a *New York Times* correspondent who told him about his 1923 interview with an insignificant man named Adolf Hitler, whom he remembered mostly for his insistence upon referring to himself in the third person. Or across the table might have been Josef Israëls II, with his story of how, in the summer of 1935, a beautiful blond Danish aristocrat named Baroness von Blixen who ran a coffee plantation in Kenya, whom Cros knew as the writer Isak Dinesen, had been sent by the British Secret Service to assess the strength of the Ethiopian defenses against the oncoming Italian invasion. She warned the British that the Ethiopian defenses were strong, but unfortunately they had ignored her.

Or talk would spring up about Ben Robertson, the PM reporter Cros had known in Cairo and hoped to run into in New York City. Roosevelt had so respected Robertson that he directly intervened over government bureaucracy to get him to the front in North Africa. After that he had come back to New York briefly, but then accepted a job as chief of the *Herald Tribune*'s London bureau. On his way there in February of 1943, his clipper crashed during a fierce storm and he was killed, four months shy of his fortieth birthday.

Cros had a way with audiences. He could be urbane and jovial. He had been "in it." He spoke firsthand about the bravery he had seen, his hopes for spreading democracy abroad after the war, and the need to conserve rubber for the war effort by not wearing out car tires. One day he got a call from the Speakers Bureau. Would he address the British War Relief Society at the Plaza Hotel? He would. The tide of the North Africa campaign was turning. On November 1, 1942, the Allies had broken through the Axis lines at El Alamein. Eight days later, Dwight D. Eisenhower led the U.S. invasion of North Africa, the first real test of British-American cooperation. Sir Owen Dixon, Australian Ambassador to the United States, would speak alongside him at an event scheduled for February.

Cros followed events in North Africa. By the end of January, the British Eighth Army had taken Tripoli. By the middle of February, just as he was about to speak, the U.S. Army's Second Corps and Rommel's Panzers at Kasserine Pass were beginning the first full-fledged confrontation between the Americans and the Germans.

At the Plaza, Cros looked out over the faces of the men and women in the audience. Their mood was grave. The fighting at Kasserine Pass was not going well for the Allies. The Germans were advancing. Their equipment outmatched the United States'.

His voice lifted as he told them about the courage of the Rats of Tobruk who had held out for so long against such long odds. He described the wave of optimism around the tables at Shepheard's when it seemed American tanks might hold up against the Germans. He told about relieving the British Car Company and sleeping in their rigged-up dugouts; about the gallantry of Syd the tinsmith when the bombs began to drop. He spoke of his unit's dread that it might be cut off when Tobruk began to fall, the terror in Cairo when the order came for civilians to evacuate, and his despair when he learned that the Germans were breaking through the El Alamein line. And of his joy on hearing, after he had gotten home to New York, that the Allies had beaten the Axis back through it.

He did not talk about the faces in his dreams. He did not say what he thought about land mines. He told them that he knew victory would not be easy, but that it would come, and when it did, Britain and America would stand together and spread abroad the values they shared.

He followed the Battle of the Kasserine Pass as it came in over the wires. Three days later Rommel attacked again. U.S. morale dropped. The troops pulled back, leaving equipment on the field. The pass was completely open. Then, desperate resistance by isolated Allied groups managed to slow the German advance. When the battle began again, U.S. defenses were much stronger. An intense artillery barrage from Allied guns destroyed the Tenth Panzer and disrupted communications. Overextended and undersupplied, with not enough fuel for his tanks due to U.S. air attacks on German shipping from Malta, Rommel disengaged and withdrew east. By the end of February, the pass had been reoccupied.

In May, American and British forces linked and the Allies finally took all of Tunisia. Winston Churchill summed it up: "Now this is not the end, nor is it even the beginning of the end, but it is, perhaps, the end of the beginning."

Churchill was a stirring speaker and a great leader, but Cros knew that in Cairo the bodies were overfilling the ambulances, the hospital trains, the hospital ships. He kept on working at his war book. It would have two parts: first, the pictures with "word track" captions such as he had done for the Hudson River book, and then the diary, taken from his notebooks. Maybe there he could say what he really thought about war.

The calls for speeches kept coming, and he kept on giving them. At a war bonds rally in the New York offices of a large Hollywood movie company, he told about the fall of Tobruk and its recapture and the victory the Allies had gained in North Africa.

But as he looked out over the faces in the audience, he wanted to tell them about the dispatch rider who had been driven mad by war. About the bomb neurosis case who kept getting out of bed and walking like a monkey, repeating over and over that they were looking for him. The man who took off his army sneakers, put them back on, took them off, all the time saying that they wanted to shoot him for spilling a glass of water.

He wanted to tell them what a terrible waste it all was. He wanted to ask them a very simple question. "How can a war be just when it's the little people who get the worst of it?"

But he did tell them about his friend Otto, the German prisoner of war in the ambulance going away from Tobruk. With his bleeding arm, the wounded Otto had taken a picture of his fiancée out of his breast pocket, sighing the same sigh of all the soldiers Cros had ever talked with. When he learned that his mother might be dead in the ruins of Cologne, he felt the same pain an American GI would have felt upon learning his mother might be dead in the ruins of Des Moines. Men were men, all over the world.

As he was about to leave, one of the executives called him aside. "That stuff about prisoners of war . . . it's interesting and true . . . I know, I was in the last war and we know what it's like. But you mustn't tell anybody."

"Oh?"

"You've got to create mass hate. You've got to tell the people that these German soldiers are monsters and that you despise them, and they must despise them and buy war bonds so as to help kill them."

Cros left without shaking the man's hand.

When spring came, Cros drove out to Connecticut and spent long stretches of time at his farm. He swam in the cool lake he had dreamt of in the desert and ate simple food by kerosene lamplight. He slept deeply, surrounded by forests and fields, enclosed by four walls built out of horsehair plaster by hardscrabble sheep farmers scratching a living from the thin Connecticut soil. War had shown him the shallowness of his routine, self-centered life and how little possessions really meant. He felt closer to the simple Yankee ways of his neighbors, to the gentle quiet ways of his friends at the Quaker meeting nearby, than he did to the world of his youth as a rich man's son.

More than anywhere else, this farm was where he wanted to be. He had yearned for it lying on his back on the hospital train out of Cairo, not knowing if he would ever be able to walk again, not really even knowing if he would live to see it. But he was here.

As Africa fell to the Allies and the field of war moved away to Europe, Cros thought about what would happen after the fighting ended. Victory would give the Allies an opportunity to spread their conceptions of freedom and respect for the dignity of man to the world. By the end of summer, he had finished his war book. He made prints of his best photographs, mounted them on heavy paper, and wrote captions for them. He told the stories of suffering he had not been able to tell in his speeches. As he drove back into the city with the manuscript and the prints, he wondered if the book he had written was right for the mood of the country he had come back to. The publicity flyer had seemed to want to make the book out as something other than what it was. On it was a picture of him in a tin helmet, pointing a camera. "Ace photo reporter Cros Bowen's battlefront dispatches from the scorching sands of Libya," read the blurb. But the book he had written was about seeing the horrors of war and yearning for peace.

The responses were gentle and polite, but they all said the same thing—no.

That fall, he loaded his photographs and the typed copies of the book into his old Ford and drove back out to Connecticut. He put them in the barn and drove back into the city.

In those struggling New York years right after Tobruk, Cros very much needed a wise mentor, and he found one. The war news in the fall of 1943 was mixed. The Germans had occupied Rome and put Mussolini back in power. But by October the Allies had entered Naples. Victory was not certain. Democracy was at stake. Before the war, Hastings House had shown interest in *Democracy in Action*, a book of photographs he would shoot showing how a democracy functions. He had begun lining up Eleanor Roosevelt, Felix Frankfurter, and Wendell Willkie to write the text. Hastings House was still interested in the democracy book, so he went to Washington to interview Felix Frankfurter.

Frankfurter was a short, spry man known for his brisk style, an Austrian Jew in a childless marriage to a Yankee woman named Marion whom he adored. He had been brought onto the Supreme Court by Roosevelt. Before that he had taught law at Harvard, and together he and Marion had become an institution in Cambridge, Massachusetts, opening their home for weekly salons. Frankfurter lavished brilliance, charm, and affection on a generation of bright, ambitious young men he inspired to make their careers in government implementing the New Deal. They were called his Hot Dogs.

Instantly, Cros liked Frankfurter. Notebook and pencil in hand, across from him in his chambers, he asked him about the role of the press in a democracy. Public discourse on issues is essential to informing citizens, and informed citizens are essential to a democracy. But would the public listen? "Mastery of a subject, sincerity, stout-hearted humanity: the public always responds to these qualities. If it were not true, there would be no basis for the democratic view," Frankfurter would write to him, and he would post the Justice's words by his typewriter.

But how could he get pictures for the democracy book? He was getting around well now, but he still couldn't do the hard physical work of climbing up riggings, tromping for hours carrying his cameras, the kind of work it took to get really good shots.

If he couldn't do it, maybe he could find pictures by other photographers that would tell the same story. He found them, and he wrote, "We have noticed a series of patriotic pictures which have run in *Fortune* and think them excellent. I am wondering if it would be possible to reprint some of these pictures in the book, *Democracy in Action*."

Wendell Willkie would pull out of the project and eventually Cros would drop it, but he again interviewed Felix Frankfurter. The talk turned to the Associated Press suit that had been moving through the courts. In 1942 the antitrust division of the U.S. Department of Justice had filed suit against the AP, charging that the news-gathering cooperative was a monopoly whose membership regulations made the establishment of competing newspapers almost impossible. A nonmember paper could not use the news the AP produced. To cover the story it would have to send its own reporter, putting it at a cost disadvantage.

The interests of the pro-FDR *PM*, the newspaper Cros had admired since its inception, were at stake in the suit. Col. Robert McCormick of Chicago was the owner of an AP member paper, the *Chicago Tribune*. To him, "freedom of the press" meant the freedom of newspaper owners to operate however they chose. He was also against interventionism, in favor of Axis governments, and anti–New Deal.

Marshall Field, McCormick's enemy on many fronts, had funded *PM* in New York, and then in 1941, on McCormick's home turf, started the pro-Roosevelt interventionist *Chicago Sun*. Both of Field's papers had been denied AP membership. Such restrictions on the creation of new publications, as Frankfurter saw it, limited the availability of information from a wide variety of resources necessary for full discussion of public concerns.

McCormick did not consider Field a "legitimate newspaperman" because his great wealth made him able to fund a paper that did not accept advertising, and, even worse, he could survive financial losses while establishing a paper that would compete with his own *Chicago Tribune*. He was "a rich young man trying to kick the entire industry around with his wealth" and had started his paper solely to advance a "political faction," the FDR administration.

Marshall Field, on the other hand, saw McCormick as a member of a "privileged class with tremendous power and exclusiveness" that connived to corrupt and distort freedom of the press.

In McCormick's view, the First Amendment set an absolute bar against government interference in any aspect of newspaper operations, including business activities. He viewed the suit against the AP as the result of New Deal pressures "aided by socialistic, communistic, and paler pinks, intellectuals, radicals, lecturers, and columnists."

Ralph Ingersoll, PM's creator, thought the First Amendment did not bar government intervention to ensure public enlightenment if newspaper leaders did not respond to the needs of the American society. One of the most respected concepts in American justice, Ingersoll believed, was the "free marketplace of ideas" and the availability of a diversity of opinion to all. Artificial and unnecessary restraints on news sources could not be tolerated.

Frankfurter was elated. The AP case had gone before a three-judge expediting court consisting of Judge Billings Learned Hand, Judge Augustus Hand, and Judge Thomas Swan. Judge Learned Hand, writing for the majority, had noted that the press "serves one of the most vital of all general interests, the dissemination of news from as many different sources, and with as many different facets and colors as is possible.... Right conclusions are more likely to be gathered out of a multitude of tongues, than through any kind of authoritative selection. It is only by crosslights from varying directions that full illumination can be secured." The expediting court ruled against the AP.

Journalists were crucial, Frankfurter told Cros. Their work was essential to a democracy.

Frankfurter uplifted and soothed Cros, but he also challenged him and gave him a mission. Cros would write to him, "Yours is the most civilized mind it has been within my experience to have known . . . and the most interesting."

Cros was still keeping a close eye on PM. If a PM reporter was at a table at the Overseas Press Club with a group of other reporters, Cros would head for that table. PM reporters were politically liberal, idealistic, professional, and hardworking. The great I. F. Stone wrote for PM, carrying on in the tradition of the courageous investigative truth tellers of the Progressive era. To stay there meant you were the best in the business. And PM reporters seemed to be having fun.

Cros knew it was risky. The Newspaper Guild was fighting management at every turn. The paper wasn't making money. The masthead was filled, so an opening would have to come up. But he wanted to work at PM, so he waited, and kept in touch with Bill McCleary, who might need him for the Sunday Section.

On New Year's Eve in 1943 throngs gathered. The mood was joyful. The war was edging toward victory. In the Village, sit-down dinner parties were the new rage, tables boasting menus unheard of in Britain. Cocktail parties, a more long-standing rage, featured the clatter of ice in a shaker, chilled gin poured out into martini glasses and topped with a green olive stuffed with a strip of pimento on a toothpick. On the table, a large ham, a brick of cheese, and a long loaf of French bread. Women looked their best. Men wore their uniforms.

Cros dropped in at the Carmers'. Bill McCleary would be there, and he'd make sure McCleary knew he was still interested in PM and was well enough to do the job. With some PM men like his friend Charles Norman away in the service but still on the masthead, and the paper committed to giving returning servicemen their jobs back, a class of staffers called "war replacements" had come into being. Cros hoped he could get hired as one.

Cros especially wanted to work with McCleary. He was known as a great "originator," an editor who came up with story ideas and sent reporters out to research them. One of the reasons why he was so great was that he had a feeling for what the ordinary man or woman would want to know—how to get or do a better job, how to get along better with the boss, how to raise and educate children, how to run the household, how to stay healthy.

So when an event that affected the whole city, such as a

strike, happened, McCleary would have his staff get out the phone book and call all the Smiths on Staten Island for their opinion. The Staten Island Smiths stories were often just very funny, because people said such funny things, but they were also serious and worthwhile without being highbrow.

The Carmer circle knew McCleary was dismayed that too many ordinary readers identified PM as a Communist paper. As he saw it, it was one thing to stand up for freedom of speech and another to allow the paper to be perceived as Communist dominated. Ingersoll had refused to do anything that could be perceived as anti-Communist, but he had brought a sense of mission to the paper. Now, with Ingersoll drafted and serving in the army, some of the staff felt restive about hanging on when the paper hadn't gotten the circulation it needed to be self-sustaining. But still, it was a paper that was too good to be true.

Cros said good-bye to Carl and Betty, shook hands with McCleary, and left. Outside, a salty breeze mixed with wood smoke from Village chimneys. A clump of cheerful soldiers crossed the street toward him. A sauntering policeman saluted as they passed. Inside the warm rooms of the restaurants, men and women in each other's thrall leaned forward and back, tilting their heads in amusement, shaking them in laughter. Arms linked through their heavy coats, they squeezed out through doorways and glided as one down the crowded side-walks. Cros's mind wandered back to the day he'd left for the Middle East. He'd been glad to be single then. But now he was lonely. He thought back to summer weekend house parties at Hidden Hollow before the war. Elizabeth was married now. Most of the women he had known back then were married. He wanted to find a wife and have children.

Inside the crowded apartment, voices rose and fell in a chorus. I see Cros making his way to the center of the room. An older woman, polished and suave, took a cigarette out of a case and turned toward him. He steadied his drink, cigarette, and napkin in one hand, flicked his lighter with the other, and held it toward her.

She smiled at him. He looked past her. Standing in one corner of the room, her shoulder turned away, was a young woman with long, cascading brown hair.

He put his lighter back in his pocket, nodded, and moved toward her.

The woman turned toward him. She had Bette Davis eyes and a discontented look on her face.

"You look submerged," he said.

Marjory Hill was.

She was twenty-one, just out of college. She was angry with her fiancé, a Williams man she had been engaged to who wanted to wait to get married until after he came back from the war because his mother had told him they should. She was angry with her father, a civil engineer with the firm of Ford, Bacon & Davis, and in her view a capitalist pawn, for having built TNT plants for the government. As her father saw it, he had not paid for her fancy women's college instruction in the ideas of Karl Marx in Vernon Venable's course on political philosophy for her to throw it all back at him. When she told him she wanted to become a philosophy professor, he told her he had no intention of supporting the education of a daughter who seemed only to be learning to criticize his politics. He would not pay for graduate school in philosophy. Her hopes for a teaching career vanished. She was working as a secretary, "stuffing envelopes for American Tobacco."

In his desert uniform, Cros was handsome. He was also weak from the war and the long trip home, and needy. He was older than she, and worldly. His eyes were brown and liquid.

They talked about his war, of course. They talked about politics. She was impressed that he knew as much about communism as she did. He listened quietly to her opinions, too. He wasn't like her father, who dismissed them without knowing anything about them at all.

It was the way he listened to her that made Marjory feel Cros knew her very well. Better than anyone else in the world, in fact. He was everything her father was not—a man with a wild imagination and a joyous sense of possibilities, charming and outgoing, a political liberal. Marx did not scare him. He was full of idealism. He made her feel alive.

To Cros, Marjory was young, beautiful, and smart. He was amused by her young, fresh, fiery radicalism, but he was captivated, too. That she had gone to Vassar gave her a special place in his heart. While doing the research for his Hudson River book, he and Carl Carmer had spent many happy hours there with Nick Strelsky, Ukrainian nobleman and ex-captain in the Russian Imperial Army who had fought in the White Army against the Reds in Sevastopol, escaped to Constantinople in 1920, and been brought to Vassar as a "Distinguished Displaced Scholar." He'd gone on to found the Russian Department, but Cros remembered him most gratefully for having introduced him to several attractive Vassar undergraduates, all opinionated and outspoken, one of whom, the beautiful Theodora Finney, had broken his heart. Marjory was just like them, opinionated and outspoken.

She admired him and could tell he wanted to be a father. They went back to 144 West Twelfth Street together.

The wedding took place on March 11, 1944, in Marjory's hometown of Larchmont, New York, in a Catholic side chapel, with Marjory quietly pregnant. Her sisters were bridesmaids. Louise was also there, having come from Los Angeles, where she'd gone to be near Billy's new wife, Mary, while he was in the Pacific war. Billy had prepared Louise for the news of my incipient arrival. Cros had sent it to her via him, to put it to her as he would. Billy had written back, "Mother was shaken by the news, but she said she had wondered if that was the case. She does not think you can support a family, but I know she will be a good grandmother."

Marjory, who would have chosen the consolations of philosophy over religion any day, did not convert to Catholicism, as Croswell has asked her to do. But after the wedding, she wrote effusively to Louise, thanking her for coming, adding that she'd forgotten her hat. Should she send it to her or would she be back for it soon?

Marjory had hoped her family might like Cros, but she suspected they might not, and if they didn't, she was prepared to defy them. Mira Hill was, indeed, slow to warm to Cros. "The Look," Cros called it, and he would come to know it well. His mother-in-law's raised eyebrows, the set of her jaw, and her pointed stare to him meant she took a very dim view of the whole situation: of the writing trade in general, of Cros Bowen in particular. He had no financial prospects. It didn't matter that he had gone to Choate and Yale and was a gentleman, because it was on new money, and even worse, most of it had disappeared in the Crash. On both sides, the Hills were a family with a somber New England pedigree Skull and Bones would have found acceptable. Mira Hill did not quite trust this flamboyant, happy-go-lucky Irishman.

Edgar Hill was cool toward his new son-in-law. He was a man's man who expected a traditional courtship and a chaste request for his daughter's hand. Instead, Marjory had told him she was in love and proud of it and would get married in due time. That did not make Edgar Hill happy.

Cros, though, was very happy. What made him happy was Marjory's courage. Her courage gave him courage. True, Louise's admonition that he could not earn enough money to support a family had cast a pall over him. But now, home from the war, wanting to be a family man and then suddenly becoming one, it was all fading away in the face of the blunt fact of the new life he and Marjory had created.

I was just sprouting eyebrows and fingernails and closing in on only eight inches long, so it could be said I was there as they stood together and said their vows, quite unaware of the storm my father was about to create. In June of 1944 the invasion of Europe began on the beaches of Normandy. The German army was in retreat. In August the French resistance rose up and the Americans marched into Paris, Charles de Gaulle leading them. But the NBC job had begun making him uneasy. The higher-ups wanted him to treat a known U.S. propaganda shortwave radio station as a legitimate news source. He would have to quit on principle. Marjory would probably love him even more for it. Her parents would be aghast. In July Cros quit NBC. He quickly got in touch with Walter Winchell, whose syndicated column announced to the whole country that "Croswell Bowen (he served in the Libya campaign) was injured at Tobruk. He has quit as foreign news monitor at NBC after protesting the use (by the network) of an Allied psychological warfare shortwave radio station as a news source."

He'd acted according to his principles, but now he was a family man who no longer had a job.

His hopes were on *PM*.

Then, on September 21, bending over the oven at West Twelfth Street, Marjory felt the first labor pains. It was a short ride from West Twelfth to Second Avenue and Eighteenth Street, and Cros struggled to pay the cab and pull together the doctor's fee. I came into this world on a rather high note, an eight-pound pudding of soft girl flesh delivered at the New York Lying-In Hospital in the early morning of the day the Allies liberated Boulogne.

The Bowen family went back to West Twelfth Street. A born glutton, I sucked my mother dry until she resorted to cow's milk. Cros mastered the changing of diapers. This Bowen baby, he boasted, smelled like Chanel No. 5. He would send for the rare oil of the Himalayan Xerxes for her toilette. "Marjory was saying the other night that she wished that just with us and this first baby these last weeks would go on and on and on," he wrote to Billy. "It has been good and brought me stillness and deep happiness. I am telling you all this because you have seen me troubled so much in my life and it has upset you, I know."

Marjory was stalwart. If it was a difficult delivery, she didn't speak of it, well schooled in "Never apologize, never explain, never complain." She wrote to Louise that the delivery had been easy, anesthesia had come at the very last, and Cros had hired a nurse so she was swaddled in comfort. "Dearest Mother," she wrote again to Louise, "I'll say once and for all time that we both are deeply sorry for any grief or disappointment we may have caused you, and know that we more than deserve any amount of reproach. And yet, I'm so tremendously thankful to have Cros's child that I cannot sincerely say that I regret anything that has happened, except the fact that one cannot act in this world without affecting those who love you and hope for you. With fondest love, Marjory."

Just as Billy had predicted, Louise returned east to help with the baby. She took a room nearby at the Holley Hotel, overlooking Washington Square Park. She lived on the monthly income from her late husband's insurance policy. The check from Goodbody and Co. was steady, and she usually had a bit left over. She took strolls pushing a baby carriage through Washington Square Park so that Marjory could have time to herself.

A family man needed a job, but for Cros it couldn't be just any job. He wanted one he could believe in. So he was elated when *PM* asked for an interview.

"Why do you want to work here?"

Cros quoted Felix Frankfurter. "Fertile endeavor in society means an unremitting process toward concentration on the essentials by which the great body of people of goodwill can be united." *PM* published journalism that helped people concentrate on the essentials. His work could contribute to that.

What were his goals as a writer? Again, he quoted Frankfurter's words, the ones he'd pasted on his typewriter: "Mastery of a subject, sincerity, stout-hearted humanity: the public always responds to these qualities. If it were not true, there would be no basis for the democratic view."

Was he a Communist?

No.

Was he a member of the Newspaper Guild?

Yes.

PM hired him. Cros exulted. This job would bring out his best. Only two and a half years ago he had lain among the sick and dying on a hospital train out of Cairo to Suez, not knowing if he would ever walk again. Now Marjory and he were happy together and they had a baby. And he worked for a paper he believed in. He soon was writing to Louise in Dallas, "At the moment I am keeping the wolf from the door by doing feature stories for PM. I am okay." Later, he wrote to Billy, "I want to tell you how very happy I am these days. I know you want to believe this and it is very true. My work is getting recognition and acclaim at PM. The piece I did in last Sunday's PM called 'A Bad Night at GOP Hq.' seems to be more and more admired."

At West Twelfth Street Marjory was determined to live frugally and make peace with her new life. She knew Cros was full of wild enthusiasms and fervent opinions. He was an idealist and a crusader. He would disappear for long streaks of prodigious work and leave her to herself, but she could be happy alone, wandering the city, reading and thinking. His world had important people in it. He lived in a hubbub of activity. Hers was all inside her head, but that only made her love the world of people he brought home with him more. She still wanted an academic career, but for now she was putting that aside. If she suspected Cros would not be the kind of husband who would provide a large income, she didn't care. It was not all she would ever want, but she could live frugally, and she gave herself to it.

If Louise worried about Cros losing his job, Marjory would smile and say, "We'll just have another baby."

And Louise would say, "Oh, horrors."

Cros was on top of the world. He was a lucky man.

PM's offices were a three-story industrial warehouse building on Duane Street in Lower Manhattan. From the street floor, a staircase led up to a landing. At the top of the landing to the left was McCleary's Sunday Section newsroom. Things there were quieter than to the right, the newsroom of the daily section, where people yelled and screamed over the clatter of typewriters. Both newsrooms were large open spaces, floor-to-ceiling windows all around, desks where the staff worked, and filing cabinets pushed into rows. Editors had outside offices with windows. Black upright typewriters, black telephones, and stacks of papers crammed every flat surface. At the end of the Sunday Section side was a morgue—a library with facts on well-known people, ready to be used for obituaries. The GI Bill was giving veterans who wouldn't otherwise have made it a chance. Many on the staff were women, doing jobs they knew they could not have gotten in peacetime. They all felt inspired to do their best work.

In the basement was the darkroom. Photographers gathered around the developing baths. Down there was the paper's own printing press. Before the recent move from Brooklyn, the paper had rented a press from the *Brooklyn Daily Eagle*. "The print job back then was always better when the foreman wasn't there," one of the photographers told Cros, "so we bought our own press." Up on the third floor was the engraving room, where photographers took their negatives to have the plates made that the printers would lock into the presses.

PM encouraged reporters to originate story ideas and run them by the editors. Photographers got their assignments from photo desks or from John P. Lewis, the editor of the whole paper. If it had "MUST" written on it, the photographer got what the editor wanted. If it didn't, he was free to be creative. Traditional photographers used to doing only what they were told were uncomfortable with the system.

Cros's first assignment was to do a story and a picture on *Bloomer Girl*, the new huge hit on Broadway. It was a *PM* kind of musical, a lighthearted take on liberal themes—the emancipation of women and slaves—in an 1861 setting. Bill McCleary, with his theater contacts, would have known that Joan McCracken, the young comic lead, had just gotten word that her brother had died in the service. She was a vivid presence, singing "T'morra T'morra" in the musical, but could she hold up her comic role in the face of her grief? It had the makings of a "feel-good" story. McCleary as editor of *PM*'s Sunday Section, under Ralph Ingersoll, promoted the jaunty *New Yorker* reporter-at-large style.

Cros brought his camera. Watching the young actress from the audience as she sang, Cros observed a flicker of pain cross her face. He went back with her to the small apartment she shared with her mother and talked with them both. Mrs. McCracken served Joan Ovaltine and Cros a beer. By the time they'd talked for a while, he knew he could make the sturdy young trouper into everyone on the home front who had lost a loved one and moved forward with courage.

He developed the photograph he'd snapped of her down in the darkroom, drinking up the photographers' talk about the way things had been in the old days. It was the first story he'd put on McCleary's desk, and he was proud of it. It appeared in *PM* as "The Comedienne Gets a Telegram."

Later, Cros wrote again to Frankfurter, "I am a full-time staff member at *PM* taking my own pictures. You summed up what a writer should aim for and I quoted the sentence when I was discussing going to work down here as a writer-photographer. My stuff has pleased them very much and they've run it at length. Am sending along some clips so you can glance at them—if you have time—to see whether you are glad or sorry you exerted this influence."

He closed, "I hope you'll have time to spare a minute or two. I'd like to tell you in person something about the new journalism I'm trying to project down here. Of one thing I'm very certain and believe in very much—the nonadvertising newspaper."

Around New York, a "war's almost over" feeling was beginning to grow. The news reports were good. The Allies were closing in on Germany from both east and west. Bill McCleary sent Cros off to do a byline story with an upbeat slant to it. Lauren Bacall, who had volunteered to dance with GIs while waiting to make her name on Broadway, and Humphrey Bogart, the man who had played chess with GIs by mail, were an item. Or was it press agent hype? Bogie and Bacall were staying at an uptown hotel. Cros arranged an interview.

When he arrived at the hotel, he traded jibes with the three publicity agents Warner Brothers had assigned to the two stars. Warner Brothers, they told him, had a policy that any publicity man who got his name in the paper would get fired. Cros promised he would name them only as Mr. Alpha, Mr. Omega, and Mr. Trench Coat.

"Does Warner's have anything to do with publicizing the romance between Bogart and Bacall?" he asked Mr. Alpha, holding out the copy of an Earl Wilson column he'd brought along in which Bogart announced he was in love with Miss Bacall and was leaving his third wife for her.

Mr. Alpha appeared greatly surprised. Then amusement came into his eyes and the corners of his mouth for just a flash; then his expression went blank. "What do you mean?"

Cros held out the Earl Wilson column again.

"Oh, that!" Mr. Alpha exclaimed. "That's not our responsibility."

1. Bowen family portrait: Bowen, sons Cros and Billy, and Louise in front of fireplace at Westmoreland, c. 1922.

2. Louise Connor Bowen, c. 1928, probably as chaperone on Paris trip.

3. (*Opposite top*) Cros during Sorbonne year, Paris, 1928. Oil on canvas.

4. (*Opposite bottom*) Cros, self-portrait, c. 1936.

5. (*Above*) Cros on the Hudson River shooting pictures from a Chris-Craft for his book, *Great River of the Mountains: The Hudson*, 1939.

6. Cros in American Field Service uniform, 1941.

7. Publicity material for *Back from Tobruk*, c. 1942. Croswell Bowen Papers. Yale Collection of American Literature, Beinecke Rare Book & Manuscript Library.

8. Marjory Luce Hill, Vassar College yearbook photograph, 1942.

9. Cros in *PM* news-room, c. 1946.

10. (*Opposite top*) Betsy Bowen, girl
reporter, by Cros, 144 West Twelfth Street,
c. 1948.

11. (*Opposite bottom*) Cros pouring
from sideboard, Star House, Sherman,
Connecticut, c. 1948.

12. (*Above*) Bowens (Cros, Marjory,
Lucey, Betsy) at Yale class of '29 twentieth
reunion, 1949.

13. (*Opposite*) Betsy, Peter, and Lucey, Christmas in Irvington, New York, 1952.

14. (*Above*) Betsy and Lucey, with Marjory in car, c. 1954.

15. (*Right*) Cros as hard-bitten crime reporter, author photo for *They Went Wrong*, 1954.

16. (*Opposite top*) Marjory, Irvington, c. 1954.

17. (*Opposite bottom*) Cros reading to Betsy
and Lucey, c. 1954.

18. (*Above*) Eleanor Roosevelt and Marjory at
NYC function, c. 1958.

19. (*Opposite top*) Cros as distinguished
author, c. 1959.

20. (*Opposite bottom*) Molly playing with
swing at Hidden Hollow, c. 1959.

21. (*Above*) Betsy and Cros on steps of 6
East Seventy-sixth Street, NYC, 1965.

22. Marjory at Chappaqua, c. 1968.

Then Mr. Trench Coat ushered Cros into Bogart's suite. Bogart greeted him cordially, seated him in the most comfortable chair in the room, answered the phone, mixed a scotch highball, and sat down beside him.

"How will teenage kids be affected by the publicity you are getting?" Cros asked.

Bogie bolted up, walked over to the mantelpiece where there were two large unframed pictures of Bacall, paused to glance at them, then sat himself down in front of the fireplace.

"What's wrong with her being a friend of mine?" Bogie asked, leaning over toward Cros. "Listen, I got a good notion. . . ."

A chance to play straight man to Humphrey Bogart might never come again. Cros put on a sardonic smile and lumbered over to face Bogie eye to eye. "Are you going to bump me off?"

"Frankly," Bogie said, curling his lip, "I doubt if you'll ever get out of this room alive."

Then Bacall came into the room—white silk blouse and blue woolen slacks—and arranged herself on a chair. The two toughs sat down.

"Be careful of this guy, Betty," Bogie called out, flicking his hand in Cros's direction. "He's from *PM* and a college man."

In February of 1945 at Yalta, the Big Three, Roosevelt, Churchill, and Stalin, met to plan the postwar reconstruction of Europe. Roosevelt secured Stalin's commitment that Russia would participate in the UN. However, like many newsmen, Cros had had a feeling that the old and tired president, speaking on his return from a seated position, acknowledging for the first time ever the ten pounds of steel he carried on his legs, might not have long to live. Roosevelt went to Warm Springs, Georgia, to rest up before attending the UN's founding conference in San Francisco. At Warm Springs, on April 12, 1945, he died of a cerebral aneurysm.

FDR's death stunned the *PM* newsroom. It was a blow to the nation, to liberalism, and to Cros. He had admired the man since childhood. The one third of his life during which Roosevelt had been president were years in which he had learned to be a writer and a political reporter. Roosevelt had inspired his belief in the common man. He had inspired him personally in his struggle to overcome polio and go on to do work he believed in. It was a very personal tragedy.

It would also be the biggest story Cros had yet covered for *PM*. He had started out as a writer for the Local News section with no byline. Then he was doing bylined feature stories. Now he was a full-time staff reporter writing about the funeral of the president.

But first, McCleary sent Cros to the Little Red Schoolhouse to report on how the children were taking news of the president's death.

"How did you hear the news?"

"I was trying to listen to Tom Mix adventures on the radio."

"Me, too," another said.

"Me, too."

"I thought, 'Gee, we're gonna lose the war.'"

"Nah!"

"Shhh."

"Because he was a good president during the war."

"My mother came back with some groceries. She said, 'Your president is dead. He was a dear friend to the colored people.' Tears were in her eyes."

In retrospect, Yalta would be seen as having framed an uneasy peace. Stalin wanted Russian influence to extend past Russian borders into Eastern Europe, to form a buffer to protect it against Germany. He wanted the Allies to divide Poland, Finland, Romania, Germany, and the Balkans and give over the eastern parts to the Soviets. Churchill did not believe Stalin's promise that he would allow those territories the right to national self-determination and feared that the

United States would return to its prewar isolationism, abandoning Europe to Soviet domination. Roosevelt, however, gave Stalin the benefit of the doubt, perhaps trusting that if he conceded him what he wanted, he would respond like a gentleman, not try to annex anything. He ordered Eisenhower to allow the Soviets to reach Berlin first. Stalin, however, saw nothing stopping the Soviets from imposing Communism in Eastern Europe. Another world conflict was shaping up. In the newly forming United Nations lodged the hope for a world that would remain at peace.

Would Truman carry out the course FDR had set? Left liberals at PM, who had supported Wallace's belief in coexistence with Russia over Truman, thought Truman ill-equipped for the job and far less inspired by the same hopes. But back in the office, Cros read that Truman's first act as president had been to inform the press that the San Francisco UN founding conference would go forward in twelve days as scheduled. He was heartened.

The morning following Roosevelt's death, a Saturday, Cros took an early train out of Grand Central, traveling the same tracks that the president's funeral train would pass over later. He stopped at the Hyde Park gate to discuss his credentials with the sentry and then went a mile and a half farther into the town. He spent the rest of the day talking with people there who'd known FDR.

He woke up early on Sunday and took a cab to the local St. James's Church, where he talked with the sexton who had helped to dig the president's grave the morning before. Then he went to the burial site and stationed himself on the front lawn in a spot where the sun pierced through the morning cold. When he caught sight of a horse-drawn caisson carrying the flag-draped coffin up the back road to Hyde Park, he slipped back through the hedge surrounding the garden where the dignitaries had assembled.

The ceremony began. He watched the coffin being lowered into the grave. He heard the funeral service spoken. The bugler sounded "Taps." Mrs. Roosevelt straightened. She handed the flag that had wrapped the coffin to her son Elliott, embraced her other family members, and walked out of the gate of the garden.

It was 10:49 a.m. and still cold. Cros decided to stay. The soldiers standing at attention limbered their legs, squatting and kicking. Troops and civilians both breathed on their hands to warm them. Cameramen began packing their telescopic-lens cameras. Justice Douglas stood on tiptoe as if he were searching out a certain person. Dignitaries helped their wives adjust their coats and scarves. Justice Frankfurter turned to his wife and reminded her to speak to someone he had recognized. Secretary of War Stimson pulled his old felt hat squarely on his head and threw his shoulders back. A sailor next to Cros passed around a bag of peanuts.

Cros slipped back through the hedge and watched President and Mrs. Truman leave in a limousine, and then he went back into the garden. Most of the crowd had gone. He stood beside two men who seemed to be trying to find something in among the flowers heaped nearby.

"I hope they understand about the Cuban earth," one said.

Cros asked what that meant. The two men said they were from an airline and had flown a box of earth from Cuba sent by the Cuban, Dominican, and Haitian governments as a goodwill gesture to be buried in the grave.

Cros suggested they speak to Will Plog, the gardener, whom he knew from a previous visit to Hyde Park. Among the flowers, Plog found the box of Cuban earth and emptied it into the grave.

"You look tired and hungry," said white-haired Anna McGowan, one of the maids from the house. "Would you like to come into the house and have something to eat?"

"I would be very happy to, if it's proper."

"I asked you, didn't I?"

The kitchen was long and rectangular, with a big coal stove at the end and a long metal-covered table in the center flanked by cupboards. Anna seated Cros, set a pitcher of cream beside him, poured him a cup of coffee, and gave him two big pieces of angel food cake with lemon filling.

It was almost five p.m. Cros thanked Anna and the others for their hospitality and went out to the front lawn. He took one last look at the grave, asked one last question of the sentry who, entirely alone, would guard it all night, and left.

PM was full-throated in its coverage of FDR's death. Looking at a *PM* piece on how other papers had handled it, Cros read that William Randolph Hearst had immediately wired all his editors cautioning them not to attack or criticize FDR. "As a result, the Hearst papers carried an eloquent, ungrudging tribute to the man they had fought all along the line," *PM* said. Both the *New York Journal-American* and the *New York Mirror* had been against FDR, but as the *PM* piece noted, "We didn't run across a sour note anywhere in their pages."

However, while the whole country had elected Roosevelt four times and now mourned him deeply, the majority of its newspapers still spoke against him. Joseph Patterson's *New York Daily News* and Eleanor Patterson's *Washington Times-Herald* made no comment but ran a column of excerpts from speeches, giving the impression that Roosevelt had deliberately led the country into a war he had promised to avoid. The Sunday *New York Times*, in contrast, printed a page of quotations that were "fairly and thoughtfully selected."

Some spoke as if a providential act had reversed the results of last November's elections. The *New York Herald Tribune* wrote with ill-concealed contempt that "[w]ithin a few hours of the death of Mr. Roosevelt, some of his most devoted disciples in the 'inner circle' of the New Deal began to scurry for cover. By today they seemed to be in full flight." The *Daily News* said, "There is little in Truman's record to bolster the hope of some financiers that there will be a sharp or substantial reversal in New Deal domestic policies."

Roy A. Roberts, managing editor of the *Kansas City Star* and a Republican, wrote in support of Truman: "Harry Truman was as far apart from Roosevelt as Hyde Park is from Independence, Missouri. Truman has humility, loyalty, common sense, deep patriotism, abiding faith in his country and its democratic system." He was not, like Roosevelt, a "patrician brother of Churchill, working the liberal side of the street."

PM's eulogy was heartfelt. "No other president in our history, neither Washington nor Lincoln nor Wilson, carried a heavier load of care and responsibility. None acquitted himself more nobly than did Mr. Roosevelt. We owe him so much. He brought our country out of the worst depression in its history. In an age of dictatorship, he demonstrated that free government and democratic processes could cope with the sharpest of crises. He was leading us to victory in the greatest war of our history when he was taken from us."

In the days that followed, the mood in the *PM* newsroom was grim. The staff felt themselves going on alone, without their leader. They comforted each other. Cros wrote to Frankfurter, alerting him to his piece on the burial and reminding him of how much he admired him.

Frankfurter wrote back: "Of course you warm my heart by what you say about our meetings, and it is hard to believe that we have had only two talks in our lives. But such things are not measured by numbers. I read your piece on the funeral in *PM*, even before you called my attention to it. I think FDR would have been delighted by your effort to make even a funeral a part of life. Wasn't it an extremely gracious occasion—a most fitting leave-taking of that vivid and zestful personality. Come down here soon again, and it will be a pleasure to see you."

The president who had led the country through the war was not alive to see its last days. A string of German surrenders across Europe, the execution of Mussolini, and the suicide of Hitler culminated on May 7, 1945, in the unconditional surrender of the entire German force.

Cros went out on assignment to West Forty-ninth Street to interview for a piece that would be titled "How West Forty-ninth Street Took the Victory News." The idea was to find out how New Yorkers along one street—West Forty-ninth, which ran through a slice of New York from East Side tenements to Rockefeller Center on the west—were reacting to the victory. Cros reported, "The blocks on West Forty-ninth Street west to Tenth Avenue looked about as usual. Just across Eleventh Avenue though, rows of tenements began. American flags dotted the fronts of them." Cros counted twelve flags. By mid-afternoon he counted twenty-seven. Then, on the next day, Tuesday, May 8, America celebrated Victory in Europe Day. Cros found the block almost deserted, but seven more flags had been added to the display. A little girl of about four was playing in front of the houses. Cros asked her if she knew it was V-E Day. She wiped her nose on her sleeve, and then said disdainfully, "That was yesterday."

"How come all the whistles blew this morning?" Cros asked.

The girl looked as though she thought he was very stupid and answered matter-of-factly, "My mother had a baby in the middle of the night."

The country began emerging from beneath the weight of the mightiest struggle the world had ever seen. The war had killed more people, cost more money, damaged more property, and affected more people than any other war in history. The Pacific was still to be won, by what means nobody yet knew, but once it had been, fifty-five million people would have died.

Cros, though, was soon in the middle of another war, a domestic one of dangerous racial conflict. It was in New York, where Irish American neighborhood gangs sought out young

Jewish boys to attack and Father Charles Coughlin's "Christian Front" was arming itself in secret to battle communism and "unchecked Jewish influence in American life." It was in the South, too. Among many Southern whites, anti–black race hatred ran very deep. Southern conservatives were already appealing to Truman to cease attacks on white supremacy or face their full-fledged revolt. The forces that had put the South behind the New Deal would weaken if they became a stronger political faction.

In May of 1945, the William and Mary story came in over the wire as an AP dispatch. The situation was that *The Flat Hat*, the student-run paper at the college in Virginia founded by Thomas Jefferson, had been asked by its president to accept faculty supervision because of an editorial on the "Negro question" written by its editor, Miss Marilyn Kaemmerle of Jackson, Michigan. It hit two big PM chords—freedom of the press and civil rights. Since the AP suit was still in the courts, PM hadn't been able to run it as fresh news, but the paper could do a more in-depth look.

McCleary sent Cros on a week-long research trip to Williamsburg to cover it. Did the people involved feel differently now that things had quieted down? Had they learned anything? The paper would run it as a three-part series, which was unusual.

Miss Kaemmerle's editorial, titled "Lincoln's Job Half Done," had said that although Lincoln undoubtedly hoped the Negroes would someday be accepted as equals, they had not yet been. Equality would mean integration into schools and clubs, being roommates, even intermarriage. Bodily differences were only on the surface. Differences in intelligence occurred not because of race but because of environment. The idea of white supremacy was as groundless as Hitler's Nordic supremacy idea. Nazi race tactics must be eliminated from the everyday life of the country before victory would bring peace for the "Universal Human Race of One World." A few days after the editorial was published, President John E. Pomfret announced his decision.

Cros took the train south and traveled toward Virginia. In Washington DC, he stopped to visit former PM-er Hodding Carter. Carter was a liberal Southerner who had gone back home to run the family paper, the *Greenville Delta Democrat-Times*, in Greenville, Mississippi. Cros wanted to get his view on the story.

Carter told Cros he believed what had really upset the South about the editorial was its suggestion that miscegenation was possible, even desirable. Preventing intermarriage between the races and maintaining the purity of white womanhood, Carter said, was what Southerners built their culture around. And Carter just happened to have recently written a book on the Negro problem, *The Winds of Fear*, in which an unpleasant town sheriff calls a fictional PM reporter, which Carter once had been, a "Yankee butt-in."

"Take it easy, Bowen," Carter said.

In Richmond, Cros met with the AP reporter who broke the story, Virginius Dabney, and he asked Dabney if he would really be regarded as a "Yankee butt-in."

Dabney smiled and said that was unfortunately true.

Cros took the bus from Richmond to Williamsburg. Whites were at the front of the bus and blacks at the back. He sat down behind the bus driver, and after a bit of lazy conversation in which he tried very hard not to be a Yankee butt-in, asked, "Is enforcing this difficult?"

The driver allowed as how it wasn't all that hard, at all. "In the case of an empty seat being up front and a colored gets on, I takes a white from in back and puts him up front," he said.

The William and Mary campus was bright with spring. Flowering trees were everywhere. Students sunned themselves on the grass. Cros's first call was to John E. Pomfret, the president. "So far as I know, the significance of the story rests on the fact that *The Flat Hat* is undergoing faculty censorship as a result of the controversy," Cros asserted.

"There is no censorship," said Pomfret.

"Aren't two faculty members now supervising *The Flat Hat*?"

"Not faculty supervision, but faculty advice. Most college publications have faculty advisers."

Had the administration terminated Miss Kaemmerle as editor?

"The staff of *The Flat Hat* acted themselves. There was never any question of the girl not continuing as editor. It's all in the record."

Cros telephoned Kaemmerle. He met her at her sorority house. She was dressed in a simply cut blue dress, with shoulder-length brown hair and deep, serious eyes, open faced and poised, though she seemed slightly sad. They walked toward a modern brick restaurant built as a part of the restoration of Williamsburg and waited for a table.

"People are being kind, but I wonder if they feel sorry for me," she said. She loved William and Mary. She had thrown herself into being a student, been very active in many honorary societies and clubs and been listed in *Who's Who Among Students in American Colleges and Universities*. But now she wanted to finish her senior year quietly and get her two degrees, one a BS in Home Economics and the other a BA in English.

Pomfret had told her, she said, that he thought the publicity over the editorial had hurt the college. "President Pomfret said, 'If you feel you have to be a crusader, I think you'd be happier at some other college.' I don't want to seem a crusader." But she thought some good might have come out of the controversy. It might have made people think about the race problem.

Cros asked her to tell him exactly what had happened.

"The whole thing began on the Saturday after the editorial appeared," Kaemmerle said. She received a call from President Pomfret, who told her not to get excited, but the Board of Visitors had just passed a recommendation that corrective and disciplinary action be taken because of "Lincoln's Job Half Done." On Sunday President Pomfret called her to his office and told her that the current unprinted issue of *The Flat Hat* should be immediately submitted for censorship. Subsequent issues would be supervised by faculty. She should resign as editor. The alternative was no more *Flat Hat*.

She discussed it with her staff. "Most of them said freedom of expression was one of the things the war was being fought for. They voted not to publish *The Flat Hat* rather than publish a censored paper." Early in the next morning, at one a.m., the men on the staff went the round of the men's dormitories spreading the word that a mass meeting would be held the next morning at ten.

That morning, Kaemmerle said, nine hundred of the thousand-strong student body gathered at a meeting advertised as "Freedom of the Press or No Press." A stuffed figure labeled "Board of Visitors" was hanged. The AP estimated that fifty students spoke, and the students adopted a resolution protesting the "infringement of the doctrine of freedom of the press as laid down by our honored alumnus Thomas Jefferson."

A swarm of news media descended on the campus and on Miss Kaemmerle. On Tuesday afternoon, Pomfret called a faculty meeting. His position was that supervision should be established over student publications and the editorial author could not continue as editor. He asked the faculty to choose among three courses of action: vote to back his stand; vote against it and censure him; vote against it with a request for his resignation.

By now, the evening darkness had gathered. There was sadness in Kaemmerle eyes. "The paper was not printed that week," she said. "President Pomfret made it sound like there was going to be violence. The staff got anxious and began working on a compromise agreement." The compromise was that they offered to consult a faculty counselor if they felt doubtful about any article scheduled for publication.

Kaemmerle and Cros sat quietly together for a while. "Pomfret accepted the compromise," she told him. Then Cros walked her back toward her dormitory. They stood together for a moment beside her door, and Cros asked her what she had learned. She paused in thought for a moment, and then said, "I might leave the 'marry among us' part out because it startled people too much. But the basic problem is to get people to think. If people would think when the big problems arise, we'd find the way to create a world of peace. You see, I can hardly remember the years of my life when there was no war."

For his final interview, Cros returned to Pomfret, who motioned him into his office without offering him a chair. "Freedom of the press had not been the issue," Cros was thinking. Hodding Carter had been right. Miscegenation was the issue.

"Did you learn anything from this?" Cros asked.

"Nothing I didn't know before," Pomfret said.

Cros had learned something. He had learned that men like Pomfret could make people like Miss Kaemmerle, who really wanted to make people think, not want to be a "crusader." Journalism needed crusaders, but it was not a job that those like Miss Kaemmerle would seek out.

On June 18, 1945, there was real joy in the PM newsroom. The Supreme Court decision on the Associated Press suit came down. In three separate opinions, a five-justice majority ruled against the AP. PM would be able to join the AP if it chose to. Justice Frankfurter stood behind Judge Learned Hand's argument that the public had an interest in a free press and that the AP, by offering its services only to a few member newspapers, diminished the dissemination of information in society. "The business of the press, and therefore the business of the Associated Press, is the promotion of truth regarding public matters by furnishing the basis for an understanding of them."

Justices Black and Douglas found that the AP bylaws constituted a restraint of trade hindering competition. Black wrote, "The widest possible dissemination of information from diverse and antagonistic sources is essential to the welfare of the public."

McCormack still did not give up. Supporting him were people who called attempts to interfere with the Associated Press "communist-inspired." In 1946 after the election, in a Republican-controlled Congress, an association of conservatives in the newspaper industry— Annenberg, Gannett, McCormick, Copley, and a representative of Hearst—lobbied for passage of a bill supporting exemption from the law, but it died in committee. The victory was complete.

In those years, as soon as I was big enough to climb into his lap, whenever my father came back home after being away, we would settle down into a game he had made up for us.

"Who's the greatest writer in the world?"

"Daddy!"

In time, he taught me to answer "Shakespeare!," but still he would always pull me to his chest for big hugs. His job was to protect the country from fascism on the right and communism on the left, and to spread American values abroad in the world. He would grip me by the shoulders, straighten himself up, and give me a stern look. I was to speak the truth that was in my heart.

"Whose side are you on?"

"The side of truth and justice!" I would call out. There were always more big hugs.

After the AP decision, Judge Learned Hand entered into the game. "What do you believe in?"

"The free marketplace of ideas!"

Another big hug.

If the Supreme Court decision was good for *PM*, another event that at first looked like it might be, turned out not so. On July 1, 1945, newspaper delivery workers struck. Only

PM, which had not been granted space on the nearby papers' shared delivery trucks since its inception and therefore had to supply its own, was alone on the newsstands. All eight of the other New York City newspapers were not. Circulation shot up from 100,000 to 500,000, the most the PM presses could produce. In a show of liberal values, the paper ran a column to explain the striking workers' grievances and summarized the important news from each of the competing papers. PM drivers helped man the picket lines in solidarity. PM's circulation rose, and along with that, hopes that the paper might gain enough permanent readers to keep afloat on its own.

Staffers exulted, but then after the strike was settled, circulation dropped back down. The fear grew that Marshall Field would stop financing PM. Roosevelt's death had been bad enough. If the paper could not sustain itself even after the increased readership during the strike, rough times were ahead.

Cros's next big piece was a heavily researched investigative one on an attack being waged against the New Deal's government programs, or what conservatives were calling "social planning." An alliance between business and the publishing establishment was giving a big buildup to Friedrich von Hayek's *The Road to Serfdom*. According to the publisher's blurb, von Hayek's thesis was that social planning "may eventually cause the end of individual freedom."

Cros wrote, "In recent years, *Fortune, Look*, the *Reader's Digest*, the Hearst newspapers, the National Association of Manufacturers, General Motors, the New Jersey Power and Light Co., and many smaller groups and less thunderous publications have helped to spread its rather vague antiplanning message to millions."

Look had printed a flyer to introduce the book. It read, "Today, individuals and groups bent on planning our future are a feature of American life. What happened in Russia, Italy, and Germany can happen in America, too, if we ignore the warnings outlined here."

Look heavily distributed the flyer. *Reader's Digest* ran a twenty-page condensation of it as a lead article followed by a condensation of an article from *Newsweek*, "What Is Being Planned for You," which told the reader, "Those who are making these plans are as smart and clever and ruthless and determined as any group in this country. Remember that this same program when it was in effect in Italy was known as 'fascism.' And today in Germany it goes under the name of 'Nazism.'"

Von Hayek came to the United States, held a press conference in New York, and then went on an eleven-state lecture tour. Cros tracked down sources who had listened to what von Hayek actually said on his tour. In fact, von Hayek had said that his book was not an argument against Roosevelt-Wallace-Truman planning and a return to Harding-Coolidge-Hoover principles. At a University of Chicago Round Table radio discussion panel, in response to the observation "It seems to me that you do allow far more of public planning than most of the readers of your book in this country have assumed," he replied, "I have noticed this." Then he flatly stated that some kinds of planning were justifiable, that "socialistic" central planning led to fascism, and that his "whole effort was to distinguish between legitimate and illegitimate action." As far as the government plans for competition or stepping in where competition could not possibly do the job, he had no objection.

"I am somewhat mystified at finding myself under attack by liberals for having aligned myself with reactionary elements in the United States," said Hayek. "I have always considered myself a liberal, a nineteenth-century liberal."

DeWitt Wallace was the *Reader's Digest* publisher. Cros called on him at his offices in Pleasantville, New York. His sun-tanned face reminded Cros of one of the "Calvert Men of Distinction" photographs in an advertising campaign then being run by a liquor company.

"Are you aware that, in giving von Hayek's book so much promotion, you're aligning the *Reader's Digest* with the reactionary forces behind von Hayek's antiplanning ideas?"

"The von Hayek condensation was the best attempt so far to examine the principles of nineteenth-century liberalism in light of our current problems and the chief alternative to those principles," Wallace countered.

Then he put Cros on the spot. "Despite its past and present shortcomings, are not the achievements of American business and the things those achievements made possible—among them *PM*—sufficient to merit some justifying? Does the justification of New Deal planning require the discrediting of American business?"

Cros replied that he thought the aims of big business and the New Deal were incompatible. Did Wallace really feel he had fairly presented both sides on the issue of planning?

Wallace replied that the *Digest* had indeed "presented both sides." It had published a seven-page lead piece by Henry Wallace, then the new secretary of commerce. It was an "able statement of the other side by its most eloquent spokesman."

And then he added, "May I express my amazement at the effrontery of this assertion of our responsibility to 'present both sides' from a periodical which day after day makes bias its business and picks, chooses, and distorts the facts to serve its own prejudices?" As one of the few papers in the country that regularly took a liberal stance, and in fact tried to shape it, he said, *PM* was certainly not in the business of "presenting both sides."

Cros had met his match.

"In my opinion," Cros said, "*PM*'s job is to examine closely the workings of American business and politics. We are interested in objective reporting. I think we are serving the truth."

With that, they parted.

West Twelfth Street was getting tight for the Bowen family. A new baby was due the following May. A move was well in order. Cros had often walked along Bedford Street in the Village on his way to Chumley's, passing the narrowest house in New York City, where Edna St. Vincent Millay had once lived, built in an old alleyway, and farther down, at 17 Barrow, the carriage house where Aaron Burr had hidden after shooting Alexander Hamilton with a dueling pistol.

Now 66 Bedford Street, one in a row of brick town houses, was for sale. The three floors each had kitchens and baths, so each could be a separate apartment. There was a basement, and a walled garden in back. With Louise's help, Cros pulled together the money, and the Bowen family moved into the first floor.

Marjory found an antique Victorian sofa for the living room. She pulled out her sewing machine and whipped up a slipcover that fit perfectly every curve of its ornately carved wooden frame. Billy, home from the war, lived on the second floor, and produced radio programming for Radio Free Europe.

In January of 1946 Ralph Ingersoll came back to *PM* from the Army with "as big a splash as he could." He wrote a long letter to Marshall Field enumerating the newspaper's faults. He said the paper had become ideologically predictable. Major staff changes were in order. It looked like he was trying to upend the John Lewis/Rae Weimer organization that had run the paper for three years. He began a flurry of "economy firings," although as Lewis remarked, it seemed incongruous to fire dozens of people for financial reasons before embarking on the major expansion he planned.

Ingersoll started out with the Washington office. Lewis tried to head off a confrontation but Ingersoll demanded that several of editor James Wechsler's protégés be fired. Wechsler advised the fired protégés to seek protection from the American Newspaper Guild, founded in 1934 by crusading journalist Heywood Broun to improve wages and working conditions in the news industry. Then Wechsler asked the rest of the Washington staff to resign. He went public with the opinion that the quarrel lay in Ingersoll's susceptibility to communist domination. Wechsler then left *PM* to become editor of the *New York Post*.

Ingersoll moved on to reorganize the New York office.

On March 11, 1946, with a wife seven months pregnant and in possession of a new house, Cros came home to Bedford Street to tell Marjory that he had just received notice that the whole class of war replacements, of which he was one of seven, had been fired.

Marjory was indignant. The Newspaper Guild filed a grievance. Cros and the six others kept working. On April 3 the Guild heard the war replacement firing grievance. The Guild argued that it would be better for *PM* to expand than to retrench, and that editorially *PM* favored full employment. Management, with Ingersoll as spokesman, yielded nothing. The Guild requested that all war replacements be made permanent. No promises were made.

Cros's future was uncertain, and so was the future of the United Nations, upon which hung the hopes of liberals like Cros that the democratic ideals men had fought and died for would spread throughout the world. The UN, he hoped, might develop into a worldwide representative government. In March of 1946, nine days after the first UN sessions adjourned in London, a planeload of twenty-nine key people from the UN Secretariat landed in New York and began preparing for a meeting of the Security Council, which would open in ten days in the Bronx gymnasium of Hunter College. Cros did a photoreport to introduce the UN to the city. He took a picture of the building they would move into and got headshots of eleven of the staff. "One percent of the city's transient and semitransient accommodations are being reserved for UN delegates, their staffs, and members of the Secretariat," he wrote. For the next Sunday Section, he did a brief follow-up piece on the first UN Secretary-General, "Random Facts on Trygve Lie," of Norway.

Winston Churchill was in the United States at the time. What he had to say was a dash of cold water in the face of the hopes for peace. In his "Sinews of Peace" speech, delivered on March 5 at Westminster College in Fulton, Missouri, he first used the term "iron curtain." Cros read the text in the newspapers. As Churchill warned, "From Stettin in the Baltic to Trieste in the Adriatic an 'iron curtain' has descended across the Continent. Behind that line lie all the capitals of the ancient states of Central and Eastern Europe: Warsaw, Berlin, Prague, Vienna, Budapest, Belgrade, Bucharest, and Sofia. All these famous cities and the populations around them lie in what I must call the Soviet sphere, and all are subject, in one form or another, not only to Soviet influence but to a very high and in some cases increasing measure of control from Moscow."

Cros was not convinced. The United Nations would provide the framework for a universal federation of democracies in a world without war. Churchill was alarmist. The first confrontations of the Cold War were not yet palpable facts, and the Iron Curtain was quite invisible.

The second Bowen child, Lucey, was born in May 1946, just as New York had begun bracing itself against an epidemic of polio expected to break out in the summer. Families were advised to stay away from crowds, away from people outside their circle of friends. Children should stay out of parks and pools and not drink from public water fountains.

Marjory took the newborn Lucey and me, twenty months old, out to Sherman, to Hidden Hollow, to spend the summer. She spent the week alone taking care of us, washing our diapers in the brook across the road and getting along with Louise and Bill's wife, Mary, when they came to visit. Cros commuted out to Sherman on weekends.

After one such weekend, Cros woke up sad. Marjory drove him to the Brewster station. He usually waved to her from the train window, but this time he did not. Cros wished he could have stayed in the country. The weekend had shored him up. They might have seen Muriel and Malcolm Cowley, now living full-time in Sherman, Malcolm writing. They seemed happy there. Now the city faced him again. He was beginning to dread work. The train stood still for a long while at the Bethel stop. Out the window, Cros noticed a thin, tired baggage man pulling a wagon heavy with suitcases and trunks down the tracks. Watching him, he felt himself become that thin, tired man. The problems of the world were the suitcases and PM's problems were the trunk and there he was, that very same tired man, pulling them all on a wagon.

Looking out through the window up the bright green lawn that swelled up from the tracks, he saw a long, low factory building. There, standing in the doors and windows, talking and laughing and smiling, were a whole lot of happy people. Over the door of the factory, somebody had erected a sign. It read:

THE ONLY TRUE FORMULA FOR WORLD PEACE
I—YOU—ME
YOUR RIGHTS—MY DUTIES
YOUR DUTIES—MY RIGHTS
100% RIGHTS—100% DUTIES—PEACE WITH JUSTICE
THIS IS GOD'S WILL

What was the secret of this happy place? Did the sign have anything to do with the smiles on people's faces? Cros ran the story by McCleary and the next morning took the 8:08 a.m. from Grand Central back out to Bethel. He got off the train and walked up the green lawn onto the ground floor of the factory. The workers were singing and whistling. The foreman came over and introduced himself.

"Why is everyone so happy?" Cros asked.

"We're all whacky around here. But we have a lotta fun."

"We've got a good bunch of kids here."

"We make good money."

"Who made the sign?"

"Mr. Vaghi, who owns a woodworking shop."

Cros found Mr. Vaghi. What did he mean by the sign?

"Men must live in peace and they can live in peace by respecting each other's rights, regardless of race, creed, or color," he said.

Cros had his story. The people in Bethel had come to understand a very basic truth and, quite simply, that truth made them happy.

Then the factory whistle blew and Cros went back to New York. He called the piece "The Happy Factory." Later he would look back to it and remember that time as the time a long depression had first set in.

Routinely those days, the mood in the *PM* newsroom was tense. Fruitless arguing between the Guild and management over the problem of war replacements continued. Meanwhile, forty-seven more veterans returned and took up their jobs. In July, management capitulated and offered to abolish the classification of war replacement, giving permanent status to all. The Guild accepted *PM*'s offer.

Cros's job was now as safe as *PM*.

But *PM* wasn't very safe at all.

Henry Wallace was the favorite of the left wing of the liberal party. *PM* endorsed him. Ralph Ingersoll opined that after he had met with Truman, he believed the man was "no president of the United States at all, no president with a brain, personality, and a character of his own." A Lerner *PM* editorial titled "Seven Choices to Replace Truman in '48" had Henry Wallace at the top of the list.

That fall Wallace came to New York City as Truman's secretary of commerce, campaigning for the Democratic ticket.

In a keynote speech in Madison Square Garden, he called for America to commit to the elimination of racism and the industrialization of the undeveloped world. He warned against letting American foreign policy merge with British imperialism. He claimed to be neither anti- nor pro-British and neither anti- nor pro-Soviet. He compared the Soviet interest in Eastern Europe to the American interest in Latin America. He proposed a peaceful competition of the two systems, communism and capitalism. He predicted that Russian ideals of social and economic justice would eventually govern a third of the world.

PM devoted the first four pages of its September 13 issue to Wallace's Madison Square Garden speech, affirming that the remarks summarized the paper's views. Then both *PM* and Wallace came under a barrage of attacks—from the Communists, from other members of the Truman cabinet, and from Truman himself, who fired him. In Lerner's words, the Democrats became "a party without a leader, while Henry Wallace is a leader without a party....

"But in personal terms," Lerner continued, "Wallace emerged from the ordeal a more massive figure than he had ever been, with a more distinctly presidential stature than any man in public life today." That year Wallace took on the editorship of *The New Republic*, which Cros's Sherman neighbor Malcolm Cowley had formerly edited, and in whose pages he vociferously criticized Truman's foreign policy. Truman presented the Cold War as a choice between freedom and oppression. If America let one country fall to communism, all would follow, falling like a line of dominos.

Truman's wariness toward the Soviet Union resonated with the nation in ways that Wallace's enthusiasm for peaceful coexistence did not.

As the 1946 Congressional elections got underway, domestic problems were foremost in the minds of the electorate. Huge numbers—twelve million men—were still in uniform, waiting to be reintegrated into the society and the economy. Wartime controls, particularly of wages, had to be loosened. The right to strike was restored, and in one year, from 1945 to 1946, the total production time lost to strikes tripled. Wages went up and prices followed. Inflation hit in full force, and despite prosperity, people felt their dollars shrinking. The public placed the blame at the feet of the Democrats.

When the ballots were counted on Election Day in November of 1946, the Republicans controlled both houses of Congress for the first time since 1928.

That very day, *PM* announced it would accept advertising. The campaign for subscribers to support the paper had failed. Marshall Field's money was still holding it afloat. Ralph Ingersoll resigned. In the early days of the paper, FDR had written to Ingersoll, "Your proposal to sustain your enterprise simply by merchandizing information, with the public as your only customer, appeals to me as a new and promising formula for freedom of the press." Ingersoll quoted that when he wrote to Field that Roosevelt had hoped that the paper might add a notable chapter to the history of the free press, and he thought *PM* had fulfilled that hope. Advertising, even if it might not alter the paper's editorial stances, still went against his principles. "There should be at least one mass newspaper in this country supported solely by its readers," he said, and that had been FDR's hope, too.

But now that formula was no longer to be. It had not made money.

Bill McCleary left *PM* to write plays. As he was clearing out his desk, he came across an April 28, 1942, "think" letter he had written to Ingersoll and never sent. He passed it on to Lewis. "If you can make use of it, take it. If not, let's discuss it briefly when you've read it."

What McCleary said in the letter was what he had wanted to tell Ingersoll all along—that it was one thing to stand up for the free expression of ideas, including communist ones, but his refusal to combat the paper's reputation as a "communist sheet" had hurt it. "What the American Communists are is one thing; what the American people think they are is another thing. And in a democracy we must take into consideration not only what the truth is but what the people believe the truth to be. What is important is the fact that for various reasons, some valid and some invalid, the American people are extremely distrustful of native Communists. And this feeling of the American people, if not fully understood, can lead to trouble."

McCleary thought it had indeed led to trouble. He saw Ingersoll as a hotheaded idealist who had refused to compromise in the face of reality. "Now maybe you take the position that it is better to state the truth baldly and take the consequences and to play along with people's prejudices," McCleary wrote. "The only hitch is that this kind of head-on attack may isolate so many potentially understanding but presently prejudiced people that the newspaper is stamped as pro-communist and left strictly alone by enough people to cause it to fail."

McCleary signed himself "William Jennings O'Brien." Then he left *PM*.

SEVEN

Ahab in Seersucker

Back in those early years while we still lived in Greenwich Village, as I grew old enough to be taken by the hand and walk beside my father, he and I would set out on "expeditions." If the wind was from the west it brought damp salt air off the Hudson. If it came from the east, it carried the sour smells of the open-air Italian market on Bleecker Street, where gutted rabbits hung upside down in butcher shop windows. After the stalls closed, huge street-cleaning water hoses washed rotting fruits and vegetables down through the city's drains.

A different smell would be in the air when we headed over to Washington Square Park to board the Fifth Avenue bus. There, the air was strong and bracing. It smelled of serious and important things I didn't understand. The bus would grind to a halt, its tail pipe sending out a huge plume of gray exhaust, and we'd climb the steps. Grinning broadly, my father would greet the Irish bus driver.

"I have with me a fine colleen and she has the map of Ireland written all over her face. Would you like to take her home with you?"

I cowered beside my father. Would he give me away to

just anyone? But the bus driver would smile and steer the bus out into traffic.

"Top of the morning to you, sir," my father would say, reaching into his pocket for the fare.

"And the balance of the day to you, sir."

With that, the two Irish gentlemen would part.

One day, as we took our seats and the bus gained speed, Dad was lost in thought. Coming out of his reverie, he said, "The up shall be down and the down shall be up with the rising of the moon."

What exactly he meant by that, I didn't ask. I just wondered.

Those bus encounters piled up and he didn't give me away to a bus driver, so I became less afraid. One day he told me about the bogtrotter Irish and the shanty Irish and the lace curtain Irish. That was a big advance.

"Who are the lace curtain Irish?"

"The people who have lace curtains at their windows, and that's more than the bogtrotters have."

"So the bogtrotters will have lace curtains when the moon rises?"

"With the rising of the moon, they will."

"Will you still be a king?" That was why a fine suitor would come to me. He had told me that.

"In Ireland anyone is a king who has a pig in his backyard."

"But we don't have a pig in our backyard." The only animals I knew were a flock of pigeons in Washington Square Park. Our backyard was a tiny sliver of mostly paved, brick-walled garden behind the Bedford Street house, where in summer we would go out with spoons and a cup to dig in the thin strip of weedy black earth that edged the wall and smelled of motor oil.

"In Ireland, we would have had a pig. Everyone in Ireland is a king," my father said.

But once he had told me that being Irish had nothing to do with the sod you trod on. It did not make sense. I began to suspect this mystery had something to do with my father's feeling about who is on the top of the heap and who is on the bottom, and the wrongness of there being a heap at all. Now he was more of a mystery than when all this unraveling had begun. But I was going up Fifth Avenue in a bus, so there was something far more important to understand than my father. I let it go.

I could tell, from a look that would often come into my father's eyes, that he believed he was a lucky man. I first saw that look on a raw spring day when we still lived in Greenwich Village. My father took his young family uptown and seated us in the bleachers that had been put up along Fifth Avenue. He disappeared, only to blow past us much later with his lumpy gait, grinning and waving, wearing a green shamrock in his lapel, at the tag end of the St. Patrick's Day parade.

Afterward, as if his lucky card had been renewed, his tank of luck refilled, his glass refreshed with luck, he was more carefree, more willing to take risks. Even the very painful things that had happened to him were a path to something good. There would be more terrible things to come, but there would always be more luck, too.

So I asked my father more questions about luck. I didn't always believe what he told me, but I didn't disbelieve it, either. He told me in Ireland there are little people that live under the earth. Some of them are good and some evil. The evil ones and the good ones watch the race of men carefully. They mostly bring luck, but sometimes the evil ones do rise up to cause trouble. Then terrible things happen to you. But when luck is with you, it is often because you are Irish.

In those last years of *PM*, Cros became an "Ahab in Seersucker," a phrase he'd used to title a profile he'd done on his friend Charles Bolte of the American Veterans Committee. "Seersucker" came from a term of scorn devised at its first annual convention, held in Des Moines in the spring of 1946. A California group faction trying to unseat Bolte and his friends, among them Franklin Roosevelt Jr., called them "the seersucker set," referring to the cotton suits the Eastern liberal delegates wore.

"I really think what [Bolte] wants is to help his fellow man, to [be the Ahab who slays] the white whale that stands in the way of social justice," Bolte's wife, Mary, had said when Cros asked her what made her husband tick. She could just as truthfully have said that about Cros.

In Bill McCleary, Cros lost a skilled editor, a mentor, and an ally. But his career at PM was only just getting going. After McCleary's departure, he became an associate editor, with responsibility for originating other reporters' pieces as well as his own. In those years, he did a great number of long feature articles on political subjects and assigned many to other reporters.

He was coming into his own as a political reporter, but it was just as the power and unanimity of the liberal center and the viability of PM were waning. Two major domestic issues threatened to divide the party and heavily impact the politics of the 1948 election: communism, both domestic and foreign, and civil rights. Around both, splinter parties coalesced that could divert strength from the liberals.

Cros wrote major pieces on each.

Cold War fear was not the only fear that had begun to infect the country. Equally strong was the fear of communist influence inside the United States, a fear exploited by powerful domestic forces in ways that destroyed lives, not with guns or bombs, but with words. In the late 1940s it was the House Un-American Activities Committee (HUAC); later it shifted to the Senate, led by Wisconsin Senator Joseph McCarthy.

In March of 1947 James Francis O'Neil, head of the American Legion, was called before the HUAC. Its chair was J.

Parnell Thomas; its junior member Richard M. Nixon, then a freshman. O'Neil advocated outlawing the Communist Party. He would deny use of the mails to all communist publications, continue the registration of aliens and authorize a check of their activities, and discontinue federal aid to institutions that refused to purge their faculties of Communists. Cros caught a few moments to speak with him. He suggested that it was un-American to outlaw any political party.

"I don't think the Communist Party," O'Neil snapped, "is a political party. It is a subversive international conspiracy. It is a cloak for their operations."

Thomas's committee then began nine days of hearings into alleged communist propaganda and influence in the Hollywood motion picture industry. The committee interviewed forty-one people, friendly witnesses. They named nineteen people they said held left-wing views. Ten of them refused to answer questions posed by committee members. They became known as the Hollywood Ten.

As the HUAC chairman, Thomas presided over the hearing on the Hollywood Ten. He was a short roly-poly man with chubby cheeks, bald head, and a reddish complexion. He smoked nervously. He was a gavel banger. "Take him away!" Thomas would cry out when he wanted an unfriendly witness removed from the stand. One little girl, before the opening of one of the sessions, asked her mother, "Where are the prisoners?"

Thomas had a lot of clout. He had been elected a state representative and given the chairmanship of a committee that was poised to become an anti-communist juggernaut with the power to destroy lives and careers and spread fear throughout American life, all on very little hard evidence. Just as fascists had manipulated the fears and insecurities of Germans, Thomas, the anti-communist crusader, seemed to want to do the same in America. If that was true, the public had to be warned about it. Someone had to look into this man's past, find out what he was really like, where he came from, and what he was all about.

Cros took on the job. He went to Thomas's hometown of Allendale, New Jersey, and did his usual gumshoe work, searching out the names of people who had known him, asking them questions and listening very carefully to what they said. He spent several days there, and then he went to Thomas's office in Washington DC to get his reactions to what he had gathered. At a press conference outside the HUAC room, Cros had a chance to talk with him.

He need not have introduced himself. "I know about you," Thomas blustered. "You've been investigating me. You're out in my hometown, going into stores and things and asking about me. I had reports. I know the kind of stuff you've been getting."

"Could I check what I've gotten with you?"

"Write what you want to," Parnell said. "You will end up doing that anyhow. *PM* wouldn't have anything good to say about me."

Then he turned and walked away.

Was this anti-communist crusader a man who genuinely felt he was battling the forces of evil out of a love for America? Or a self-promoter looking for a chance to get power? An early source, Thomas's old neighbor in Allendale, said flatly that power was what he wanted. Thomas had told him, "I'm going places now that I'm the Chairman of the House Committee on Un-American Activities and we have a Republican Congress. Now is the time. Going after the Reds is going to make me."

Sitting through the committee hearings, Cros watched Thomas carefully, the same question on his mind. Thomas emerged as a man of many small inconsiderate acts. A Hollywood Ten witness who had been sitting in the hearings for several days was about to be sworn in. Robert W. Kenny raised his left hand. Thomas glowered and said, very firmly, "Raise your right hand."

Kenny stirred his right arm slightly.

Again, Thomas cried out, "Raise your right hand!"

Bartley Crum, an attorney for the Hollywood Ten, walked over to Thomas and whispered, "Everybody in Washington knows that Kenny's right arm is paralyzed."

J. Parnell Thomas, Cros discovered, was a skilled image maker. His raw material was himself. Early on, he had set about reconstructing himself into the kind of man to whom, he believed, other people would hand over power. He had been born in an Irish Catholic family as John Parnell Feeney. He had attended the University of Pennsylvania and New York University law school, leaving to join the army. His first job out of the army was as a bond salesman in New York. At twenty-four he petitioned to change his name to Thomas, his mother's last name, because he believed he could get recognition and business under it that he could not get under the name of Feeney. He began to claim Noah Webster and Nathanael Greene as forbears on his mother's side. And he became a member of the Episcopal Church.

At thirty he decided to enter politics. He ran for mayor of Allendale, where you couldn't get elected unless the Ku Klux Klan supported you. The Klan never opposed Thomas. In 1928 he was elected mayor for a second time on the Republican ticket. But allegations of overspending on a water system, the police department, and roads caused a good deal of bitterness among those who later took over the management of the town, so he did not run for reelection in 1930. In 1935 he ran for the state assembly seat for his district. He made his name when a group of unemployed people moved into the New Jersey assembly and camped out in the legislature. Thomas spoke to the press. "This demonstration is communist inspired. It is an open revolt against the state government by forces which seek to overthrow the United

States government. I call upon you to throw them out. Or if they are to be treated as guests of the state, let's do the job properly. Feed them caviar! Feed them chocolate éclairs!"

As Thomas himself later said to a *Chicago Tribune* reporter, "My fight against communism dates from the day I saw a yelling mob pour into the legislative chamber."

In 1936, when his district's representative died, Thomas lined up support to take the seat over. He succeeded. In 1938, when the House Un-American Activities Committee was organized, he sought and got an appointment. He began his 1939 congressional year with a big noise, asking for the impeachment of Secretary of Labor Frances Perkins. In a speech to bond salesmen in New York City, he said, "The time is coming when it will no longer be considered criminal to be a businessman," and went on to expound on his favorite theme, that there was a direct "link between the New Deal and radical subversive groups in this country." He voted against the WPA and public works. He spent the next seven years battling the New Deal and accusing people whose politics he disliked of being Communists. After the war ended, he continued doing the same. When the Republicans gained control of Congress in 1946, he was reelected and named to head HUAC. His ascent to power as an anti-communist crusader was complete.

A Washington political reporter told Cros that the groups in Thomas's gerrymandered district did not know one another and were served by different newspapers, so Thomas could tell each faction a different story. Thomas understood the subtle difference in class between them, the subtle lines of snobberies. "He plays this up, trying to make each feel superior to the next class down, then pitting one against the other. I think he is doing this on a national scale now, by saying to various groups, 'You're good Americans, but there are others who are not.'"

A political official who helped get Thomas a job as a state

relief administrator during the Depression said, "I didn't realize it at the time that he was building up a political machine. Everything he does is for a reason—to get votes. His appeal is always to emotion, never to the mind."

Cros called the piece "The Americanization of J. Parnell Thomas" and let Thomas's mother have the last word. "I don't know what's happened to him since he went into politics," his mother had said. "I don't know what he's about. You know, sometimes these days I don't think Parney has any real friends left at all."

The Cold War had begun, although liberals like Cros had been slow to see it. With Stalin's purges, executions, and deportations still concealed from the West, many liberals viewed him as a mirror image of themselves, committed to a more egalitarian society. By September 1947 the UN had moved to Flushing Meadows, and Truman was getting ready to carry out an armed conflict in Korea under its auspices. Notebook in hand, Cros fretted in the bullpen reception room in the nineteenth-floor suite of Two Park Avenue, then the home of the U.S. Mission to the UN. This was a place he had hoped would be the seedbed for a world government under which men could live at peace, but now he was here to get a view of the two sides that were shaping up in the Cold War—the United States and Russia, Marshall and Gromyko. Heels clicked in the hallway. An elevator door opened and shut. Five men in single file walked into the room. The man in the lead, shoulders back, hands swinging infantry style, brown tropical suit and highly polished shoes, was George Catlett Marshall, secretary of state and chairman of the United Nations General Assembly, reporting to work. Behind him was his special assistant, Brig. Gen. Marshall S. Carter.

The next day, the second regular session of the General Assembly would meet at Flushing Meadows. Marshall and Carter would face Andrei Andreyevich Gromyko, the Soviet

Union's UN representative since April of 1946, who would come to be called "Mr. Nyet" for the frequency with which he used the Soviet veto in the General Assembly. World peace was the UN story Cros had hoped he would be writing. War in Korea was not, but things were shaping up that way.

Would the Democrats retain the presidency or would the Republicans capture it? General Dwight D. Eisenhower was on the sidelines, serving as president of Columbia University, but his name held a special place in the hearts of Americans. He could be a formidable opponent. An Eisenhower draft had been contemplated by both the Republicans and the Democrats, but in October of 1947 Cros heard that it was a group of Republicans, the "Draft Eisenhower for President League," that had set up headquarters in New York.

Cros did not trust business interests to support hard-won New Deal social legislation and did not want them to regain the power in American life that had built huge monopolies and concentrated wealth at the top. He wanted to find out what kind of people these men were.

Winston H. Thornburg's offices and the Draft Eisenhower headquarters were at 270 Park Avenue, the building that housed the Henry Loudon Advertising Agency, of which Thornburg was an account executive. Thornburg was a tall, handsome man who greeted Cros with a "you and I see eye to eye" look.

Then Col. George Peabody Converse walked in. Cros introduced himself. "We've got nothing to get out of this. We're businessmen. We don't want anything," Converse said. "I'm a wealthy man and no one can do anything for me. I have everything."

John S. Dickerson, a former stockbroker now in the advertising business, joined them.

Converse continued, "The important thing to remember is that Eisenhower is not a politician. He has no ax to grind."

"We have a horse in the stable," Dickerson said, "but now our problem is to make Mr. Eisenhower drink."

These men, Cros noticed, did have a certain way with clichés. He asked about their campaign slogans. They had a list.

"I Like Ike" was among them.

"Peace and Power with Eisenhower" was another.

The last was "Eisenhower. Better even than the Little Flower."

"That's only meant for use in New York," said Dickerson. "Little Flower" was the name by which New York mayor Fiorello La Guardia had been known.

It was getting late. Cros and the three businessmen took the elevator down and went outside together. A Rolls-Royce drove up.

"Good night, gentlemen," Converse said. A uniformed chauffeur held the door open and the limousine purred away.

"I was afraid of that," said Thornburg. "For God's sake don't put that in. People might get the wrong impression."

What Thornburg had called the "wrong" impression was exactly the message Cros wanted to convey. The piece appeared in PM as "I-Like-Ike-for-President GHQ Purrs Smooth and Easy as a Rolls-Royce."

Most New Dealers, including Eleanor Roosevelt, believed that liberalism should have nothing to do with communism. They joined the Americans for Democratic Action, supporting a strongly interventionist, internationalist foreign policy and a pro-union, liberal domestic policy.

PM did not disavow the Communists. It considered them a legitimate political party, one among others. It supported Henry Wallace and the Progressive Citizens of America (PCA).

Henry Wallace had taken on leadership of the PCA after having been passed over by FDR for the vice presidency. The PCA encompassed a broad spectrum of members—on the left, communist sympathizers and on the right, establishment liberals. Its platform called for progressive taxation, federal aid to education, women's rights, civil rights, national economic planning, government ownership of the power industry, expansion of welfare and Social Security, and health and unemployment insurance. In foreign affairs, it sought negotiation with the Soviet Union and acceptance of it as having a legitimate sphere of influence in Eastern Europe. It advocated against the Truman doctrine and NATO, and explicitly pleaded for support of the revolutionary striving of former colonial nations.

The PCA became the Progressive Party. Wallace traveled the country speaking out against the Cold War and for cooperation with the Soviet Union. He attacked the Marshall Plan, blamed Truman for Stalin's takeover of Czechoslovakia, and predicted that Truman's "bipartisan reactionary war policy" would end with American soldiers "lying in their Arctic suits in the Russian snow." The United States, Wallace said, was heading toward fascism.

When the Truman Doctrine of "containment" to stop Russian expansion was declared in 1947, "to support free peoples who are resisting attempted subjugation by armed minorities or outside pressures," Wallace predicted it marked the beginning of "a century of fear."

As the November 1948 elections came closer, Henry Wallace formally announced his candidacy. Among his strongest supporters were Afro-American leaders like W. E. B. Du Bois and Paul Robeson, who foresaw that black people worldwide would want to overthrow colonial powers. The Progressive Party lost the CIO, a big labor bloc, though, when forces that wanted to purge labor of communist affiliations forced the CIO to stop supporting the Wallace campaign.

PM still refused to take an anti-communist stand. But in 1947 Lewis, perhaps recalling McCleary's "think" piece, made a weak and belated attempt to change course. "*PM* unequivocally opposes communism in the United States of America.

         AHAB IN SEERSUCKER

By the same sign, we refuse to join up with the rabidly hysterical anti-communists, whether they be disillusioned former party members, or that hysterical band of reactionaries which seeks power by attacking any and all progressive movements as communistic. Internationally, PM believes that the capitalist democracy of the U.S.A. can live in peace with the communist Soviet. PM wants to prevent war with Russia and to build a progressive movement here."

The paper continued to support Wallace. But was anybody listening? With FDR gone, PM no longer had the ear of the powers in Washington. It had never had the ear of most of the American people. Those who denounced the New Deal, labor, and the Soviet Union now did.

Anti-communist hysteria was infecting the country. The case of Alger Hiss became a flash point for anti-liberal sentiment. Cros knew Hiss as a brilliant man who had served at high levels in the State Department and been involved with the formation of the United Nations. Like Cros, he was a Frankfurter protégé. Whittaker Chambers, testifying to the HUAC, accused Hiss of being a communist spy. Hiss filed a suit against him when he made the accusation publicly. Then a HUAC subcommittee led by Richard Nixon inflamed fears of a broad underground communist conspiracy within the ranks of the U.S. government. Liberals vehemently defended Hiss. The case would reveal the depths of dissatisfaction many ordinary Americans had with what, to them, had become the "liberal establishment," for in their eyes, it had become just that. An establishment.

Truman tried to appease the country's unease, imposing loyalty oaths on all federal employees and vowing that all Communists and communist sympathizers would be, without deliberation, removed from the government. Cros was alarmed. By virtue of his association with PM, he could be branded a "Communist sympathizer."

He wanted to get to the bottom of this. Was there a pattern to why people were so vulnerable to fear now?

He found one. The country seemed to go through inflation and red scares while recovering from wars. Cros sought out one of the few men he could find who had lived through the red scare that followed World War I.

His name was McAlister Coleman. He was a man of slight build, with graying bushy hair and deepening lines in his face. His dark eyes were lustrous and gentle, and his smile was warm. He was nearing sixty, a prominent Socialist, and "a distinguished alumnus of many American jails." Cros talked to him in the offices of *The New York Call*, a weekly Socialist Party newspaper for which he wrote a column.

To understand the red scare of the 1920s, Coleman said, you had to understand the temper of those times. "Democracy was at low ebb. It was bankrupt. We were a nation of contented cows with no urge to kick the hand that milked us."

He remembered vividly the night of January 2, 1921. "Ten thousand men and women, aliens and citizens, were rounded up in police stations and offices of the Department of Justice in almost every industrial city in the nation." The raids were under the direction of one Mitchell Palmer. Half of those arrested were picked up without any warrants at all. Their homes were entered and searched. In many instances they were severely beaten, separated from their families, and held in police offices, without any word of their whereabouts being sent to their relatives. Working men and women suspected of having radical sympathies were held incommunicado for days. A group of prominent lawyers investigated what had taken place and wrote a report. Under the guise of a campaign for the suppression of radical activities, the Office of the Attorney General, acting with its local agents throughout the country and given express instructions from Washington, had committed illegal acts. The Palmer dragnet pulled in Coleman.

In October of 1920 in Meriden, Connecticut, Coleman had been scheduled to give a speech. "But the American Legion guys had machine guns mounted around the square," said Coleman. "Finally, a butcher, a Socialist friend of ours, let us have a wooden table for me to talk from."

When he got up to speak, Coleman started to read the Constitution of the State of Connecticut. "Now it so happens that the Constitution of the State of Connecticut is a very liberal document," he said. "They have provisions for freedom of speech and worship and assembly. I got through the first paragraph, just about, when the chief of police arrested me."

Coleman quickly noticed that the poor old police chief was scared to death. His hands trembled. Coleman felt sorry for him. "He was all dressed up with a new uniform, badges all shined up, and fresh white gloves."

A crowd was following the police chief to the jail. The old chief turned to Coleman and said, "Disperse this crowd!"

"Hell, I'm not going to disperse the crowd. That's your job," said Coleman.

The chief took him to jail and then, having discovered that Coleman's grandfather was a distinguished Connecticut banker, took him to his own home, where his wife made him a steak dinner.

The next day Coleman was found guilty, fined $25, and ordered to serve two weeks in jail. The case was appealed by Alberto Silva, an American Civil Liberties Union lawyer, and heard in front of the State Supreme Court in New Haven, where the decision was reversed. The American Civil Liberties Union would use the decision often during the red scare, which did not end until about 1929.

Cros asked Coleman what he learned that might shed light on the current version of the red scare.

"I learned that any repressive laws passed against any minority group cannot be administered. It is against every human right and results in more disorder than if the minority is allowed to speak and to exercise their constitutional rights. Much of the present red scare is directed against the Communists. Actually the Communists are on the wane. But any arrests of Communists will make thousands of new members, especially among the working class."

Housing was booming. Colleges and universities were full to the brim with students, freezers crammed with flash-frozen vegetables, and the airwaves on their way to buzzing with television channels. But beneath the prosperity, the country seethed with anxiety and mistrust. The Cold War, inflation, and domestic fascist groups made for an uneasy peace.

Just as J. Parnell Thomas knew how to exploit jealousies among the classes in New Jersey, a man named Homer Loomis did the same thing in Georgia. In the summer of 1946 in Atlanta, the nation's first neo-Nazi political organization, the Columbians, came on the scene. The Columbians claimed 5,000 members, although anti-fascist organizations that investigated them estimated only 250.

As they put it, their work was "to scare niggers." Intimidating the city's minorities by patrolling neighborhoods in racial transition, they threatened anyone who dared cross the city's "color line." What intrigued Cros most about the story was that Homer Loomis, their leader, had an elite upbringing and was even then living in his father's Park Avenue apartment while on bail awaiting trial in Georgia for unlawful possession of dynamite.

By what path had this child of privilege become a neo-Nazi? What did the appearance of the Columbians portend for the country? The possible answers were disturbing. Cros wanted to get some actual ones.

Cros tracked down Loomis's friends from his Park Avenue "right schools," his socialite life, and his Princeton years. He visited a friend from his St. Paul's days, now living on the

Upper East Side. They sat across from each other in arm-chairs in the man's living room.

"Homer was definitely not 'one of the boys,'" the man said, prep school manners and accent impeccable. "The interesting thing about him was that he didn't seem to mind." Most of the outsiders felt left out and inferior. "Not Homer. He took his being 'out' as a mark of distinction."

"Oh?" Cros's notebook was filling up with details.

"He actually became the leader of the other boys who were not 'in,'" the man said. "It was amazing to watch."

Sensing the man had intuitions he wasn't voicing, Cros asked, "Did he do anything as their leader?"

"Not much. He went on to Princeton. I heard he drank and partied his way through there. He got kicked out after his sophomore year, but he kept coming back to drink in the dorms and they had to order him off campus for good."

"Ever hear anything else?"

"Get this. When he got kicked off campus, he said his future actions would bring credit to the university and they would ask him back, and only then would he consider it."

Cros got a warm feeling. He was beginning to find the story. The two men stood up. The St. Paul's man asked if he would like to join him for lunch at his club, but Cros said he had to be on his way, shook his hand, and headed out.

As the elevator door was about to close, the man held it open. He'd remembered one last thing. "My Princeton friend said old Homer read Gibbon's *Decline and Fall of the Roman Empire* and started telling everybody that if you read that one book, you'd understand everything you'd ever need to know about the world."

Cros filled up more notebooks. Loomis had married twice, both times to heiresses; both marriages failed. He persuaded his second wife to set him up as a moviemaker in Florida; then as a gentleman farmer in Mississippi, which he decided was no good; and finally in Virginia, on another farm. There he

came to see that the poor white workmen he hired were dominated by a continuing fear, that of racial equality. They bitterly
resented the increasing wages paid to Negroes. He read *Mein
Kampf.* He told everyone it was the greatest book ever written. Impressed with Hitler's asceticism, he stopped drinking.

Meanwhile, on Park Avenue, Mrs. Loomis was having a
hard time finding guests to fill up her dinner parties. Her
husband's boring tirades about the inevitability of fascism,
which he had foreseen as an associate of Mussolini's government while general counsel for the Italian Line, attracted
few repeat listeners.

Homer Loomis joined the army. His second child was born.
He began to talk about organizing a group. His wife knew
what he meant. "If you come back with any more of your
strange ideas, I'm going to divorce you," she said. When he
came back with even stranger ideas, she did.

Now, it was time to meet Homer Loomis himself. Cros
tried to reach him by telephone. No answer. Two days later,
setting out early in the morning, armed with the only photograph he had of the man, he headed for Loomis's Park Avenue
address. Noon came and went and he was still waiting. Then,
unmistakably, Homer Loomis emerged from the revolving
door. Cros moved toward him.

"Are you Homer Loomis?"

The man tried to move away.

Cros followed him and held out his hand. "Look," he said,
"I just want to know all about the Columbians."

Loomis put his hands in his coat pockets and kept walking, but Cros kept up with him and looked straight into his
eyes. "What are they planning? What do you want to do?" He
turned his palms upward, tilted his head, and grinned. "I'm
very interested. I figured if anyone could tell me, it'd be you."

Loomis softened.

Then he spoke for three hours. Loomis had something to
say about everything. The Jews: they have a plan for world

domination. The Nazis: if their plan had succeeded we'd all be speaking German. We want to speak American. America: the United States has just three enemies—the Japs, the Germans, and the Communists. The UN: "This international stuff is just selling America out to anybody, to nigras [as he put it] and to anybody. It's not natural. Man is an animal and animals like their own. . . .

"I'm a nationalist," Loomis said. "There's nothing wrong with loving your country, is there?"

"I guess there's nothing wrong with loving your country," Cros mumbled. Loomis was looking at him so intently that Cros shifted uneasily and moved away.

Loomis's talk became disjointed. He jumped around quickly and his words flew out so fast Cros stopped trying to take notes. "There can't be a real nationalism without blood unity," he was repeating to himself as he walked away. Back in the office writing the story, Cros got a call from one of his early sources on Loomis, a Princeton friend Loomis had solicited for money for the Columbians. Loomis had gone straight to his apartment after talking to Cros, arriving at his door incoherent and distraught.

"What's happened to you?" the friend had asked Loomis. "You weren't like this before, this Jew stuff. When did you start thinking up all this stuff?"

"I guess it was down in Virginia," Loomis said. "I'd stopped drinking and the farm wasn't using up my mental energies."

"But look at you. You could end up in jail."

"If I go to jail for a while, it'll give me a chance to think and to write a book, *Thunder in the South*. I'm going to have a mighty army and we're going to march on New York," Loomis said. "I'm going to be the Hitler of America." Loomis stood up suddenly and headed for the door.

"Frankly, Homer," the friend called after him, "I think you've gone nuts." Down in Georgia, Loomis faced multiple indictments: usurping police powers, inciting to riot, possession of explosives, and accessory charges in the brutal beating of a black man. Cros watched as Loomis's defense, managed by his father, who knew nothing of criminal law, failed. By the time the jury's verdict came in, Loomis faced three years in jail on the first charge, and on another, a year's hard labor at the Georgian State Penitentiary. Trials on the other charges brought his sentence to a total of three years. But as the appeals process dragged on, Loomis and the cofounder of the Columbians, Emory C. Burke, a railroad draftsman who had been Loomis's fellow "race warrior," were free to walk Atlanta's streets. The Columbians fell to fighting among themselves and faded out. By the spring of 1950, Loomis and Burke began serving their chain-gang sentences.

The American white supremacist movement, of which the Columbians were only a chapter, continued under other names.

It was two years after Cros had reported on Victory in Europe Day from West Forty-ninth Street, and European cities still lay in ruins. People were homeless and starving. The transportation infrastructure was in shambles, leaving the countryside isolated. *Time*'s Man of the Year in 1947 was George C. Marshall, former Army chief of staff and now Truman's secretary of state. He had emerged universally admired for his contributions during the wartime years. Truman called him "the greatest living American." Winston Churchill said he was "the organizer of Victory." He would go on to win the Nobel Peace Prize.

Early in 1943 *PM* had advocated for massive American economic aid to Europe, including Germany. George C. Marshall organized such a program and spearheaded it. On June 5, 1947, he announced a plan to rebuild and modernize Europe's economy along American lines. The plan offered the same aid to the Soviet Union and its allies, but the Soviet Union forbade its satellites to participate.

Henry Wallace opposed the Marshall Plan. His view was that money lent to Europe would support American-style capitalism and divide the world into hostile camps competing via their two different economic systems. Exporting capitalism would strengthen the influence of American business abroad and exacerbate economic inequalities at home.

PM's peace liberals continued to support Wallace for the 1948 Democratic presidential nomination while still endorsing the Marshall Plan. But there was concern that Wallace's candidacy would split the Democratic vote and throw the election to the Republicans, just as Republican Theodore Roosevelt's Bull Moose Party had led to the victory of Democrat Woodrow Wilson.

Cros supported Wallace, but he was very drawn to Marshall. He liked the style of this "Southern gentleman" from "lineage-proud Southern gentlefolk." Pretty much a full biography on him had been written in the recent news, but PM sent Cros to Uniontown, Pennsylvania, to fill in a missing chapter, the boyhood story of the man who had such power to affect the postwar world's future. What Cros would find reassuring was that Marshall's father had been "a splendid organizer" but had too much a Southern gentleman's "faith in his fellow man" to beat out the likes of Frick and Mellon. Maybe somehow under the junior Marshall, the cutthroat brand of capitalism might not be the hallmark of a postwar economic reconstruction of Europe. Cros began tracking down everyone he could find who had known him.

Marshall's father had moved from the South to make his fortune as a coal and coke operator in Uniontown, seventeen and a half miles north of the Mason-Dixon Line. Marshall called his youth a happy one. Cros took pictures of Marshall's boyhood haunts—the stream he swam in, now edged with industrial buildings; the backyard where he had played. He found out the names of the boys in his boyhood gang. His old friend Alex Mead, the only one left, told of their exploits.

The gang, with Marshall the leader, had explored a great natural cave with candles and a roll of twine that they fastened to a rock and paid out, and had searched for honey and gotten stung by hornets. They built locks and canals and a water wheel and a raft on Coal Lick Run. "The stories of the trouble George Marshall used to get into, of his schoolboy pranks, have increased with his fame and achievements," Cros observed.

But strikes in the coalfields grew more frequent, and violence touched the Marshall family. Strikers came to shoot his father. The young George Marshall heard them coming down the street. One of the strikers took a shot at the end of his father's lighted cigar and missed. Marshall Sr. stubbed out his cigar and hid in an alleyway until they went away.

When young Marshall was nine, his father lost his fortune. Marshall Sr. and his partner Arthur Weir Bliss had amassed some three thousand coke ovens, but men like Frick and Mellon outcompeted them. Marshall and Bliss sold out their holdings to Frick, invested the funds, and overexpanded, while a depression tightened money. The banks called in loans and Marshall was wiped out. His wife sold land that she had inherited, and the family survived. "If Bliss and Marshall had been anything but Southerners, they'd have made fortunes in coal and coke," the junior Marshall said.

Even without a fortune, the Marshalls lived a gracious life. On Saturday nights there was a cotillion at the Laurel Club. The ladies wore silk, brocade, or velvet. Marshall Sr. drove a horse and buggy, had a "back like a ramrod," was a rector at the Episcopal Church, and wore a cutaway when he passed the plate on Sundays. He carved a turkey as skillfully as a surgeon. "A gentleman never stands to carve a turkey," he loved to say.

Then came the day when, at seventeen, George C. Marshall's family drove him to the railroad station. George took the train for Charlottesville, waved good-bye to his family and to Uniontown, and went off to Virginia Military Institute, returning only for short visits. After that, his was the story of a man who rose to the highest levels of power serving his country.

Another thing pleased Cros. He loved, especially at Thanksgiving, to tell the story of how Marshall Jr., who, like his father, believed that "a gentleman should never carve a turkey standing up," had in later years been the object of a complicated trick played on him by his family. The cook had prepared two turkeys, one young and succulent and the other old and tough. The old one came first to the table. Sitting down, Marshall tried to cut into it but could not. He tried and tried again until finally he gave up and stood up. As he sliced the knife down into the bird, it slipped off the platter and landed in the lap of the lady to his left.

Then the cook brought in the young bird. Marshall sat down and carved like a gentleman.

Of all the men Cros wrote about, he seemed to like George C. Marshall the best.

At *PM*, staff morale was plummeting. For a long time the paper had been doing more with less. Although as associate editor, Cros had responsibility for others' work as well as his own, the number of bylined pieces he did skyrocketed. Then a mass economy firing of twenty-three went to arbitration. At the Guild meeting, management contended that monthly losses had gone from $24,720 in November to $35,190 in March, despite the new advertising income. Although the Guild had finally acknowledged that *PM* should not be used as a trailblazer because of Field's wealth, it still made its case against the economy firings on the grounds that *PM*'s desperate situation must always be considered "in the light of the fact that Marshall Field is, as far as this record shows, indefinitely committed to meeting *PM*'s needs and obligations." Neither side made any real concessions.

Marshall Field was indeed most definitely not committed to meeting *PM*'s needs and obligations indefinitely. Since mid-1947, managing editors John Lewis and Rae Weimer had been in discussion with Field about what to do about the paper. The two proposed a national newspaper on the *PM* model, perhaps a weekly instead of the daily. Field dismissed the idea. He was concentrating on his own newspaper in Chicago and told Lewis and Weimer he was looking for a purchaser for *PM*.

The New York City newspaper *FrontPage* reported on the result of Field's search. Clinton D. McKinnon was a California publisher and a Democratic congressional candidate who was willing to take over. The sale was announced at two p.m. on March 15, 1948. At the March 18 Newspaper Guild meeting, Zinny Schoales, former personal secretary to Ingersoll and still at *PM*, didn't even take minutes because she felt she was "neither fish nor fowl," the paper having been, in effect, sold.

As the winter progressed, even the sale of *PM* looked chancy. The Newspaper Guild objected to it because McKinnon was not willing to abide by contract guarantees to the employees. McKinnon said that he could not meet the terms of the existing workers and withdrew. The sale fell through.

Things were getting tight on the first floor of 66 Bedford Street. I was a handful, a whopping three-year-old with boisterous energy, and Lucey was beginning to crawl, an age needing constant supervision. The rooms that had once seemed so spacious to a couple with one child and another on the way now were cramped. Cros was often restless and agitated, touchy and irritable. He bore the troubles of the world on his shoulders. He was often on the telephone about a story, and when at last he hung up, he would begin expostulating about something that was wrong with the world. Bickering was becoming background noise. Nobody seemed to really know what it was all about.

But Marjory and Cros, Louise said, could bicker over the color of the sky.

"O horrors, Croswell," she would say.

Cros would go to work and Mom would be alone with us, but if the weather was good, Louise would come to take us for a walk. She would pile Lucey into the baby carriage, take me by the hand, and we would all head for Washington Square Park to feed the pigeons. I was a young duckling eager to be trusted to look out for myself, straining at her hand, so I loved it when she said, "Now run along to the corner and then stop," which I did.

Marjory was grateful for the respite Louise's help gave her. She would go uptown on a few errands, or maybe to Central Park with a book to read. Then the whole family would meet up for dinner that evening, usually at the Blue Mill, two blocks away, where the menu was written in careful European handwriting on a floor-stand chalkboard. My favorite was grilled chopped sirloin that came with fresh, fat green peas. There was a bar at the back, and behind it a wooden telephone booth my father would spring toward to make one last call to a source, then a few more.

Those could be jolly times. But sometimes Dad's mood was grim. The Democratic Party needed fresh leadership. He had pinned hopes on his old friend Charles Bolte, who was idealistic and eloquent, but in the end, he could tell, Bolte really wanted to retire to the country and write. Franklin D. Roosevelt Jr. was promising, but underneath Cros sensed he did not have the compassion for the little guy his father had, and would probably settle down to a lucrative law practice and dinners with good china and crystal on the table and his prep school friends as guests.

But there was Cord Meyer Jr. Like Bolte, he had been injured in the war, losing an eye to a Japanese grenade. Like Bolte, he had written about the experience eloquently in *The Atlantic Monthly*. Like Roosevelt Jr., he came from a wealthy family whose politics were liberal. Meyer Sr. had made money in real estate and the family rose to prominence in diplomacy. Meyer Jr. had gone to St. Paul's and Yale, graduating in 1942 and enlisting as a Marine. In 1945 he married Mary Pinchot, daughter of Amos Pinchot, a wealthy progressive who spoke out against communism, big business, and America's entry into World War II. Then Meyer became an aide to Harold Stassen at the 1945 San Francisco UN conference, helped found the United World Federalists in 1947, and became its president.

Cros wanted to write an article that would advance Meyer's career and the goal of world peace, but even Meyer himself was skeptical about the chances for that. "Meyer thinks the only time world government is achievable is when we've got the bomb and nobody else does," Cros would have grumbled, and then gone silent.

Cros spent a long time on the telephone with follow-up calls and typed his story late into the night. "Young Man in Quest of Peace" was the last political profile he wrote for *PM*, and appeared in the March 21, 1948, issue. Later, he would express his disgust that Meyer had rebuked his own ideals and become a CIA man.

Cros had known for a long time that *PM*'s days were numbered, but he was determined to hang on until the bitter end. A news release announced that a press conference would be held by two Romanian royals deposed by the Communists, King Michael and Queen Mother Helen of Romania. As was the custom when dignitaries arrived, the press conference would take place on the ocean liner as it pulled into New York harbor. Reporters rode cutters out into the harbor. Cros knew his days of nimbly leaping from cutter to liner were over, but he wanted to prove to himself he could do the story. Besides, two deposed royals made good copy. He took his camera and as soon as the cutter was lashed to the *Queen Elizabeth*, boarded her on a gangplank and found suite 77, a throng around its entrance.

The royals traveled royally. They had two trunks and forty-four smaller pieces of luggage. The king was tall, his carriage graceful and military, his age twenty-six, but there was a worried frown between his eyes. The throng moved into a room where the royal pair mounted a dais, the sort where an orchestra would sit. The reporters shot questions at them.

There came a zinger. A young reporter held up the front page of the *New York Times*. "Have you heard of the suicide of Jan Masaryk?" Masaryk, son of the first president of Czechoslovakia and, since 1940, foreign minister of the Czech government-in-exile, had returned to Prague after the war as part of the National Front government, but the Czech Communists had opposed participation in the Marshall Plan and seized power in the "Czech coup." Masaryk had just been found dead in his pajamas, below his bathroom window, in the courtyard of the Foreign Ministry.

The young king looked incredulous. Then a grimace of terror crossed his face and he grew pale. Someone thrust the *Times* in front of him. "Masaryk Funeral Is Held in Prague. Czechoslovaks Weeping at Funeral of Jan Masaryk," the headline read.

The King looked up in wonder.

Did he have any comment?

No.

"When do you think you can get your throne back?"

"That," remarked the Queen Mother, "is a stiff question."

Cros snapped a picture and the boat docked. The royal pair disembarked, limousines and a motorcycle escort's engines humming. Cros had come a long way since the time he had lain flat on his back on a train out of Cairo, believing he would never take pictures again. *PM* had given him the chance to do work he believed in. It would be hard to see it end, but he and many of the staff suspected it was going to. What no picture could have shown, but he was beginning to understand, was that Churchill had been right. An Iron Curtain was indeed descending across Europe, a thought he'd have shaken from his head as the motorcycle engines roared and the limousines headed off for the Waldorf Astoria.

Cros's last two PM pieces, brief ones, appeared on May 2 and 3, 1948.

At PM arguments between labor and management had continued. At its April meeting, the Newspaper Guild had asked to reinstate several winter vacations that had been canceled. Management refused. With morale in its present condition, it required all hands on deck to put out the paper.

Marshall Field called upon another possible buyer, a Californian by the name of Bartley Crum, a well-known liberal lawyer whom Cros knew from the House Un-American Activities Committee as counsel for the Hollywood Ten. Crum had been very much involved with the Wendell Willkie campaign and was a peace liberal like Cros. He was a one-of-a kind man who put his legal abilities, often pro bono, in service to the causes of the far left, meanwhile making a substantial living defending wealthy clients in corporate America. Field felt Crum "might be attracted to a lost cause." He was. Crum deliberated, hoping he would be able to raise money in time to take over the expense of running the paper before the million dollars Field offered to see it through the transition ran out. The plan was that Joseph Barnes, another Wendell Willkie aide and a friend of Crum's, would become the new editor.

On April 23 PM had new owners. Bartley Crum and Joseph Barnes took over. The mood in the pressroom was "a second honeymoon." On June 23 PM was renamed the *New York Star*. At the eleventh hour, Crum and Barnes steered the paper toward Truman. Lewis and Weimer left in June. Cros did, too.

On the day PM folded, I was a small, quiet, unnoticed presence on a New York City sidewalk gripping tight my mother's hand in the midst of a cluster of agitated adults. My father, in his fedora and reporter's trench coat, paced the sidewalk. He was elated. Impassioned. Effusive.

"The labor union saved me!" he called out.

All those months while the war replacement case had been in arbitration, he'd been able to hold on and do his work. But now the paper was finished, and he had no job.

Looking back, I know it was in the PM years that the Stanley Lincoln inside my father finally stood tall. I think of him as he was then, press card stuck in the brim of his fedora, in his trench coat, reporter's notebook in hand. "Always be thinking of ledes," he'd tell me, and he was. He'd be mustering up every ounce of charm he had to get the source to say more. He was listening, really listening, and if the source came up dry, he'd flash him a grin and thank him and ask for a steer on the next one. He channeled everything he thought and felt into getting those stories and telling them true.

I wasn't sure what being fired meant, although I could tell it was bad. But I knew my father still was a lucky man. And I knew exactly why. The little people were still on his side. Things would always get better.

He had told me that.

Luck did not leave my father with PM's demise. It left him later.

There were close ties between PM and *The New Yorker*. It had been clear for a long time that PM might fold. Cros's reporting showed Shawn that he had mastered the "Talk of the Town" subject and had a deft hand with the "reporter at large" style. Certainly he had the ability to do a profile. The occasion for his 1947 PM "Sidelong Glance at a Profiler" had been the publication of Geoffrey Hellman's first collection of *New Yorker* pieces, *How to Disappear for an Hour*. Geoffrey Hellman was a *New Yorker* profiler himself, a man "whose humor was the driest in town and than whom no man had made a finer thing of writing about the foibles of other people." Cros had asked all the right questions and done up Hellman in fine style, missing nothing.

His tryout for *The New Yorker* paid off with a staff job. The offices were uptown, at 25 West Forty-fifth Street. For now, he had landed on his feet. The Bowen family began looking for a year-round house in the country. Marjory was the strong one. She felt she could get by during the week alone, and wanted to. Louise's bottomless benevolence had been a great help, but Cros's expectant attitude toward it troubled her. Cros would be free to do his work in New York, staying at 66 Bedford and taking the train out on the weekends. Mom told me that we wouldn't go back to the city much at all, but if we did go and we got to go to a park, we were not to drink from a water fountain. You could catch polio that way, and polio was what made Dad walk with a limp.

Sherman was a sleepy country town. Its center was a general store and a post office. Up the hill were a gas station with one gas pump and a red Coca-Cola machine, and a church. Hidden Hollow was nearby, but it was too cold to live there in the winter, so we found an old colonial farmhouse with lots of land that had been fancied up in the Victorian era with white gingerbread trim and a star-shaped window in the attic. We named it Star House, and went out there on fall weekends, moving in furniture. Mom cooked a Thanksgiving dinner in the farmhouse kitchen, and I devoured the whole drumstick.

The Cowleys were still in Sherman, and there were other friends Cros had made in the ten years since he had bought Hidden Hollow. There were Dan and Marion Gerow, gentle Quaker farmers who named a cow after each of the Bowen girls. There were neighbors up the hill from Hidden Hollow, the Damrosches, with four daughters, and close by, their relatives, the distinguished but slightly fearsome Tee Van husband and wife, both naturalists. And down the road from Star House was Alice Rogers, the mother of two children older than us, who became Mom's dear friend.

With Roosevelt dead, would there be a liberal in the next White House? Cros kept a watchful eye on the 1948 elections. On the day of the voting, the polls and the newspapers were confident that the Republican Dewey would win. In the South, Strom Thurmond had led the States Rights Democratic Party, or Dixiecrats, on a platform of upholding segregation and the Jim Crow laws. The party was not on the ballot in enough states to win the election, but they hoped to draw votes from the Democrats and send the election into the House of Representatives. In the North, the Progressive Party, with Wallace leading, mounted a passionate platform of leftist liberalism that might also draw strength away from Truman.

Dewey had deliberately run a low-key campaign, thinking himself to be a shoe-in. Newspapers across the country, all Republican, supported him and predicted victory. The pollsters predicted victory, too.

But Harry Truman believed none of it. If he had heard it, he ignored it. He crossed and recrossed the country, speaking at whistle stops, giving 'em hell until his new nickname became "Give 'em Hell Harry." The *Chicago Tribune*, Col. Robert McCormick's pro-Republican newspaper, archrival of *PM*, was so sure of Dewey's victory it printed the next day's headline, "Dewey Defeats Truman," on election night.

Dewey did not defeat Truman. Truman won 49.6 percent of the popular vote to Dewey's 45.1 percent and won in the Electoral College. The States Rights Democrats and the Progressives together won only 2.4 percent of the popular vote. The Democrats regained control of Congress. The Democratic Party had four more years to show what it could do.

PM's successor paper, the *New York Star*, had only months.

We moved out to Star House for good in the winter of 1948. On a snowy day we took the train out to Pawling and all piled into the Ford, which got stuck in the snow going up Quaker

Hill from the railroad station, so Mom and Dad left us together and trudged ahead to a neighbor's house, coming back with a snow shovel and a bucket of sand. They found us curled up on the backseat, huddling together for protection. That evening we all ate together at the large dining room table and slept upstairs, my sister and I in separate bedrooms for the first time.

In the big farmhouse kitchen Mom made creamed chipped beef on toast with margarine—I kneaded the orange dye in the middle of the package until the white mass turned yellow. There was pineapple upside down cake, and sugar frostings for our birthday cakes out of beaten egg whites with a stream of boiling sugar whipped in. She upholstered furniture and sewed her clothes and ours, and taught us our prayers and put us to bed and was there in the morning when we woke up. She and a few other mothers started a cooperative nursery school in the local church. The mothers took turns reading stories to us and, come spring, watched over the outdoor sandbox where we played. At night on the lawn of Star House, there were fireflies. Mom taught us to catch them in glass jars with a hole punched in the cap for air, and to put in twigs and leaves for them to perch on. I pretended I could read by their light.

I was growing fast, and when Dad came home, I could no longer really jump into his lap for stories. Our conversations took place while he was driving. There was no more gas rationing, so he would take me on trips just for fun, even though they were a big luxury. Off we would go, into the rolling foothills of the Connecticut Berkshires, to visit some friend of his or another. There was Charlie Duell, who kept a gentleman's farm and ran the publishing company he had founded, Duell, Sloan, and Pearce. There were trips to Lake Mauweehoo, where Pier Lund, an old Provincetown Players hand, would tell the stories about the Viking ship he'd seen come down out of the sky and land on the lake. There was

AHAB IN SEERSUCKER

Leapy Patterson. Rides in Leapy's black Model T Ford were a big money raiser at the church fair, most fun of all when he blew a tire and got upset. There were polo matches on the hill behind the lake, rather grand affairs for a country town but a harbinger of the upscale community Sherman was on the path to becoming.

Dad did not really enjoy the new breed of Sherman people at the polo matches. The Depression had shaped him. Their fancy ways made him uncomfortable. He never bought a newspaper in a luncheonette if he could find one left behind by a previous customer. He routinely bummed cigarettes. To keep the phone bill low, he'd devised a scheme he made sure all his friends knew about. To reach someone, he would call by the more expensive "person-to-person" first. The operator would ask if so-and-so was there, but if he was, Dad had instructed so-and-so to say, "No, but he'll be back in about ten minutes." Dad would then hang up and call back the cheaper way, direct. Once, at a dump, he found a stash of clothes that fit him just right, the wardrobe of a well-dressed man who had just died. He wore the man's smoky green cashmere V-neck sweater for quite some time. The speed limit then was around thirty miles per hour, and he decided that speed was the most efficient. On trips, he would cut off the engine and coast down the hills to save gas, but the brakes would not work until he started the engine up again, which he always managed to do just in time.

In New York, Louise left the Holley Hotel and moved to 66 Bedford. Bill had gone to Munich to work with Radio Free Europe. She lived on the first floor; the second and third were rented out. There were two large rooms front-to-back, with a small kitchen and bathroom at the far back, and a small brick-walled garden. She hired a decorator to make curtains and slipcovers for the front sitting room, and installed a daybed, and had floor-to-ceiling curtains made for the living room windows out of the same linen as the upholstery, a pattern of long-armed monkeys holding onto jungle foliage. She arranged her favorite pieces of furniture from the house in Toledo in elegant style around the fireplace. In the back room, where she set up a card table for our meals, were a wardrobe, closets, and a small single bed.

Sometimes, after we moved to the country, Mom would bring Lucey and me back into New York for a visit with Louise. It was a great treat when she took us on the uptown bus to Best's Department Store, where we'd have our hair cut, eat lunch in a lunchroom, and come home with Best's helium balloons tied to our fingers. Mom had hinted that Louise barely knew how to boil water, but she set up her card table and produced bacon and toast and orange juice for breakfast. For dinner, it was the only dish she knew how to make—chicken cacciatore. We were wriggly children, and the card table was unsteady. "Please don't shake the table," she would say. But chicken cacciatore quickly lost its appeal, and I had a hard time staying still anyhow, so usually it was a choice between the Captain's Table and the Blue Mill. We always chose the Blue Mill.

In the UN preparation for a conflict in Korea had begun back in December of 1948, when "The Problem of the Independence of Korea" resolution was passed in the General Assembly. The Soviet Union refused to cooperate with UN plans to hold general elections in the two Koreas. As a result, a Communist state was permanently established under Soviet auspices in the north and a pro-Western state was set up in the south according to "free and democratic elections." The resolution called for a commission to oversee withdrawal of forces from the country and support unification with independence. By 1949 both the United States and the Soviet Union had withdrawn the majority of their troops from the Korean Peninsula.

But unification was going to be impossible. In early 1949 North Korea was on a war footing. Kim Il Song's New Year's speech was bellicose, excoriating South Korea as a puppet state. The North Korean army expanded rapidly, soldiers drilled in war maneuvers, and bond drives began to raise money to purchase Soviet weaponry. The thirty-eighth parallel was fortified, and border incidents began breaking out. Neither Seoul nor Pyongyang recognized the parallel as a permanent legitimate boundary.

The winter of 1948–49 was, for me, a winter of sledding on the hill in front of Star House, of wet wool mittens and cold fingers, and of coming inside to more wool mittens steaming dry on a clothesline over the big kitchen stove. Mom was occupied with Lucey so I could go exploring. Then came spring, that first and final spring in the country. Dad wanted us to have a "gentleman's farm," so he borrowed a few sheep and grazed them in the field across the road. Lambing time came, and we all went across to see the miracle of a new, young lamb. I peeked into the shed where the ewe had given birth. I smelled the rancid, rank, and bloody afterbirth, and it made me afraid. But then Mom held up the baby lamb for me to see. She was young and fresh-faced, with her arms around the ewe, as if the three of them shared in the glory of this creation. Her smile was full of the joy of new birth.

The day Dad's luck left him was a day in May of 1949. We had been chasing our duck, Quack-Quack, across the front lawn. A fox had broken its neck, but Mom had improvised a splint and fastened it to the duck's long neck with a strip of white sheeting. The duck's neck healed, but the splint fell off and the sheeting, all muddy now, trailed behind the duck. We wanted to catch Quack-Quack and get rid of the muddy bandage, but the duck was having none of it.

Dad was home from the city, agitated. From the farmhouse porch, he shouted, "The country is going to war!"

Mom came out of the house onto the porch to find him there, and I went up to listen. "Von Hayek warned about the military industrial complex!"

A battle had broken out on the border between North and South Korea. President Truman might send General MacArthur to command the troops.

That evening at Star House, the evil faeries came out from under the earth. Like the bombs of Tobruk, the danger came from above, unexpectedly. Walking around the farmhouse that evening, Dad saw that a slate from the roof had worked loose with the spring thaw and fallen onto the ground below.

In bed that night, Marjory next to him, he startled awake.

The time-delayed land mines of war exploded.

Boom! Another slate was falling off the roof.

Boom! And another. Boom! Where were his children?

Boom! He saw the bloodied, broken faces of dead and wounded men.

He struggled out of bed and ran to our bedrooms. We were safe. But only for now. The bombs could come again.

Cros cracked.

Mom drove him to the hospital. Later that day a neighbor visited, bringing an armful of yellow forsythia. She and Mom talked in the kitchen. I overheard her ask if my father was better.

After she left, I asked, "Is Daddy sick?"

"Yes."

"Why did he get sick?"

"He was afraid."

"Why?"

"A slate fell off the roof."

"Did it hit him?"

"No."

"Why was he afraid?"

"He was afraid a slate might hit you and he wouldn't be able to protect you."

Star House was a big house, with a big roof and lots of slates. I had never been behind it before. But that afternoon I decided to walk the whole way around it. I wanted to see if

I could find any slates. I looked up at the roof edge and then down at the ground where a slate would land if it fell. There were no slates there. I turned the corner and began trudging along the back of the house. I heard Mom call my name. She was frantic, but I didn't care. I needed to find out why my father was gone. Then I felt Mom gather me up from behind, lifting me up into her arms, turning me around and crushing me to her, and I could tell she was afraid. She was afraid of slates, too.

That night Mom read to us from our picture book of Greek myths. She read the story of Daedalus and Icarus. Daedalus made wings so his son Icarus could fly, but he warned him that they were made of wax. If he flew too close to the sea, they would grow heavy and he would die. If he flew too close to the sun, they would melt and he would die. But Icarus didn't listen, and he died.

"Why did he die?"

"He flew too close to the sun."

I could tell Mom was trying to teach us to be careful in ways Dad had not been, about not flying too high or too low. She wanted us to learn that so something terrible would not happen to us, too.

A few days afterward, she put us in the care of the nursery school mothers and drove into New York to see Cros in the Payne Whitney Psychiatric Clinic. I see her finding Dad lying on a small bed covered by a white spread. He was completely still. He did not speak. His face was pasty white. There was a chalky whiteness on his lips. His eyes were dull and motionless. He had not eaten or slept for days.

She sat on his bed and tried to be as close to him as she could get. He did not move. He said nothing.

Then he spoke. He spoke very slowly. She did not interrupt him for fear he would stop.

He said he could not go against a commandment and kill himself, but he did not think there was any reason to live anymore. He could not love her. He blamed himself for not being a good father, for *PM*'s folding, for not being able to earn a living. She would have to take care of the children, but the world was unsafe and she should know that. He had tried to do work that would keep the world at peace, but all his work was a failure. The country was going to war again.

She was three months pregnant. Bleeding, she made her way back to Star House, and the pregnancy held.

On the advice of the psychiatrist who treated him, Dr. Brooks, Cros spent a few weeks in Key West, Florida, to recover, and then came back to family life. That June, the four Bowens with a fifth on the way attended his twentieth Yale reunion. The Class of 1929 had decided to broadcast its support of organized labor by wearing workingmen's clothing. Afterward, on a field outside the class dinner tent, a classmate snapped a picture of us, Cros in a pair of blue-and-white-striped bib overalls looking like a locomotive engineer with a Rolleiflex slung around his neck. Mom wore a dress she had made with her sewing machine and stood with one hand on my shoulder and the other around the string of a blue helium balloon. Lucey clung to Dad. With his young, pregnant wife and two children, Cros was the family man he wanted to become. Peter Croswell Bowen was born in September 1949.

EIGHT

The Fifties and Its Discontents

I n the 1950s Cros saw flocks of sheep everywhere. From a crowded New York City subway platform, waiting for a passenger inside to exit, he would call out, "Will the inside flock of sheep please exit this subway car so that this outside flock of sheep can enter?"

All around him, writers he had known and worked with seemed to be choking on the full-throated public political speech they had once gloried in. Bartley Crum from the PM days, and New York liberal writers such as Lillian Hellman, Dashiell Hammett, and Dorothy Parker had been severely attacked, their careers damaged.

Red scare tactics he'd seen in operation at the trial of the Hollywood Ten were having a broad effect, even greater than those old McAlister Coleman had lived through after World War I. Joseph McCarthy and his Senate subcommittee flouted individual freedoms and rights in the name of combating Communist influence. Fear instilled a sheepish conformity. Liberals in general, as well as government employees, the entertainment industry, and left-wing activists, fell under suspicion of being subversive.

Cros suspected he was considered guilty merely for having

written for PM and *The New Yorker*. He was. In 1946, researching a piece for PM, he had come afoul of J. Edgar Hoover's FBI.
Needing their cooperation, they denied access. He protested.
They were "favoring some reporters over others." The accusation went unanswered. To Cros, this was more than personal;
it was an affront to the free press, vital to the democracy.

If "guilt by association" made you watch what you said,
did, and wrote, the *New Yorker* headquarters were a refuge,
serious and businesslike on the surface, but underneath offering the comfort of sharing the struggle with other writers,
most of them liberals of one stripe or another. His office was a
small room with a desk, a typewriter, stacks of paper, carbon
paper, and a screw-top jar of rubber cement, a brush fastened
into the top for cutting and pasting when he edited. He took
his daughters in to see it; they'd loved it. At first he was just
a no-name staffer. That didn't stop him from giving a talk at
Yale about the inner workings of the classy magazine, getting in a few jibes about Skull and Bones having passed him
over. To his delight, the undergraduate reporter described
him as "everything a Bonesman should be."

Cros's first piece was a Talk of the Town assignment titled
"The Seabury Druids," an account of a visit to a Festival of
Sacred Trees held annually by a group of Jungian nature-
worshippers called the Source Teaching Society, whose
purpose was to "permit modern man to have religious and
mystical experiences despite materialistic pressures." The
festival took place in a Midtown brownstone. In Eustace Til-
ley style, Cros got himself there, asked a few questions, wrote
down the answers, and then drifted over to the buffet table,
on which were spread several jugs of juices and an assort-
ment of figs, dates, almonds, acorns, vanilla beans, tama-
rinds, apples, and bananas. A lady wrapped up in a terry cloth
bathrobe pattered to his side, explained the upcoming ceremony and the symbolic significance of trees, and offered
him a choice of passion fruit, peach, or pomegranate juice.

"Do you dare to mix your drinks?" she asked tenderly.

"I'll have a belt of the passion fruit," he whispered, ducking past her in retreat upstairs to the library, where he immersed himself briefly in Jungian arcana and then left. The piece appeared in the December 3, 1949, issue of *The New Yorker.*

Writing about Jungian tree-worshippers might make the world a more interesting place, but it would not make it a better one.

The Bowens moved to a small house in Irvington, New York, on the banks of the Hudson, a shorter commute to the city than Sherman had been. A wide Main Street led up from the railroad station to the top of the hill, lined with shops, a school, a library, and a town hall. The new house was smaller than Star House, with one bedroom with bunk beds for the two girls and room for the new baby's crib in the master bedroom. There was a backyard with a sandbox for the children.

Cros found an office on Irvington's Main Street, but he missed the tight deadlines and regular appearance in print of the newspaper world. He signed up to write a weekly column for the local *Irvington Gazette*, and joined the volunteer fire department, rushing out on his gimpy leg to follow the big fire truck with the other volunteers. Carl and Betty Carmer, who had moved to Irvington after selling West Twelfth Street, lived close by, and the Bowens visited them in their vast, sparsely furnished old Hudson River Octagon House, with a cupola on top.

Cros wrote more Talk of the Town pieces. Then he began a series of bylined longer Annals of Crime profiles of criminals. It was crime reporting in the style he'd seen done at *PM*, but the slant would be different. He wanted to give these "little guys" a profile as searching as any he'd done of the high and mighty. These men whom the world treated as discards were fully worthy of attention.

The official *New Yorker* tone was breezy, sophisticated,

kindly if irreverent, and he did it well for his Talk pieces; but the crime pieces were hard-hitting, thoroughly factual, and exhaustively researched. His style was film noir influenced, embittered but deeply truth-seeking. His editor was William Shawn. Shawn's editing was a hymn to detail, a thirty-page list of questions for one piece.

Cros called his subjects his "bad boys." Listening to him tell of his struggles writing about them, fellow *New Yorker* writer Niccolò Tucci said, "To write well about a scoundrel, you must really love him." Cros tried to. He searched for some deep flaw in their childhoods that might have led them to "go wrong," something that a better environment—a strong family, more law-abiding peers—might have prevented. The stories could have ended with, "You ain't such a bad guy, after all."

The "bad boy" Cros felt closest to was Bob Brown, an orphan, sentenced to life in prison for killing a man on an impulse. "I expected them sooner or later," Brown said of the officers who came to arrest him hiding in a Times Square hotel room. He was twenty years old. What had begun as a hotel cash register stickup had ended in the murder of a man whose three-months-pregnant wife was lying asleep in their Brooklyn apartment.

William J. Keating was the New York assistant district attorney assigned to the Bob Brown case. Keating had assembled Brown's records, noting in particular one probation officer's assessment that the boy's "present antisocial inclinations are at least partially due to the frustrations and inadequacies stemming from his unfortunate rearing" by foster parents and in orphanages. He wondered if the boy should end up in the electric chair, but he could not justify assigning a staff investigator to a case that seemed ready for a swift delivery to the jury.

Then his investigator appeared. Cros Bowen, a man long celebrated for his meticulously detailed reporting on stories like this, walked into his office. Keating couldn't discuss the case; it was pending; but he did give Cros a few leads. Cros said he wanted to go deeper, to find out what was driving this boy. Something that, if discovered, might help society understand men like him a little more clearly.

Before he was finished, Cros knew more about Brown that Brown himself knew, winning access to files that had been closed, even uncovering the name of the birth mother whom Brown had spent much of his life looking for. He compiled the long story of Brown's sad life, shunted from one foster home to another, from one institution to the next, committing petty thefts with increasing regularity.

Keating hadn't had the manpower to investigate and would have had to let Brown go to the electric chair, but with what Bowen was telling him, perhaps he could be rehabilitated. He decided to accept a lesser plea, Murder Two. The opinion of a psychiatrist who interviewed Brown was that he had been driven by an obsessive search for his mother and was acting under "such a defect of reason as not to know that the act was wrong." The judge rejected the insanity defense but accepted the lesser plea. Brown was guilty of Murder Two.

On the day before Bob Brown's sentencing, Cros faced Brown over a two-foot counter in the counsel room of the Manhattan House of Detention, known as the Tombs and infamous for corruption and brutality. A guard stood by who showed no interest in the four or five similar conversations going on in the room. Cros told Brown the sentence could be as low as twenty years to life, but it might be fifty to life. "Brown's head jerked slightly when he heard that, as if he had been struck, and he closed his eyes for a while and then smiled nervously."

"But fifty—I'd just as soon go to the chair. . . . Fifty years with good behavior means . . . I'll be too old to get married, too old to have children. I think I'll say something to the judge when he sentences me tomorrow."

Bowen was at the sentencing. Brown "seemed to be the least noticed person in the courtroom." He looked up at the judge but he said nothing, his head seeming to sink between his shoulders, as if he were expecting a blow. The blow came. The sentence was for a term "the minimum of which shall be not less than forty-five years and the maximum of which shall be the defendant's natural life." Two guards grasped Brown by an arm and a shoulder and rushed him out of the courtroom.

Brown wrote to Cros from jail for the next twenty years.

Some bad boys were not so easy to love. There was William Tierney, a brutal cop who severely beat a mild-mannered Phi Beta Kappa engineer, was defended by the police and his family, and had gotten off lightly. But Fred McManus, loner though outwardly normal, serial murderer, fire setter, and problem child from the beginning, well-liked in jail: might even he somehow be redeemed? John Resko, serving time for murder but emerging a talented illustrator and solid citizen, had been. Cros gave them each the same treatment he'd given all his subjects, from George C. Marshall to J. Parnell Thomas to Homer Loomis. He searched out detail until he believed he knew what made them tick, put the puzzle pieces together, told their stories. *The New Yorker* ran them in the Annals of Crime section and McGraw-Hill would publish them as *They Went Wrong*, the jacket copy calling him "one of America's top-ranking reporters."

By 1953 the H-bomb had been tested, far more powerful than the one that had devastated Hiroshima and Nagasaki. A negotiated cease-fire had begun in Korea.

But the price of everything was going up. The *New Yorker* job put the Bowen family on a slender footing financially. Cros would get assignments that might or might not end up in print. He wasn't earning a salary; he was paid on a "drawing account." If the magazine didn't like a piece, it was "bought and killed." Marjory could not run the household on what he could earn. He'd write post-dated checks that bounced, or forget to sign them. His financial prospects had been shaky when they were first married, but Louise had been there to help out. Now they had two growing daughters and a house to keep up. It loomed large that she depended on a man who, deep down, simply did not care about money. She reasoned, she pled, he would promise to do better, but nothing changed.

When a milk strike hit, she decided she had had enough of labor unions. It was Halloween. Our Halloween costumes usually had something to do with old sheets, but this year, she made two pairs of sandwich boards, painted the Borden's milk seal on them, dressed us up as picketers, and entered us in Irvington's Halloween costume contest. She pushed us out onto the stage of the local high school auditorium.

"Just walk across," she commanded, and we did.

"Where's our milk?" the signs read.

In those years, the increasing commercialization of everything became one of Cros's subjects. A bestselling novel was Sloan Wilson's *The Man in the Gray Flannel Suit*, about a man bearing the scars of war who had to choose between his human values and success in the world of business. Cros, similarly scarred, felt it was his calling as a writer that put him in conflict with the men in gray flannel suits. They were corrupting the culture.

For what?

For money.

He kept on writing.

Dad hated advertising. George Orwell had called it "mind control." Cros mocked the plastic smiles of the Betty Crocker housewives pulling casseroles from bright white ovens. He cursed the whole damn culture and its surfeit of gleaming kitchen appliances. He did a piece for *Harper's*, "Reputation by Sonnenberg," on Benjamin Sonnenberg—perhaps genius but also charlatan, father of the new corrupt breed of public relations experts—those liars spinning fictions for coin. Businessmen were luring people into supermarkets to buy things they did not need—more and more home appliances and frozen TV dinners—all of it advertised by the newest bad thing, the television commercial. In 1958 Cros would write a piece for *Science Digest* on the new findings in psychology that the designers of supermarkets were using to market their wares.

Cars had tail fins and air conditioning, four-speed transmissions and v8 engines. The Bowen family had a battered Ford, and was proud of it. Marjory made clothes with a sewing machine, disdained supermarkets, and shopped at the Gristedes, up the hill on Main Street. Sometimes she would send one of the girls up to fetch something she'd forgotten from "Mr. Gristede," who would find it, hand it to her, and mark it down on the bill.

All up and down the street, families gathered around *Arthur Godfrey's Talent Scouts* and *I Love Lucy*. Art Carney of *The Jackie Gleason Show* had even driven through the neighborhood in a top-down convertible to visit his nephews, the Carney kids. Everyone lived for *Hopalong Cassidy* and *Lassie*.

The Bowens watched nothing.

"Why don't we have a television set?" I asked one day.

"Television is middle-class," Dad grumbled.

"What class are we?"

I turned toward Mom. Dad saturated his talk with feeling. He could spend a whole ten minutes on why something was unethical or corrupt. Mom's pronouncements were less impassioned, more evenhanded, if a bit snippy. With her, you knew it was the straight facts.

"The intelligentsia," she said.

"That means we're useless." Dad winced. "We're not. We're the intellectual class."

Was there a whole group of people whose job was to sit around and think and write about things? Was that the way the world worked? If so, it was very risky, being in whatever this intellectual class was. Most fathers had jobs in companies that made things or helped people do things they wanted to do anyhow. The father of one of my friends down the street was a banker. Dad wrote books and articles about things he really cared about. Money wasn't important.

But even though money wasn't important, there was never enough. Maybe that was why there were always arguments about it. And how could something not be important if there was never enough?

Then, early in the summer of 1954, a television set arrived in the Bowen household without warning, an awkward but stolid presence in the tiny living room, bringing in people we'd never known before, only to vanquish them in a storm of flickering and buzzing until Mom jiggled the knobs back to normal. It was the size of about four shoe boxes, but Dad spent hours in front of it. He was watching the Army McCarthy hearings. Many of his old PM pals had been open Communists. He might be suspected of being a Communist, with the FBI compiling a file on him.

Dad didn't tell us any of that, though. All I noticed was that after the hearings ended, he seemed less anxious. Something had gone right in his world. It wasn't that we had a television set. He never watched television again. But he would often recite, word for word, the exchange between Joseph McCarthy and Joseph N. Welch that set off the fall of the senator from Wisconsin.

It went like this.

McCarthy and the smarmy Roy Cohn, a favorite of J. Edgar Hoover for his anti-Communist prosecutions, had accused the U.S. Army of harboring Communists. The Army hired the Boston law firm of Hale & Dorr and its gentle, patrician senior partner, Joseph Welch, as special counsel to defend it.

The hearings dragged on for weeks, Welch patiently putting up with McCarthy's boorish posturing. Then McCarthy went too far. He insinuated that Fred Fischer, a young lawyer at Hale & Dorr, had communist sympathies.

At this point in telling the story, Dad came alive. He was Joseph Welch fixing his glare on an imagined McCarthy. His voice was gentle and plaintive. "You've done enough. Until this moment, Senator, I think I never gauged your cruelty or recklessness. Have you no sense of decency, sir, at long last? Have you left no sense of decency?"

This was great stuff.

Quietly and with dignity, Dad would then fix us with a moral eye and orate, "If there is a God in Heaven, it will do neither you nor your cause any good. You, Mr. Chairman, may, if you will, call the next witness."

The hushed gallery erupted in applause. McCarthy turned to Cohn and asked, "What happened?"

Later, Missouri Democratic Senator Stuart Symington told McCarthy right straight to his face just exactly what had happened. "The American people have had a look at you for six weeks. You are not fooling anyone."

The mood changed in the Bowen house after that. McCarthy's canned news conferences and pompous addresses to the nation had concealed his demagoguery. Live television had unmasked him. For a while, Dad was happier. Television could be a brave new world for writers, and he wanted to be in it. He put together a proposal for a TV series on criminals based on his *New Yorker* Annals of Crime pieces.

"It's not for the money," he wrote.

"How can I motivate a man who doesn't care about money?" the TV executive who read it must have thought. The proposal went nowhere.

The New Yorker had its share of eccentrics. Cros was one. There were quarrels with Marjory. He took to sleeping in his office, shaving in the men's room sink. Sometimes he'd be spotted in his blue Brooks Brothers boxer shorts, headed back down the hall. Management objected. He pestered a source with phone calls; the source sent an angry letter to the higher-ups. Again, management objected. Out of his pain over Peter's death, he began a long piece on the desperation of parents with children dying of leukemia in research hospitals who placed their hopes on experimental cures. *The New Yorker* bought it and killed it, another death to bear.

His connection to *The New Yorker* began to weaken and then ended. He wrote articles for the middlebrow *Pageant* magazine. They paid better than *The New Yorker*. He was proud of the most ambitious of them, "The Invisible Death Around Us," on low-level radiation from nuclear power plants that could cause cancer, in which he speculated that the controversy over controlling the nuclear bomb might bring on world government. It won him a Benjamin Franklin Magazine Citation. Writing like that could make the world a better place.

They Went Wrong's success gave Cros a place in the national debate over reform of the juvenile justice system. "New findings in psychology" showed that some wrongdoers could be rehabilitated. Releasing the convicted offender to probation might eventually bring him back into the community for good. Parole, the reduction of sentence based on a period of good behavior in jail, could too. Statistics supported it. Cros joined the national board of the American Association for Probation and Parole and attended conferences for doctors, social workers, and law enforcement personnel.

At those conferences, J. Edgar Hoover's FBI was solidly against probation and parole, although Cros thought he could educate them. He also knew that they were targeting "subversives and radicals," himself possibly among them. As a member of the press, he believed reporters had an equal right to access to the FBI. But the FBI favored some reporters over others, depending on how compliant they were. Cros had profiled criminals. He'd admired Edward R. Murrow's 1954 *See*

It Now, which portrayed Joseph McCarthy as a reckless liar. He'd do a profile on J. Edgar Hoover, find out what made him tick. But how to get access to the man? He'd have to show the FBI he could be trusted. He would have to become one of the "favorites."

Early in 1958 came an opportunity to do that. The Great Brink's Robbery case broke, the "Crime of the Century," a $1.2 million holdup, then the biggest robbery in U.S. history. Years of dogged police work had not paid off, but the Boston office of the FBI had learned that the eleven suspected participants had begun turning on each other. FBI Special Agent Edward J. Powers had figured out who the weakest link was.

Just five days before the six-year Massachusetts statute of limitations on the case would have expired, Special Agent Powers and his FBI team had approached gang member Joseph (Specs) O'Keefe. Whatever they said, worked. O'Keefe turned state's evidence. He would take the stand as a witness against his colleagues. Prosecution of the Brink's case became front page news. Eight of the robbers seemed on their way to maximum sentences of life imprisonment, and even O'Keefe, the one who'd turned on them, would go to jail.

Cros sprang into action. He got in touch with his old employer, Hearst's International News Service (INS). They assigned a six-part piece. He'd do quick *New Yorker*-style profiles of each of the Brink's criminals.

His next step was to contact Special Agent Powers and arrange an interview to get the FBI account of the case. He traveled to Boston. Powers gave Bowen some detail on the subjects and leads where he might find other information, but "absolutely no information with regard to the case itself was afforded him," Powers reported to Washington. Bowen was not a "friend of law enforcement. . . . He seems to be very naïve and the type of person that is easily hoodwinked by the criminal elements." His book *They Went Wrong* "seems to have a strong anti–law enforcement flavor and one of sympathy and understanding to the plight of the criminal." Bowen "overemphasizes the part psychiatric results can play in any case." He should not be trusted.

Hoover agreed. "It is obvious Bowen is a 'rotter' but nothing else could be expected in view of his background . . . PM and *The New Yorker.*"

What Cros had suspected, that he was being watched by the FBI, was true, and it had been going on since the late 1940s. "Bowen is a former news script writer for NBC, was on the staff of PM (defunct New York newspaper), and had written the Bureau on stationery of *The New Yorker,*" the file on him read.

And then there had been his 1954 review of *The Anatomy of a Crime,* by Joseph Dinneen, an account of a crime with parallels to the Brink's robbery. Dinneen was a newspaperman highly regarded in Boston newspaper circles, Bowen wrote, the kind who "really knew the town." As an ace police reporter, he had "friends" everywhere, sources in all circles—rich as well as poor; the underworld, politicians, law enforcement. His hallmark was trustworthiness. He was poor in dollars, but "he was rich in the currency of his trade—information." Dinneen was also fearless. He had no reason to go easy on the FBI in his *Anatomy of a Crime,* and he hadn't.

Cros asked the FBI to respond to his review of the Dinneen book, and they did, contacting him confidentially, asking him to change "two false statements about the agency." He changed only one. He did not think the other statement was false. His review endorsed the book. Yes, he was a rotter.

Indeed, the FBI favored correspondents who toed their line as a matter of course, and they would continue to. On the matter of how to handle Bowen, it was clear. The door was shut. He could not be trusted. They would check his stories, yes, but only after they were printed, and they would not tell him what they'd found. So Boston agent Nichols phoned Barry Farris, the FBI's contact person at the International News Service, the publisher of the series on the Brink's robbers. Nichols reported on the call to Hoover's assistant Charles Tolson: "I told Barry it appeared Croswell Bowen has a psychological jag on and I wanted to alert him because feeling was running high in the Bureau." At the INS, Barry Farris promised Nichols he would "not publish anything [by Bowen about the Brink's case] until we approved it."

To do the INS series, Cros spent several weeks visiting the places where the accused Brink's robbers had grown up, ostensibly searching for clues: "Why and how could such men band together? What manner of men are they? Why had not reformatories reformed them? In short, why did the eleven Brink's case defendants go wrong?"

The Brink's situation did not have the makings of a *They Went Wrong* story. The crime had had its genesis at the "JA Club" in the Jamaica Plain section of Boston, "a sort of poor man's nightclub." Eleven "toughs," all in and out of jail their whole lives, had found each other and spent a year rehearsing for a big score. To Cros, theirs was just "the dream of the sick criminal mind about to come true: one last big haul and then quit for good."

He never found an answer, nor did he even expect to, the "one thing" that might have made any of their lives different. Indeed, even if each of those men had a story that, if someone just listened to it, they might have been saved, there would not have been time to find it out. Doing a story like that could take months of building rapport with the subject. Besides, men in the Brink's situation knew enough not to trust a newspaper reporter.

But he wasn't after another *They Went Wrong* story. He was after J. Edgar Hoover. To get that story, he needed a chance to observe the FBI, to work with them, to show them he could be trusted. So in a March letter to Hoover, Cros thanked him, saying it had been a pleasure to work with the Boston office in connection with his series on the Brink's case. He would be attending the upcoming probation and parole conference in Washington and hoped to see him there. "One of my projects is to see if we can explore the idea of bringing parole, probation, AND law enforcement together," he volunteered.

Hoover would not have been interested in the prospect, nor was L. B. Nichols. "The more I saw of professional advocates of parole, the more I wondered if they didn't prostitute themselves to being in a special caste and set themselves apart from all others," Nichols told Cros.

Nonetheless, when the Brink's series appeared in print, in a fulsome display of cooperation, Bowen went to the Boston office with all his six articles in hand and took them directly to Nichols. He'd demonstrated that he could play along. This was the moment to ask for the J. Edgar Hoover story.

"Has there ever been a good portrait done on the director?"

"The director has been living in a fishbowl all his life and everything has been written that could be written."

Would the FBI cooperate with him in doing a pattern case study of a special agent?

"There is no such thing as a pattern for agents. The six thousand agents are all rugged individualists and it would do no good to single out one."

Could he do profiles sympathetic to the agency? Hoover had recently said that eleven of eighteen agents who had died in the line of duty had been killed by individuals either on parole, on probation, or were recipients of some form of clemency. Was material readily available on the eleven?

"It would take too much time to dig out the material."

L. B. Nichols forwarded the six Brink's articles to Mr. Tolson. "They do point up the sordid childhood of the subjects and in that respect could be called 'sob-sisterish,'" he said. On the other hand, they did point out the harshness of the men's actions. "I am more convinced now that in the absence of glaring factual errors, we should return the articles to him without comment; however, I suggest we withhold making a final decision until the articles are checked."

Tolson gave the articles to Director Hoover, who sent them to Edward J. Powers asking him to review them and advise the bureau. Powers found eleven inaccuracies, ranging in seriousness from the number of burlap bags carried by the subjects to the exact time the subjects entered Brink's. The FBI was a very careful fact checker.

But Cros never saw their work. In a letter, Nichols thanked him for bringing them copies of the INS Brink's series. Then came the familiar refrain, "We have come to the conclusion that since this case is pending trial it would be inappropriate for us to make any observations or comment on the articles."

Cros would knock on the FBI's door once again. He had an assignment to do a story on James Bozart, the newsboy who had discovered a hollowed-out nickel containing a chip of microfilm involved in the Rudolf Ivanovich Abel espionage case. He was told the FBI had the full cooperation of the newsboy and the detective contacted concerning the nickel before it was given to the agency. He wanted to get some detail about how the bureau had gone into action on the matter of the nickel. Surely they would comply. Hadn't he worked very well with SAC Powers on the Brink's case?

The FBI refused. In a casual conversation, Cros told an Irvington neighbor that he thought the bureau favored certain correspondents over others. The neighbor happened to be FBI Special Agent Edward Brandt, who reported it to his superiors. The agency had already pegged this Bowen as the enemy long ago, a rotter, not to be trusted by law enforcement. The letter went out from Hoover the next day. The case was under appeal. Bowen should go away.

Cros had given it his best shot, trying to get those FBI sheep moving, but he hadn't budged them. The 1950s would give him one more chance. He took it.

William Keating, the young assistant district attorney who, back in 1949, had helped him with the Bob Brown case, now, as counsel for the New York City Anti-Crime Committee, had discovered and exposed a ring of illegal wiretapping in the city. Keating chose to follow his conscience, resigned from the Anti-Crime Committee, and refused to identify the informants who had made it possible for him to bring charges against the perpetrators. For doing so, he was sentenced to jail in June of 1955.

Cros set to work. Prosecutors as well as newsmen had the right to protect the identities of their sources. He assembled an impressive roster of radio and television personalities, executives, attorneys, and writers to stand up for that right. He had stationery made up that displayed their names as members of the Public Committee for William J. Keating, which he had founded.

Cros wooed Keating by saying "Bill, it is traditional among newspapermen that whenever any of them goes to jail, his friends buy him a nice, hot meal when he comes out. We're going to throw a luncheon for you and raise one final bit of hell about the right of newspapermen and crime-commission men not to reveal their sources, and then we'll disband, I promise."

He gave the story to the *New York Times*, which ran it as "Keating to Enter Prison Tomorrow," beginning with a terse summary of the occasion and ending with the full list of notables he had assembled.

The day of Keating's luncheon, the judge who had issued Keating's contempt citation accused the Public Committee for William J. Keating of "glorifying defiance of the law."

But as the gathered audience saw it, a decade that had seen the vanquishing of Senator McCarthy had brought new stature to those who acted according to conscience in defiance of the law. The judge's words were just what Cros needed to bring the luncheon off with éclat.

All through those years, I knew nothing of what went on in the worlds my father was writing about. I was interested in other things, like Silly Putty. One Christmas, the first *New Yorker* toy craze, Silly Putty, came into our lives. Silly Putty was a pliable shiny beige substance that its manufacturer—hoping for publicity—had had liberally distributed to the magazine staff. It bounced crazily if you rolled it into a ball. If you pressed it against the ink of the newspaper funnies and then against blank paper, you could make it into a printing press. The next year's toy craze was Slinky toys, metal springs that unfolded themselves down stairs so precisely that it looked like they knew where they were going.

But things in the Bowen family were about to change, although Silly Putty and Slinkies both showed up in our Christmas stockings for years after that. Marjory's doctor had told her that her husband's financial instability was permanent, that he should not be relied on to provide a steady income, and that she should get ready for a career. She loved libraries and books. She began volunteering in the Irvington public library, planning to get a library science degree. She would look for a job in one of the Westchester public libraries. And now a fourth child was about to be born. The Bowens needed a larger house and a better school system.

The Bowens looked for a house in Chappaqua, a commuter town on the Harlem line out of Grand Central Station and a slightly longer train ride from New York than Irvington had been, near the two of Marjory's three sisters who had settled there with their families. Louise would help with the mortgage. Bill would own 66 Bedford. In the summer of 1955, with a fourth child due that fall, the Bowen family moved.

Chappaqua was grander than the working-class, sleepy Irvington-on-Hudson, where the train station had been a haphazard place. Here, the train station was the hub of the town. A swarm of dapper executives boarded every weekday headed for the city and returned, crumpled and weary, in the evening. The new house was close enough to the station that Cros could walk to it if he had to go into New York.

If he was in a hurry, he would break into a fast lope. On the ride home, he would join the Chappaqua gray flannel suits beginning their drinks time early in the club car.

Eighteen Spruce Lane was snug and sturdy, in a woodsy neighborhood, built tight against the side of a hill. It had a larger living room and kitchen than the Irvington house, a dining room, and another small room downstairs Dad could turn into an office. Upstairs, there was a master bedroom, and rooms for each of us and the new baby.

Molly was born in September. Louise came out while Marjory was in the hospital. She was a comforting influence, but her sight and hearing were even dimmer. She had left a water faucet running at 66 Bedford and hadn't heard it. A sink overflowed onto the kitchen floor and created a flood. Cros put her name on a waiting list for a room at the Mary Manning Walsh Home, a facility known for its good treatment of the aged in Midtown near the East River, run by Carmelite sisters. When a single room on the ground floor became available, he would move her there.

When Marjory came back from the hospital, it seemed like her baby and her job both gave her a new energy. Mrs. Perry, an Englishwoman who had survived the blitz by hiding with her family in the London Underground when the bombs came, took care of Molly during the day. Mom's income kept things steady at home. She paid the light bill on time and bought the groceries.

I began seventh grade and Lucey fifth in the Chappaqua public schools. At school the talk was about bomb shelters in basements and how if you had one, when there was a nuclear attack, you wouldn't die. I wanted a bomb shelter. But Dad had read *Hiroshima* in *The New Yorker*, knew John Hersey, and said that you most likely could not survive a nuclear attack in a bomb shelter, and if you did, you might well wish you hadn't. The Bowens did not build one.

NINE

A Darkness That Would Not Lift

Eugene Gladstone O'Neill (1888–1953) was America's first great playwright. All through the twenties and the thirties, Cros had "suffered and died" with O'Neill's plays; "they were a part of my life," he wrote. Here was a man whose genius transformed people otherwise scorned—the chronically unlucky, prostitutes, addicts, derelicts—into stage characters who spoke directly from the soul of humanity. At their greatest, the plays aroused in audiences the pity, fear, wonder, and awe that Aristotle in his *Poetics* had identified as the four tragic emotions. Certainly they had aroused them in Cros.

So it was, when life delivered a blow greater than any he had already borne, greater than any parent could be expected to bear, Cros's thoughts turned to O'Neill. In 1952, early in the morning, in Irvington, in his impatience to get milk for his children's breakfast, he brought about the accidental death of Peter, his only son.

It was an event so stark that it seemed ready for the plot of an O'Neill tragedy. Marjory was away when it happened, called to her seriously ill father's bedside. He was to take care of the three children while she was gone. There was no milk for their breakfast. Thinking Peter, who by then had not yet been able to climb out of his crib, was still asleep upstairs, Cros went to his car and backed it out of the driveway and over Peter. Holding his crushed son in his arms, he drove to the hospital.

Cros's mistake, the tiny flaw that unleashed a torrent of pain, was that in his haste, he did not first look to see if Peter was safe. He was not. For the first time, Peter had climbed out of his crib and crawled down the stairs, out the front door, and behind the parked car in the driveway.

Peter did not live. Marjory returned, and together they mourned their son. To her mother, Marjory was stoical. Her sister Dottie had come over that morning and told her "all the news of you and Daddy" and also about Peter's death. "I know that you have been close enough all these weeks to the dark and tragic facts of all our lives, so that you were perhaps as well prepared as one can ever be," she wrote. "I do want you to know that we are all going along well and life is still wonderful, the girls as much a joy (and care) as ever. . . . Everyone . . . has just swept us up in a tide of friendship and carried us through the hardest days, and now we are getting back to work as we should."

In fact, the Bowen family reeled. Peter's death was never mentioned. Mom kept on, chin high, my sister and I experiencing Peter's death in different ways. But I could see that my father's deep guilt over Peter's death, accidental though it had been, did not leave him. The pain was immense. Out of it, he began a long piece on children dying of leukemia in research hospitals where desperate parents place their hopes on highly experimental cures. He knew how they felt; he had held a dying son in his arms. *The New Yorker* bought it and killed it, another death to bear.

We joined the Irvington St. Barnabas Episcopal Church. For a while, Dad taught Sunday school and Lucey and I sang in the choir. I memorized the Nicene Creed. Maybe the Holy

Ghost was Peter, not in a body anymore, but floating around wearing a sheet the way ghosts do, only in Heaven. But St. Barnabas Episcopal in Irvington did not last. I kept on with choir until the spring trip to Rye Beach Amusement Park, and then I quit.

After a while, Dad stopped teaching Sunday school. What he had hoped would happen, that he and Marjory would kneel together in prayer and he be forgiven by her and by God, did not come about. I see him in a cathedral, searching again for that "strange, cleansed feeling" that was called grace. But a dark cloud had set in, and it would not lift. If no prayer he prayed, no confession he made, could put him right again, would it ever?

The dark fog remained. His faith weakened.

Back in 1947, propelled by admiration for O'Neill's plays, Cros had written a profile on him for *PM*. He had gone to New London, Connecticut, to interview "Captain" Thomas Fortune Dorsey, a huge white-bearded Irishman, the drinking pal and real estate adviser of Eugene's father, James O'Neill. Dorsey had given Cros a good steer on Eugene O'Neill. "He was a real Black Irishman. Always the gloomy one," the Captain said. "Always the tragedian. Always thinkin'. My God, when he looked at you, he seemed to be lookin' right through you, right into your soul. We're all Irish around here, and we knew the type."

To be a Black Irishman, the particular type of Irishman Dorsey meant, was a matter of temperament. A Black Irishman was a Catholic who had lost his faith and then spent his life searching for a philosophy he could believe in again as fervently as he had once believed in the simple answers of the Catholic catechism. He became brooding and solitary.

Cros well knew from his earliest years with the nuns in Toledo those simple answers of the Catholic catechism. O'Neill, like him, had been tutored by nuns to memorize the Baltimore Catechism, the obligatory means of teaching the Catholic faith. It taught "absolute predestination, original sin, and irresistible grace." Its theology came from the stern vision of a seventeenth-century Belgian Catholic bishop, Cornelius Jansen, who preached that Adam had lived in a state of innocent nature in the garden, where he loved and served God through his free will, undisturbed by the presence of "bodily desires." But he had chosen to reject a loving God in favor of the "love of creatures." He fell into sin. Sexual desire, the enduring punishment for Adam's abandonment of God, would forevermore be transmitted to posterity through the act of carnal conception. Cros, O'Neill, and anyone else who had been trained by Catholic nuns could recite the Baltimore Catechism by heart:

"What happened to Adam and Eve on account of their sin?"

"On account of their sin, Adam and Eve lost sanctifying grace, the right to Heaven, and their special gifts; they became subject to death, to suffering, and to a strong inclination to evil, and they were driven from the Garden of Paradise."

"What has happened to us on account of the sin of Adam?"

"On account of the sin of Adam, we, his descendants, come into the world deprived of sanctifying grace and inherit his punishment, as we would have inherited his gifts had he been obedient to God."

"What is this sin in us called?"

"This sin in us is called original."

Those words, invisibly engraved in the dark folding brain cells of those two young boys with questing souls, had only bound Cros more tightly to O'Neill and his plays. Into them O'Neill had poured those early teachings, confirmed into a mature world view by his experience—that man is fallen, destined to sin, and utterly irredeemable except by the unmerited saving grace of God.

Just as Cros had found in reporting in service to democracy a way to set right in his soul the moral wrong of war, it had been in writing that O'Neill had found his salvation. For O'Neill, in the tuberculosis sanitarium where he had gone to quit drinking and cure his lungs, writing had become his faith. "I kept writing because I had such a love of it. I was highly introspective, intensely nervous and self-conscious. I was very tense. I drank to overcome my shyness. When I was writing, I was alive." Wrote Cros, "The discovery of what writing did for [O'Neill] . . . was perhaps a substitute for the faith he had lost at thirteen. His life at the sanitarium was almost a religious experience in which he faced the possibility of death, looked for new faith, and found it in creative writing."

In 1956 the moment for a full Eugene O'Neill biography came. After O'Neill's death, a José Quintero–Jason Robards production of *The Iceman Cometh* had set off an O'Neill revival in America. There was still one O'Neill play, his last, as yet unproduced. O'Neill had labored for many years writing a long multigenerational cycle of plays about an American-Irish family called *A Tale of Possessors Self-Dispossessed*, only to scrap it and write the story of his family as a single play that took place in one day. He called it *Long Day's Journey into Night*. He had finished it in 1942 but placed a sealed copy in the vault of his publisher, Random House, with instructions that it not be published until twenty-five years after his death.

But Carlotta Monterey, his widow, who as holder of the rights to his work could bypass her husband's instructions that it not be produced, announced that *Long Day's Journey* would go into production. She transferred the rights to Yale, with all proceeds to go to the Drama School and the O'Neill collection at the library.

Long Day's Journey was produced in New York late in 1956 and posthumously won O'Neill his fourth Pulitzer Prize. Crowds lined up. Audiences sat transfixed by the raw human pain they saw unfolding across the stage. Something in O'Neill's dark vision was right for those anxious times.

Cros knew what the public did not know, that *Long Day's Journey* was a thoroughly autobiographical drama whose characters were modeled on the playwright's own mother, father, and brother. He knew this because the PM profile had not been the end of his interest in the O'Neill saga, only the beginning. Over the following ten years, he had watched the tragedy of O'Neill's life unfold. He stayed in touch with his eldest son, Eugene O'Neill Jr. He would sometimes see Shane, the youngest child, hurrying through the darkened streets of the Village. He interviewed hundreds of people and reread O'Neill's plays. On a research trip to New London, Connecticut, he had even stumbled upon what would become the very setting for *Long Day's Journey*, the seaside cottage that James O'Neill had bought for his family. The patriarch actor and theatrical entrepreneur had taken his whole family on the road to help him put on *The Count of Monte Cristo* over six thousand times. The rambling, unheated white clapboard Victorian summer cottage was the only real home they had ever known. It sat near the ocean, close to the sounds and feeling *Long Day's Journey* would evoke, right down to the cries of foghorns and sea gulls drifting in from offstage.

Cros knew he could write a book that would show forth the magnificence of O'Neill's achievement, one of personal fortitude as well as literary genius. Overcoming his deep depressions and his struggles with alcohol, O'Neill had transformed the dark shadows of his own life into stage characters that summoned up his own relentless domination by his father; the sad, thwarted life of his mother; his older brother Jamie's recklessness and jealousy; his own struggles to find himself as a writer; and the exponential amplification of it all by alcohol. Cros was sure he could do a very good job of telling what lay behind the dark and haunting eyes of the man who had lifted the American stage out of triviality, a man in whose veins flowed the same Irish blood that flowed in his.

Cros had a good anchor on his subject. He had met O'Neill back in 1948, in connection with the *PM* piece. Hoping to get a glimpse of O'Neill before he began, he went to the offices of the Theater Guild, a great stone mansion on Fifty-third Street near Fifth Avenue where rehearsals for *The Iceman Cometh* were in progress, in a large, high-ceilinged ballroom on the mansion's second floor. All around was much talking and hurrying and scurrying.

When O'Neill strode into the rehearsal room, a hush descended over the entire group. His glowing eyes seemed to take in the entire hallway and everyone in it. Later, as he sat at a table with the play's director listening to the actors read their lines, Cros noticed that a strange, almost ethereal mood had taken hold. "I remember that I wanted to become his disciple; I wanted to defend him against the world. His sad, intense eyes seemed to be piercing right into me. They haunted me for days after," he wrote.

To meet O'Neill's third wife, Carlotta Monterey, Cros climbed up to the very top of the highest balcony in the Martin Beck Theatre. She was watching a dress rehearsal of *Iceman*. O'Neill's youngest son, Shane, was with her. Dressed entirely in black, she was very beautiful. Cros introduced himself as a *PM* reporter writing a profile of her husband. Knowing *PM*, she said, "You mustn't interpret anything my husband says, or any of his work, in political terms. Art is the only important thing."

Cros's longest talk with O'Neill then took place on a darkened stage of the Martin Beck when *Iceman* was about to open. O'Neill was well groomed and quietly yet expensively dressed in a double-breasted blue suit, but he seemed old and sick. "He gave the impression of a down and out man who had been completely outfitted the day before by some well-meaning friend. He was still handsome. His hair was only slightly graying, a distinguished iron gray. He was thin and slightly bent over. His eyes were deep set, and occasionally he cocked his head as he eyed me. His jaw was lean and forceful."

They talked for a while, and then O'Neill suddenly got up and walked over to one side of the stage bar. "He seemed to straighten up and come alive." As if the bar were real, he motioned for Cros to join him. The self O'Neill then revealed was "the conscience of America asserting itself." "America," O'Neill said, "is due for retribution. There ought to be a page in history books of the United States of America of all the unprovoked, criminal, unjust crimes committed and sanctioned by our government since the beginning of our history—and before that, too. There is hardly one thing that our government has done that isn't some treachery—against the Indians, against the people of the Northwest, against the small farmers."

Was this O'Neill just another of all the great half-drunken Irishmen who sound off in bars all over the world? Cros observed that their talk is always the same, extravagant, rambling, full of madness and violence, but studded with enough essential truth and insight to force you to listen with troubled fascination. O'Neill went on: "This American dream stuff gives me a pain. Telling the world about our American dream! I don't know what they mean. If it exists as we tell the whole world, why don't we make it work in one small hamlet in the United States?" O'Neill fondled a prop whiskey glass and reached for the prop bottle with water and caramel syrup in it.

"If it's the Constitution that they mean, ugh, then that's a lot of words. If we taught history and told the truth, we would teach schoolchildren that the United States followed the same greedy path as every other country. We would tell who's guilty. The list of the guilty ones responsible would include some of our great national heroes. Their portraits should be taken out and burned."

Where did this deeply righteous anger come from? As Cros traveled through New England to visit the places where O'Neill had lived and interviewed as many O'Neill relatives as he could find, he looked for an answer.

In New Haven he found Eugene Jr., O'Neill's first son, who gave him a crucial insight about his father. Eugene Jr. was handsome, heavily bearded, with brooding eyes. O'Neill had abandoned him in infancy only to reveal himself as his father when he was thirteen. Now he was a professor at Yale, and seemed to have a brilliant career ahead of him. At his father's suggestion, he had taken up the study of the Greek classic plays and become a specialist in the tragedians.

Eugene Jr. said, "My father not only is the most sensitive man I have ever known but also possesses the highest idealism of any man who ever lived." He was, he said, "the most principled, idealistic social rebel" he had ever met. His anger at social injustice sprang from "a deep abiding love of humanity, from a deeply cherished dream of what the world could be."

Eugene Jr. had another tip for Cros. "One thing that explains more than anything about me is the fact that I am Irish," his father had told him. "And, strangely enough," O'Neill had said, "it is something that all the writers who have attempted to explain me and my work have overlooked."

To Cros, if O'Neill's passion for social justice had not been enough, his Irishness was yet another thing that drew author and subject together. The O'Neill clan was one of the oldest and most powerful clans in Ireland. Legend held that whenever a true Irish king was crowned at Tara, the keening of the banshees, the women of the gray cloak, would be heard, rising and falling like an ocean wave. One banshee guards each of the ancient Irish families whose names start with O': the O'Neills, the O'Briens, the O'Connors, and the O'Gradys.

Cros's family bore the name of O'Connor. The banshees follow descendants of the great families wherever they travel or emigrate. They keen whenever a member of one the great Irish families is about to die.

Irish folklore is also rife with tales in which, generation after generation, tragedy persists that originates with the utterance of a single curse, retribution for a wrong whose details may have long since been forgotten. Cros knew O'Neill could well have felt a curse had been laid on his family. His own thoughts sometimes went in that direction, too. "Perhaps because of my Irish blood," he wrote, "I became obsessed with the idea that here was a family on whom a terrible curse rested, and I wanted to search out the lives of the O'Neill family and learn about that curse."

Was Cros cursed? Would that explain Peter's death and the pain that had followed?

As sometimes happens with biographers and indeed with writers generally, a writer may gravitate toward subjects through which he can work out issues in his or her own life, sensing that the energy of the personal quest may propel the writing and the writing fulfill the personal quest. Cros felt gripped by the feeling that if he could uncover the reasons for the pain in O'Neill's life and to write about it, perhaps he could heal the pain in his.

There were other writers working on an O'Neill biography. Cros looked over his shoulder at Arthur and Barbara Gelb—Arthur Gelb with his *New York Times* drama critic job—and Doris Alexander, an academic. He envied them the time they could take to write their books. They didn't need advances to support a family.

Still, it lifted his confidence that he had already tried his hand at a full-length biography. At *The New Yorker*, Shawn had assigned him a piece on New York Tammany mayor A. Oakey Hall. He'd set up research headquarters in the New

York Public Library and immersed himself in Hall's world. "Why Shawn didn't draw and quarter me when I turned up twenty-seven months later with close to 100,000 words, I can only attribute to his Schweitzer-like nature," he wrote. "He understood when I explained I had found the subject so engrossing that I was unable to have done with it until I exhausted it." The book, his third, was *The Elegant Oakey.* Buried under long quotations and masses of factual detail, the flamboyant politician who straddled respectability and corruption never came into focus.

The book did not sell well. But in writing it, Cros had learned how to do research in greater depth and handle more detail than he had ever been able to do when writing for newspapers or magazines. With the *PM* piece and the Oakey book behind him, he thought he had a fair claim on the territory, and a good head start.

As he was starting the book, Cros learned that O'Neill's youngest son, Shane, and his family were living in Point Pleasant, New Jersey, on less than twenty-five dollars a week. Cros asked Shane to collaborate, knowing that sources might be more willing to help a family member than a professional writer working alone. Shane said he did not want to write about his father, but he agreed to contribute any letters or documents he had, tell Cros what he remembered, and read and correct what was written.

Cros wrote a proposal, signed a contract, and got an advance from McGraw-Hill. Ed Kuhn, editor on his book and also a Chappaqua resident, was a former Marine. He and his wife, Polly, cut a fine swath, holding elegant dinner parties where one hoped to shine. Whereas Shawn at *The New Yorker* had been gentle and supportive and let a writer take his time, Kuhn preached discipline. Cros knew Kuhn held all the cards.

He started out writing in the office downstairs, but when the girls got home from school, he couldn't concentrate. The master bedroom had a door in the ceiling that opened upward into the attic. You could reach it by climbing up a fold-down ladder into a small crawl space. He would sit cross-legged on the floor under an eave, bent over his typewriter, writing on long teletype rolls that he fed into his typewriter from a spindle. He called it "writing by the yard." You didn't have to change the sheets of paper. You just wrote until you dropped. He said it brought good luck. "You just let it flow."

But the attic was cramped. He had to find a real office. He persuaded a friend to lend him the use of a spare one in downtown Chappaqua.

Cros called his O'Neill biography *The Curse of the Misbegotten*. He told the story of O'Neill's life: his childhood, his years at sea, and his career as a playwright. He worked hard to find, befriend, and interview the people who could help him piece together not only the life of Eugene O'Neill, but also the O'Neill children. At the heart-wrenching core of the book he placed the interwoven threads of their stories.

Two marriages failed before O'Neill found happiness. He had left his first wife for a second, Agnes Boulton, and then left her for Carlotta Monterey, a former actress who had played the female lead in one of his plays. Leaving his children, they eloped abroad. The first of their married years had been happy and productive. Carlotta devoted herself to creating fine homes and a life in which he could write the great plays she believed were still in him.

The last years of their marriage were not so happy—rather, they were some of the most wretched years of his life. They spent his final year tearing up his unfinished plays. The plays had brought him three Pulitzer Prizes and a Nobel, but at the end of his life, they tortured him.

None of his children were with him when O'Neill died. Eugene Jr. was already dead. Oona and Shane learned of their father's death from radio broadcasts and newspapers.

O'Neill's story was redeemed by his genius; his children's lives were not. It was they, Cros believed, not O'Neill himself, who bore the greatest burden of the "curse of the misbegotten."

Eugene Jr., after early achievement, succumbed to despair, alcoholism, and finally suicide. Oona, the daughter, somehow had a talent for self-preservation. She endured her father's decision to cut himself off from her and found happiness as a wife and mother, albeit with a man her father's age. Shane and his story, though, tugged hardest at Cros's heart. A lonely child raised largely by servants, Cros had seen him scurrying around the Village in the forties, where he was a regular in a bar, eventually becoming addicted to more serious drugs. By the time of his father's death, he had given up heroin but took Benzedrine every day. "Benzedrine," he said, "makes life just bearable. You can get by. I was sorry to give up taking heroin because taking it gives you something to live for."

Cros finished the O'Neill book in less than two years. Marjory compiled the index. He delivered the manuscript. It was dedicated to Cathy Givens O'Neill, Shane's wife, to Oona, and to the playwright's ten grandchildren "with the sure knowledge that they have all escaped the curse of the misbegotten." His book (minus footnotes; those were to come later) came out ahead of the other biographies that were in the works. Shane O'Neill, gaunt, with searching eyes, came to the Chappaqua house for the book party. *Curse of the Misbegotten: A Tale of the House of O'Neill* was a 1958 National Book Award finalist for nonfiction. The reviews were good. The sales were good. Cros had changed the way the country looked at its first great playwright.

Though the book was a success, things continued not going well with Marjory in Chappaqua. For long stretches, Cros would be away, sleeping at 66 Bedford, which belonged to Bill, who was living abroad, in Munich, Germany. All three floors were rented out, so Cros slept in the basement. Sometimes he stayed at Hidden Hollow, "living on saltines." Marjory was doing work she clearly loved. She seemed happier without him.

Chappaqua was a Republican town where men dressed in business suits and took the train to corporate jobs in the city, collected their paychecks, had health insurance, and built up their retirement savings. Cros did none of that. He wrote things that he thought would make the world a better place. He didn't care about the money. Maybe Marjory wanted a Chappaqua husband and a Chappaqua life, although when he accused her of that she brushed it off like a bothersome insect.

When he came home, it was to "see the children." The arguments would begin, the patter of raindrops at first. They might end up loud and long and principled, like parliamentary debates tinged with theatricality and bloodlust, or they might be short and anguished and end with the slamming of a door, but anything could set one off. Cros would crumple up and take on a hurt puppy dog look. After a while, he would utter some complaint or other about the life of a writer. Arching her eyebrows, Marjory would throw him a look that said, "Stop moaning and get on with it." His anger was always above ground, with damaging winds and pelting rain. Then the sun would come out. Her anger was always there, like lava, bursting out at random, in sudden fiery eruptions.

The arguments ended, I would hear Dad's limpy gait coming up the stairs. He'd go first into my sister Lucey's room and sit on the bed and talk. Then he'd knock on my door and quietly present himself, love rays streaming out of his chest. He'd sit down beside me and ask questions about my life and listen to what I had to say, and I'd melt. When I had no more to say, he'd tell me something that would suck me up into the drama of what he called his "poor tormented soul." The deep inner core of me that believed what he'd said, that I was his Irish princess, would stand a bit taller. Then he would leave.

I was fourteen in 1958, the year my father won the big award for his book and finally "took his place" in the "Establishment." This was not the Toledo business establishment his early life had pointed him toward, but a literary establishment, one a writer could be proud to join. One weekend, he brought a copy out to Chappaqua and laid it on a table in the living room. Of course I read it. My generation was listening to the Beach Boys and getting ready for Elvis. Things were happy. It seemed to me that O'Neill had such a depressing view of life that I agreed with what O'Neill's father had said—"My God, son, do you want the audience to go home and commit suicide?"

But I had to hand it to Dad. Something was making people line up for an O'Neill play. My father had caught a wave. The book had found a big-name publisher and was selling well. He could consider himself a "distinguished man of letters."

The truth was, though, that I didn't really care about any of that. I just wanted him to stop blowing into our lives only to leave again, trailing pieces of my heart. I wanted him to go away for good or stay home for good, and if he stayed home, I wanted him to do things the other fathers in our neighborhood did, like grill outdoors, watch sports on TV, wear clothes on the weekend that were for home instead of from Brooks Brothers, and mow the lawn.

That Sunday evening, as he was about to leave to go back to New York City, we found ourselves in the living room together.

"Do I tilt at windmills?" he asked.

I knew he wanted to take on another project he believed in, but I also knew his endless crusading was exhausting my mother. I'd heard it in her voice during those fights. He wanted me to say I believed in him because she didn't anymore. I did not want to be pulled into a conflict between them.

I turned away from him, picked up the book, and opened its pages. I had read the elegant dedication, the grateful acknowledgments to so many people who had passed through his life, none of whom I knew. It was all so high-minded, so graceful. If only we could live like that. I got up the courage to ask him a question I had been pondering for a long time.

"How can you be so wise in your books, but when you're home everything falls apart?"

He looked at me. His face crumpled.

I wished I had said nothing.

The shadows Eugene O'Neill cast on his family were indeed very dark. Having peered more and more closely into them, Cros, his disciple, had drawn so close it was impossible to know whether it was the darkness of O'Neill's life or the darkness of his own life that enveloped him.

Was being a Black Irishman truly beyond repair? Was it true, what the nuns had taught? That the curse was "that sin in us which is called original"? That it came from being born human? That it was inescapable, universal?

In this darkness that would not lift, Cros felt only what O'Neill had so well articulated, "man's agonizing loneliness, his feeling of not belonging, of wanting and not wanting to belong, of being cursed to remain alone, above, and apart."

TEN

A Writer Attends to His Soul

After the O'Neill book, things changed in the Bowen family. Mom was a "never apologize, never explain, never complain" Yankee who figured out the right thing to do, set her jaw, and did it. She kept the family afloat with her job; Cros should put in his oar. She was proud of his O'Neill book, but the right thing for him to do now was to earn enough money to send his three daughters to college. He would have to do just that. Otherwise she would go empty-handed to her mother, Mira of "the Look," the accusing stare, impossible to deflect, that was "unutterably painful but you couldn't look away," and ask her to support the children's educations.

Cros acquiesced. If writing for money only was his duty as a father, he would do it out of love—for the girls, and for her.

His first project for money only was a commission to coauthor an "autobiography" of the Japanese actor Sessue Hayakawa. Hayakawa had played the role of the Japanese general in *The Bridge on the River Kwai*. He was a Zen Buddhist and a member of the Japanese samurai warrior class, according to whose code of conduct, Bushido, it was his duty to kill himself to preserve his honor. He had attempted suicide by hara-kiri, cutting out his intestines, but been saved from bleeding to death by his faithful dog. The otherwise rather long-winded, bumpy story told, among other things, about his growing up, his Zen Bhuddism, and about being a Japanese actor who starred in American movies.

Cros tried to make writing *Zen Showed Me the Way* interesting. He had read the work of Thomas Merton, the social-activist, pacifist Trappist monk, and considered joining his order, but when he thought about how difficult taking the vow of silence Merton had taken would be, he decided against it. Then he began studying Zen Buddhism, reading Alan Watts and talking about "the sound of one hand clapping." Sessue Hayakawa visited, serene and detached, for the book party, but after that Cros spent more and more time in the city, except for holiday visits.

My father did not like having to write only for money. Nothing he had written had ever been just for the money. He had persisted in becoming a writer despite his mother's admonition that a writer could not support a family and therefore should not get married. After the breakup of his first serious love affair, he had recommitted himself to being a writer. When he and Marjory met, she believed in him, and *PM* paid fairly well, but now he was the father of three daughters who would have to be educated.

So if he had to earn money, he would go where there was real money to be made—the business world. He began writing a series of profiles of businessmen for *Madison Avenue Magazine*. He became fascinated by the psychology of these practical, worldly, disarmingly charming men who were motivated by profit, not ideals. He stayed away from Chappaqua for longer and longer stretches.

One fall, back to us for Thanksgiving dinner, it was clear things had changed. I hugged him endlessly and stuck close by as he went from one room in the house to the next. The dining room chairs had not been pulled to the table. Marjory was in the kitchen. Nobody was helping her. She erupted in a sudden volcanic burst. A look of terror fell over Cros's face. He did her bidding and brought the chairs to the table. He sat at the head of it, but slumped in his like a schoolboy who had been punished. He carved the turkey, but it was not the same. He didn't even talk about George C. Marshall. He left, and came back even more rarely. When he did, the arguments were less and less about money. They were about pain.

We still had Christmases together. Mom cooked Dad's Southern brunch—ham, grits, and ambrosia—as she always had. Everybody was very polite with one another. We ate quickly. Then we sat around the tree and opened presents. Dad had never wrapped his, and he still didn't. That was about all that was the same. When it was over we all separated.

Cros's guilt over leaving his family and his hopes for a new life after Marjory made for a volatile mixture. He had his first heart attack. From his bed in New York Hospital, it was not Marjory he asked to come to visit him. It was a woman he had recently met, Dody Stevens, a thrice-married widow who was working on a biography of her father, a noted theoretical physicist. She was a few years younger than he, but not many. Her third husband had just died of cancer. She had gone to Miss Porter's, "Farmington," a finishing school attended by generations of heiresses and debutantes, after which some considered further education unnecessary. She was wealthy, with homes in New York City and Watch Hill, Rhode Island, and more money, she told him, than she knew what to do with. She wanted him to help her with the biography, and he had said he would. She brought flowers and a copy of *The Atlantic Monthly*.

As she left, he felt for a moment that they ought never to meet again. She was from a different world, content with the way things were, happy in her own good fortune, childlike and carefree, utterly unconcerned about social injustice.

But he cast that feeling aside. There might be more great

work for both of them, and a happier life. Could she be to him what Carlotta had been to O'Neill? Inscribed in the copy of *Mourning Becomes Electra* he gave to Carlotta, O'Neill had written, "Sustaining and comforting, a warm, secure sanctuary for the man after the author's despairing solitude and inevitable defeats—a victory of love-in-life. Mother and wife and collaborator! I love you!"

As he was about to check out of the hospital, Cros wrote to Dody Stevens that *Madison Avenue* had said to get well, to take two weeks' convalescence and two weeks' vacation. After he got out, he would probably find a room at the Overseas Press Club. He would look for a place of his own. He would see her soon.

But the Overseas Press Club was not what he remembered. People talked about writing rather than doing the agonizing labor of getting it done. Things were gaudy and expensive. "Mirrors. Carved this and that. Doormen rushing to help you from the cab." So Cros found a room in one of the new "fabulously expensive apartments." His landlord was Princeton, class of 1949, and very rich, "but I have a hunch he is not too interested in women. . . . Anyway, it is nice. The linen is from his household, and the sheets are of the first quality, even hems, the towels are so soft and thick, a lovely soft daybed with pillows that are what they call eiderdown or something. I may buy a little portable air conditioning unit. The bath is luxurious with very hot water."

Such luxury was tempting, but it was not his. The search for a home intensified. The basement of 66 Bedford Street was no longer available. Billy, whom by now he called Bill, had come back to New York from Munich with his graceful, aristocratic new wife, Jutta, and her young daughter, Arabella. He did not want his brother sleeping in the basement while they were there. Soon they would rent out 66 Bedford again and live abroad on that and his dividends. He would pursue his painting.

Cros borrowed some of Louise's stocks as collateral for a mortgage and pulled together a down payment on a co-op apartment in a subdivided stone-front mansion on the Upper East Side, formerly the main drawing room of a house at 6 East Seventy-sixth Street—one of a pair owned by relatives of Teddy Roosevelt. It seemed Eleanor and FDR had been married in the grand drawing room, now subdivided into two large rooms, his and an adjacent one, but when they went to another room to cut the cake, they did it entirely alone. Teddy had stolen the show and everybody hung around the Bull Moose, the gentleman-politician of the hour.

"I do love the big room," he wrote Dody. "I want it to have an air of decayed elegance." He would live out his days here. "I will live as one of the 'irreconcilables'—an aristocrat of the old South—who lives in memories of former splendor—the ancien régime." On the mantel above the fireplace, Dody advising, he put the pair of silver candelabra and the large silver tea service Louise had presided over at ladies' luncheons in Toledo. On an end table went a 1923 framed picture of his father with Franklin D. Roosevelt, taken when he passed through Toledo on a Liberty Loan campaign. Ancestor portraits hung on the walls.

A gleaming antique wooden armoire bought from the Parke-Bernet auction house around the corner and hoisted in though a front window held his clothes—a few cotton poplin summer suits, light wool blue pinstripe for winter, all thrift store Brooks if he could find them. A pair of cordovan leather lace-up shoes. A tan cashmere overcoat, growing threadbare, and his fedora from the 1930s. A stack of button-down Oxford shirts, mainly white, but a few in the daring new colors of pink and blue worn by the TV news anchors coming along, the worst of them "actors, not newsmen," he would mourn. Ties from Brooks, on sale after Christmas.

After he recovered from the heart attack, he lost a great deal of weight and wrote with an unlit cigarette between his teeth, on the portable typewriter at a big partner's desk he had set up beside one of the long windows. When the *Madison Avenue* job ended, he signed on as a speechwriter for Barton Cummings, the president of a New York advertising agency, Compton Advertising. He called advertising "being a paid liar for corporations."

On an August morning in 1963, Cros woke, crossed the big room, sat down at his desk, skimmed the *New York Times*, and considered his life. Dody and he still saw each other. It had been a new kind of love. He had been writing an exploration of their love. "When my devotion for US never decreased (only increased) as we came closer and closer to a complete relationship—then I feel I have the duty and responsibility to really explore to find out—so I can say with all my heart and all my soul—from the depths of my being—Dody, I love you."

If she stiffened at being "mother," complaining that he made excessive emotional demands on her, he still hoped she would be "collaborator," and in the future, perhaps "wife." He had to admit, she had not warmed to the collaboration idea. Still, there was something between them, and he wanted to keep it, so he had been treating her gingerly, trying not to smother her with his need for affection, controlling his effusiveness at parties.

Cros pulled out a sheet of letterhead. In a few days a "March for Jobs and Freedom" would take place in Washington DC. He planned to attend. He would write to his old mentor, Felix Frankfurter, retired after twenty-three years on the Supreme Court because of a stroke a year earlier. Frankfurter had inspired his work at PM as a reporter. He wanted to look back on that chapter of their lives together.

John F. Kennedy's presidency had revived Cros's hopes for liberalism. Kennedy was committed to the people, to health care, housing, schools, jobs, civil rights, and civil liberties.

He and Frankfurter could both recall, twenty-eight years ago, FDR speaking words very similar to the ones Kennedy had: "If a free society cannot help the many who are poor, it cannot save the few who are rich." And Kennedy did not want "a peace that came by force of the weapons of war." Both had seen men walk the world stage who had wanted to overthrow colonialism and spread democracy abroad. Now a new generation was flooding into Washington, taking the reins of power. But the forces aligned on the right and on the left were just like the ones Cros had seen back in the forties; the jealous rage of Homer Loomis's Columbians was the same rage that was fueling Southern racism now. All of this was on his mind as he wrote Frankfurter, "Great events keep coming up. I need the sustenance of your telling me— as I am sure you will—the Republic will survive."

And so, on the morning of August 28, 1963, Cros headed with the crowd toward the Lincoln Memorial. People of all races and all classes, from all across the nation, had come together. The mood was mellow. Mahalia Jackson sang, and a sea of faces swayed as the crowd sang with her. Martin Luther King Jr. rose to speak, and a thunder of applause poured from the audience. Cros would have recalled FDR's inauguration speech, his voice crackling over the radio. But this was a man with a black face speaking now, a man whose voice had all the controlled passion of the great leader he was.

There was greatness in that day. And then it was over. People went back where they had come from. There is no indication in Cros and Frankfurter's correspondence that they met. Frankfurter felt himself an aging man; he would die a year later. The next morning's headline read "200,000 March for Civil Rights in Orderly Washington Rally; Pres. Sees Gain for Negro."

But it was their own generation Cros referred to when he wrote back to Frankfurter, "Our times were the best, weren't they? And our people were the greatest."

. . .

That fall, on November 22, 1963, John Fitzgerald Kennedy was assassinated. A man Cros saw as having nowhere near his vision became president. His thoughts went back to FDR's death, and he feared for the future.

Soon after Kennedy's assassination, Cros and Dody Stevens broke up. He wrote to Marjory, "At my age, I suppose I must accept the fact that I cannot live with anybody or rather get along with anybody. My job is to do two things—to make money and to try to get some more worthwhile writing done. I need you to wish me luck—and to wish me well."

He and Marjory wrote to each other and talked on the phone from time to time, and there was a kind of love still. Molly visited. She was a bond between them, and a delightful child. But then Dody came back to him, wanting to continue on. She was not "mother," she was not "collaborator." Perhaps she would be "wife." Cros told her he would leave for El Paso to get a Mexican divorce. Would she come down afterward and meet him? No, she would not; she did not want to marry; he did not earn enough money for them to be married. "You put a price on love," he told her. She wrote back that she had begun to understand him better. She had just bought a copy of *Brave New World*. "I suddenly find the source of your complaints about the world. You seem to limit your accusations to the advertising business and to science, though you're always chafing at government and the police force." But she was different. "I feel at home in the world and essentially a part of it. I accept it, I enjoy it. I have never been able to accept the Christian doctrine 'conceived in sin.'"

That summer Cros went into "the silences." He despised his work at Compton Advertising. "I got two more Cummings speeches off the ground, but this job troubles me," he wrote to Carl Carmer. "My heart is not in it. I do not have the self-discipline to work on the side. I'm going to try and jack myself up and get a new plan—a sum of what I've been doing. Reports, etc. That's what they go by. I need to get my teeth into something specific. If I had to freelance, I don't know what market I'd hit for. I'm like a horse that's been out to pasture for a few years." He hung around the corridors at Compton Advertising telling everyone how unhappy he was writing speeches for people he did not like. He got fired.

He wrote an angry article for *The New Republic*, "Cigarettes and the Ad Man," on the rationalizations Madison Avenue men used to continue making money while causing cancer. He began a biography of JFK with a working title of *The Irish Prince*, touching on how being from an immigrant Irish family had influenced Kennedy's character and political goals, but got not much further than an introduction, chapter outlines, and a dedication to Molly. He wrote an article on the scrimshaw collection Kennedy kept on his White House desk, its first line "The sea was never far from John Fitzgerald Kennedy," and an account of an address Rose Kennedy gave at a Choate alumni event published in the *New York Post*.

He searched for another subject, and found one in a new place—his own life. His love for Dody Stevens had, he could now see, had been a sinful delusion. To join her so readily in her privileged world of wealth and social class had been a betrayal of his highest ideals. Why had he done it? He had looked at O'Neill's life with scrupulous objectivity. Should he not turn that same objectivity on himself? Was it time to look inward?

Was it time for a thorough Catholic examination of conscience, the kind the nuns had taught him to prepare before confession? What was the exact cause and nature of his sin, and how could he atone? Certainly, in leaving his family, he had disobeyed the Ten Commandments. But to consider the salvation of his soul accomplished just with that acknowledgment would be to presume on the mercy of a sometimes vengeful God. He began reading the new psychology of

Erik Erikson. Maybe this was an identity crisis. "Strange, about my identity crisis. Who am I? What do I believe in?" he wrote.

"This will not solve it," he wrote. "I will iron it out with Brooks." Floundering about over his identity was getting him nowhere. Perhaps his old analyst, Dr. Brooks, who had treated him for his breakdown in 1949, might be able to help. Cros sent Dr. Brooks the "long overdue" forty dollars he owed him and made an appointment. He laid out the fruits of his self-examination in the language of their long-ago Freudian sessions together. "Self Analysis I," he titled it. Was his depression over his rejection by Dody Stevens a repetition of his jealousy at the birth of his brother Bill? Was his love for Dody his deep unconscious wish for the love of a mother? Or was he just a typical American male inflicted with "Momism," dependency on the mother, which his friend Philip Wylie had described in *Generation of Vipers*? And his recurrent depressions. Were they brought on by the repetition of early childhood losses? Or was it post-cardiac depression? Would it lift? Or would he have to live with it until the end of his days?

Things had been changing in the world of psychiatry since Cros had last seen Brooks. Their sessions had been long periods of talk. But there were new cures, quicker than Freudian psychoanalysis. There were medicines that could lift his depressions and calm his elations. "My life would have been very different," he would later say to me.

Cros did not try the new medicines. "Once a Catholic, always a Catholic," he told himself, and fell back upon what he had been taught by the nuns, that for the sake of his soul he would have to confess and atone. Relief from his depressions would come, if at all, through grace. Of Dody Stevens he wrote, "My sin—for which atonement must be made—is that my infatuation with you resulted in my neglecting my wife—my children—my job—my mother—and my drive toward my goal as a writer. Now I know where my responsibilities to people, to myself, lie. This infatuation also involved the loss of a certain amount of my integrity, my principles, my compassion for people in pain, my faith in the moral law."

He had confessed. But how could he atone? He would do it through writing. Just as the nuns had taught, grace, if it came, would come unmerited, through an inexplicable act of divine love. He could prepare himself for that by telling his story. There was nobility in that.

So at his desk in New York, and sometimes at his place in the country, he worked on *Jocasta My Beloved*, a semiautobiographical novel, a modern adaptation of Sophocles's *Oedipus Rex*. In Greek myth, Jocasta was the mother of Oedipus, whose fate, the oracles at Delphi told him, would be to kill his father and marry his mother. Sophocles's play showed Oedipus doing just that.

The idea of basing a story on Greek myth was not original to Cros. Eugene O'Neill's 1924 *Desire Under the Elms*, about an infanticide and an adulterous affair, took plot elements from the Greeks. His 1931 *Mourning Becomes Electra*, about an incestuous love between a brother and a sister, was a retelling of Aeschylus's *Oresteia* set in rural New England. When O'Neill was awarded the Nobel Prize for Literature in 1936, *Electra* was frequently mentioned as a reason for the choice, and praised as the culmination to a remarkable career. Writing *Jocasta*, as O'Neill's plays had been to O'Neill, would be a way to atone for Cros's own fallen nature.

The central character in *Jocasta My Beloved* is Barrett Connor, in whose name Cros unified two elements that had in him been at constant war: the Anglo-Saxon Barrett and the Irish Connor. Cros developed parts of some of Barrett Connor's story, set aside some and retained others, eventually doing a chapter outline of the whole book. In the first chapters, told in the third person, Cros follows Barrett Connor at his twenty-fifth Yale reunion, drawing on his own experience at his. Now become a successful author, it still rankles Barrett that he had not been tapped for a senior society. "He had not outgrown the hurt, admits it to himself, and it is bound up with why he has come back," reads the outline.

As he mingles among his classmates, Barrett sees the same old social differences playing themselves out. The elite cluster among themselves; the others mingle on the edges. But for Barrett, as he had hoped, his success as a writer has been noticed. Paul Mellon, "the very richest and most powerful of the lot," Cros's actual classmate and Barrett Connor's imagined one, puts out his hand, tells him to sit down, and starts up a conversation. He wants to talk about books. He had once wanted to be a publisher. But, "like sharks," Mellon's elite coterie of sycophants closes in and the conversation dies.

The plot moves on. Charles Francis Beekman, a "real patrician," "probably the most inside of all the insiders," walks over to him. "Saw your picture in the papers," he says. "Didn't know you'd done all those things. Being a writer, I guess you meet a lot of interesting people." Beekman asks Barrett to have lunch in New York City the following weekend, at the Union Club.

Switching from the third to the first person, Cros has Barrett acknowledging that "looking back, now I know there were many reasons why I failed at Yale. I had not tried out for the big campus jobs. I had gone out for football but quit after a few weeks." He shows Barrett losing his bitterness. He had been wrong to have thought the Bones men nasty and cold. They could be nice, once they took you in. He even admires them for "a certain freedom that came with never having to worry about money."

Over lunch at the Union Club, Charles Francis Beekman reveals his purpose in cultivating Barrett Connor. His first wife, Victoria Fortune, "an interesting woman," is the daughter of an esteemed jurist, and wants to hire a writer to help her write his biography. After lunch, Beekman takes Connor to Victoria Fortune's house, one of the old Fifth Avenue mansions, for coffee in the library. The marble hall leads to a staircase curving to the second floor; the maids are dressed all in white. Beekman watches Connor fall under her spell. They begin to work together.

It is after a few meetings with Victoria, "Tori" as he now calls her, that she takes him to meet an old friend she knows he would like, an older man and quite ill. "He's sort of your type," she says, "been a newspaperman. Also a foreign correspondent. He has written a lot of books. Maybe you've heard of him. His name is Stanley Lincoln."

Connor had certainly heard of Stanley Lincoln. He had very much wanted to be a Stanley Lincoln, do the things he'd done, be his kind of foreign correspondent. Be a crusading journalist like he was. His memoirs had had a great influence on him. "City by city he had gone—and latched into the graft and corruption." *Profiles of American Cities*, he recalled, was the title.

One evening, after they had finish working, Tori said, they'd drop around to his place. "He's living in some kind of family hotel thing down in the Village near Washington Square. Or maybe it's above there."

Stanley Lincoln was still handsome, dressed in a dressing gown, holding a long cigarette holder, talking in bursts. He had been a muckraker. He had worked on the old *New York World*, the newspaper Joseph Pulitzer had turned into a leading national voice for the working man, publishing the work of great investigative reporters like Nellie Bly and Heywood Broun. He had covered World War I and the rise of fascism in Italy and Germany. "Young man," Lincoln said, "always stay a cub reporter. When you have ceased being a cub reporter, you will have lost your usefulness." They talk until Tori has to leave. Barrett stays; they talk into the night.

As the story develops, Barrett continues as Stanley Lincoln's friend, even as the older man is dying. Tori sees that he is

A WRITER ATTENDS TO HIS SOUL

introduced to the head of an advertising agency whose biggest account is a cigarette maker about to market a new unfiltered cigarette. He wants Barrett to help. Barrett agrees. Stock options, life insurance, a pension plan, and $25,000 a year. He "begins to get into the idea of money." He and Tori become lovers. Stanley Lincoln asks him to bring him narcotic pills. He knows they might hasten his death. He does.

In *Jocasta*, Victoria Fortune brings Barrett Connor not victory, but defeat, as had Dody. She does it by enticing him into a world where men work only for money. Then the ultimate cruelty: this woman who had stolen his moral pride rejects him as a lover, saying, "I cannot continue to be your mother and your lover both."

She directs him to look in Charles Francis Beekman's files. There he reads a correspondence in which Beekman asks Victoria's jurist father to look out for his grandson, the child of Stanley Lincoln and Victoria Fortune. Barrett Connor now knows he was that child.

In horror, Barrett realizes that hastening the death of Stanley Lincoln by bringing him narcotics had been a parricide, and his love of Victoria Fortune the incest Sophocles wrote about in *Oedipus Rex*. The oracle at Delphi had told Oedipus he was cursed. The curse had been fulfilled when he had lain with his own mother and taken on his hands the blood of his own father.

Cros wrote the acknowledgments to his novel. He thanked Dr. Brooks, his psychoanalyst, for having helped him see "the relationship of Greek tragedy to facts in my own life, and drummed into me once and for all that Sigmund Freud did not invent all the things that today we label 'Freudian.' They were there all the time." But Freud had not cured him; atonement had. On a manuscript page, in pencil, he wrote, "In my writing is my salvation."

Stanley Lincoln was a part of my father, but a part he saw as far more powerful than he himself had ever been. If he had sacrificed writing some of the great stories that were in him for the love of a woman, if he had prostituted his talents for money, at least he could make Stanley Lincoln into a character in a novel, where he would be incorruptible and immortal.

Eventually, Cros abandoned the novel, still in outline form, still wavering between the third and the first person. Perhaps it was because, locked into telling the story from Barrett Connor's point of view, he could not convincingly show Victoria Fortune's internal state of mind, moving from becoming his lover to rejecting him as her son. Perhaps it was because the act of writing it had done the job he needed it to do, forcing him to look inward, lodging his sin in the human condition as Freud saw it. "This sin in us," as the nuns had said, "is original."

By the late 1960s the Bowen family had been scattered for years. I graduated from college; then a few roommates and I took off across the country, driving a repainted New York City taxicab with a shaky transmission to a miner in Idaho who had sent for it by mail order. Then I went to Albuquerque, New Mexico, to train as a VISTA volunteer and spent the next year living in an adobe house, teaching grade school in a tiny Colorado town nestled between the San Juan and the Sangre de Cristo mountains. My escape was complete.

Or so I believed. I was back in New York for Christmas when Louise died. Dad had gotten a call from the nuns at the Mary Manning Walsh home. He went there to make arrangements for her funeral, and to say good-bye. We met at a relative's apartment afterward. He was pale.

"The end of an era," he said.

Dad wanted me to take the train with him back to Toledo to bury her, but he could only afford one sleeper berth, so we boarded one of the last Twentieth Century Limiteds out of Grand Central Station, sat in the club car, and then lay head-to-toe and toe-to-head on the top bunk of a two-bunk sleeping car compartment. After a sleepless night, the sun

A WRITER ATTENDS TO HIS SOUL

rose, and we arrived in the Toledo station, a hearse waiting at the ready for the coffin. We stood on the platform as the train pulled away, and then, down the tracks, Dad saw that the conductor hadn't put Louise's coffin off the train.

Dad was agitated and rushed inside to tell the station master to call ahead to the next stop and instruct the hearse to pick her up there.

We now had time to kill in Toledo, so we stopped by the Toledo Club, which seemed to transport Dad into some romantic past and which impressed me as cavernous and down-at-the-heels. Then we called at the home of the Stranahan girl, whom he had once thought of marrying, he told me, but nobody was at home. We went to the graveyard. I saw the large cross erected in the lushly planted family plot. Louise's coffin waited next to a fresh grave, to be lowered into the ground beside her beloved husband. Dad leaned down and scooped up a fistful of the just-dug moist earth, poured it into an envelope, and folded it into his pocket.

As we left the place where probably no more Bowens would ever be buried, I struggled to fight the tight cords my father was spinning to bind me to him, cords that more words would only tighten. Yet to break away now would be so cruel that I could not. There he was, just spinning out more cords as we moved through hours that now seem suspended in time. We drove back to the train station in the rented car and boarded the Twentieth Century Limited, and I spent another sleepless night just as I had on the journey out, head-to-toe on the top bunk of a two-bunk sleeping car.

A year later, when I was back in Colorado, Dad suffered a "series of heart attacks." I flew back to New York, sure that he had died; sure nobody survived such a thing. There he was, sitting up in a hospital bed, asking for pistachio ice cream. He told me where there was a nearby Greek coffee shop that sold it. I brought some back. We ate it together.

He got out of the hospital and went back to 6 East Seventy-sixth. I went back to Colorado. On September 28, 1968, the *New York Times* reported Uncle Bill's death. He had come home to New York to die of cancer. Cros buried him in a hillside graveyard near Hidden Hollow, next to the plot where he would be buried as well.

He asked Marjory to reunite "for the sake of the children." Neither of them had taken the steps to get a divorce. They saw each other from time to time, but she refused. "Marjory says we love each other but cannot live together." She told him they brought out the worst in each other. "Perhaps she has a point. But we are friends. We talk and communicate well at times," he wrote.

But would he die alone, like O'Neill?

And would there be no more great work? To Bob Brown, the subject of a *New Yorker* crime piece, who had written to him faithfully while serving out his sentence in an upstate New York prison, he wrote, "All the young writers seem so much smarter than me and write so much better." Brown would soon be released from jail. They had talked about his living at Hidden Hollow after he got out, but instead he would marry and have a daughter, and go on to work as an undercover agent fighting drugs and prostitution in New York City's Times Square. Cros was proud of Bob Brown's rehabilitation. It was validation of the cause he had championed in his younger days.

The New York City he had known was vanishing. Old buildings were being torn down and taller ones put in their place. He had covered the renaming of Sixth Avenue "Avenue of the Americas" for *PM*. His last piece of newspaper journalism was a brief comment in the *New York Times*, a tip of the hat to the economic prosperity that had dressed up the old Sixth Avenue lady so that now she matched the finery of her neighbors, Fifth and Seventh. As he wandered down the Avenue, his body weakened by heart attacks and the limp from

Tobruk growing more pronounced, the words for a tribute to the city he had loved ever since his earliest days as a reporter came to him. Back at his desk, in the jaunty "Talk" style he'd cut his teeth on at *PM* and honed for *The New Yorker*, he typed out his farewell.

He knew the times were passing him by, but he wrote one last piece of investigative journalism just as the Clean Air Act passed and the EPA was created. It was a piece for *The Atlantic Monthly* that took him to Donora, Pennsylvania, the site of the first temperature inversion, just as smog was enveloping East Coast cities.

As if to make peace with Yale, he went back, lived in the dorms, and listened to the young undergraduates, trying to understand what they were thinking and feeling about the world they were about to enter. Much had changed after forty years, but he found the ethic of "giving back" still in place. "Rip van Winkle Returns to Yale" appeared in the *Yale Alumni Magazine* shortly before he died.

He had, he would tell me wistfully, "lived in interesting times," taken part in their "action and passion," and "made a contribution."

He went back often to Hidden Hollow. "This place has never let me down," he said.

When the market declined in 1970 and he "might be out on the street," Cros applied for Social Security, earned what he legally could over and above it, and lived on powdered milk, borscht, Roquefort on saltines, and a bit of bourbon in the evening. That summer, he phoned over to the apartment I by now shared on the Upper West Side in a marriage that was unhappy, finishing a dissertation I had absolutely no interest in but had set for myself as a task because it protected me from becoming a tortured writer.

He asked me to go with him to Shakespeare in the Park.

I said no, I was too busy.

"Betsy does not seem to like me anymore," he wrote.

A few weeks later, he asked if I would drive with him out to Hidden Hollow. He wanted to say good-bye to the place, but his heart might give out while he was driving. He drove; I sat next to him; when we got there we rested in lawn chairs under the old beech tree in front of the house. Then he seemed seized by the idea that we should replace the aging carpet tiles upstairs in the bathroom with new ones. We began. I sat on the floor and he on the bathtub, he telling me what to do. I pulled up the old tiles and stacked them and started laying in the new ones with an adhesive spray. He began having chest pains; he said the spray was giving him trouble breathing. I followed him down the stairs and outside. He took a nitroglycerine tablet. We stood under the big beech tree. He put his arms around me.

"Let's stay here for a while," he said. "Can you hear my heart beat?"

Later that summer, we argued on the phone over who should pay to repair the broken muffler of his old station wagon. He tore off part of a sheet of typing paper, scrawled a note in pencil, and mailed it. "Life is too short for these petty disagreements. Love, Daddy," he wrote.

·I opened it the day after he died.

In Cros's novel, Barrett Connor takes his own life out of despair. He believes his incestuous love for Victoria Fortune means that true love between a man and a woman cannot exist.

But in life, Cros did not take that path. "Death sits in a little bottle on my bed table," he wrote, referring to the Valium Dr. Brooks had prescribed. "It is comforting to hold it, know it is always there. The thought that I can, with its capsules, bring eternal release from my body, helps bring on blessed sleep. But does death snuff out one's mind to nothingness? Will the agonizing dreams I suffer in sleep go on and on? That question, licking at the back of my brain like a serpent's tongue, puts a brake on my taking the final step. For it is an irrevocable act from which there is no turning back."

He spoke often of Sisyphus, a figure from Greek mythology who unceasingly rolled a huge stone up a mountain knowing it would fall down and that he would go back down the hill to push it up again, forever. He might have seen his hopes for the causes he had worked for dashed, people he had loved who did not see him for what he was, but he had kept on writing, and he had kept on loving. Albert Camus had written that Sisyphus at the foot of the mountain was a happy man. "The struggle itself toward the heights is enough to fill a man's heart." So death was a presence, a "dark angel." "When death comes to me in dreams it is always a woman, a gentle, pale, thin-faced woman dressed all in black, almost like a nun," Cros wrote. "She sits beside my bed and her cool fingers stroke my forehead. Her words soothe me. Everything will be all right. She will enfold me in those black garments and carry me back into her darkness."

It was a humid July day in 1971 in New York City when my father died. I found him in his apartment where he had fallen, freshly shaven, a towel on the floor beside him, the water in the bathtub cold. The people from the city medical examiner's office arrived, measured the temperature of his body, and told me they would require an autopsy. I did not want my father's body to be cut. I called the cardiologist who had treated him for his first three heart attacks. He told them the cause of death was his heart and there was no need for an autopsy. I kissed his forehead. There was white foam at the corners of his mouth. They told me they couldn't fit him into the body bag and I was to look away while they broke his legs, so I did.

After they left, I called my two sisters and my mother, and then I locked his apartment and took the cross-town bus to mine.

I threw myself across a bed in a darkened room and wailed. Gasps rose up from deep in my chest. When one sob ended, another welled up. I turned over, sat up, doubled down over my knees, and sat back up again. Again and again. I keened.

Were these the cries of the banshees, the women of the gray cloak, keening through me? My father had always said they would keen for us.

A few days later, the *New York Times* obituary cited my father's *New Yorker* connection and noted his books. The photograph in the obituary was from his crime reporter days. He wore the Skull and Bones tie he'd found in an Upper East Side secondhand clothing store. "It must have belonged to an old Bones drunk," he would say—and the fedora from the thirties with the hatband he'd stick his press card behind, calling out "I'm Bowen of the INS!" as he broke through police lines. His gaze was direct, burning.

He had been a mama's boy and a ladies' man, a truth teller and a charlatan, and I had felt the sting of those faults in many ways, but that didn't seem to matter then. For days after I read the obituary, his favorite Eugene O'Neill lines sounded again and again in my head. "It was a great mistake, my being born a man," he would intone. "I would have been much more successful as a sea gull or a fish. As it is, I will always be a stranger who never feels at home, who does not really want and is not really wanted, who can never belong, who must always be a little in love with death."

Oh, how I hated those lines. He'd used them to pull me to him again and again, and now he was gone, but they would not stop their rattling. If there had been a funeral service with a eulogy, which there wasn't because I had not planned one, I would have used the words that came to me on the drive out to Sherman and at last drowned out those O'Neill lines, "He had a very forgiving God inside him because he failed mightily in many ways, but he never lost faith—in himself, in the people he loved, or in humanity. Never lost faith in the power of words to make things better."

It seemed pretty much true then, and it still does.

On a hot July day, friends drove out from the city and gathered in a cluster on the Connecticut hillside where my father was to be buried. Bob Brown was there, just out of jail. My mother was not; she told me she would visit his grave alone, after the funeral. I hadn't been able to reach my sister Lucey, traveling in Europe, but I got through to her husband in Washington DC, and he got the news to her when she next called. I had reached Molly, but she was at a summer camp he had wanted her to go to, and she decided to stay there.

At the service, the Catholic priest got his name wrong—"Boswell"—but the burial service, which he read from a book, went well. I sprinkled the Toledo earth we'd brought back on the train together over his casket. Then everybody walked down the hill and gathered for a cool drink on a friend's porch and told Cros Bowen stories.

There were lots of them.

Acknowledgments

My greatest debts are to the subject of this biography himself, Croswell Bowen, my father, for having scattered pieces of his life throughout his writing in such a way that this biographer's hungry eye might someday find them, and to my mother, Marjory Luce Hill, for holding our family together through times when a woman of less determination might have given up. Also to my grandmother Louise Connor Bowen, for creating the scrapbooks and keeping the diaries that tell much of the family story, and to my sister Lucey, who painstakingly preserved family documents and shared some of the fruits of her own research. My sister Molly's steadfastness and diplomacy helped bring those papers to me. Still, this is my version of our father's story. Each of us has her own.

Other sources I have found in libraries. I am very grateful to the Beinecke Rare Book & Manuscript Library at Yale; to Judy Donald at the Choate Rosemary Hall Archives in the Andrew Mellon Library, for holding and facilitating access to my father's papers; to the Nieman Foundation for Journalism at Harvard; and to the general collections of Harvard and Yale for research I was able to do there. Also, thanks for use of the libraries of Boston University, the College of William and Mary, the University of Virginia at Charlottesville, and the Archives of the American Field Service. Thanks also to the Library of Congress; the National Archives and Records Administration; the New York State Historical Association in Cooperstown, New York; the Columbia University Library; the New York Public Library; and the Maine State Library through the Cary Memorial Library in my home town of Wayne, Maine.

To people who helped with research, my thanks—Hadassah Brooks-Morgan, Judy Donald, Arthur Leipzig, Bill McCleery, Sam McCleery, and Paul Milkman.

For encouragement and support, thanks to Josh Bodwell, Suzanne Strempek Shea, and all my friends at the Maine Writers & Publishers Alliance, Haystack Mountain, the Boston Biographers Group, and Biographers International. To the people whose skilled hands helped turn a manuscript into a book: Terri Butler, Hillel Black, Robert Astle, Elizabeth Demers, Bridget Barry, Sabrina Ehmke Sergeant, Kathryn Owens, and Bowen Ames—thank you all so much. Fondest gratitude to Audrey Marra and the late Julian Holmes, a wily truth teller himself, for their warm responses to an early draft. To the late Carolyn MacKenzie, whose encouragement with this book was only one of the many kindnesses she has extended to our family over the years, again, my gratitude. Thanks to Arabella Killander for permission to quote from her father's letters. And thanks to Felicity Yost, sharer of delight in a bond our fathers formed on a trip taken together before we were born, for help along the way.

Thanks also to my miraculous family, all of you—sisters, cousins, in-laws, second cousins, kissing cousins, and so many more —for giving me love, advice, and photographs.

As always, my husband, Bob, was my first reader. Thank you for staying at my side while I wrote this book.

ACKNOWLEDGMENTS

A Note on Sources

That a biography could be written at all about the career of a newspaperman owes a great deal to the fact that quite a few newspapers are now digitized and searchable. However, to read through a full run of *PM*, I resorted to piecing together the resources of three libraries, those of the Nieman Foundation for Journalism at Harvard, Boston University in its Ralph Ingersoll collection, and the College of William and Mary.

I am extremely fortunate that my father's family were letter writers and that my grandmother saved the diaries, scrapbooks, photographs, telegrams, newspaper clippings, and correspondences filled with the treasured details that made it possible to tell a family story. In his published work, correspondences, and other unpublished work, my father incorporated disparate chunks of his own life story that I have adapted. Certain scenes at which I was not present, I wrote as I believe they would most likely have happened, using impressions and intuitions based in what I had read or experienced firsthand.

1. Skull and Bones, Paris, Crash of 1929

Lyman Hotchkiss Bagg's *Four Years at Yale* (New Haven: C. C. Chatfield, 1871) describes much that would become traditional in Yale student life.

Archivist Judy Donald at the Choate Rosemary Hall Archives in the Andrew Mellon Library shared with me her research into Headmaster George St. John's "ask not" quotation that Choate alumnus John Fitzgerald Kennedy would adapt in his 1961 inaugural address.

I was able to obtain the alumni records of Cros's time at Yale by courtesy of the Yale University Library.

Direct and indirect quotation from Charles W. Yost's account of the trip to Russia, from an unpublished autobiography, is by permission of Felicity O. Yost. Cros and Yost would renew their friendship over lunch some thirty-five years later, in 1964, at the United Nations in New York, where Yost was then serving as U.S. Deputy Representative to the United Nations with Adlai Stevenson. In 1969 Yost would be appointed U.S. Ambassador to the UN.

2. Several Reversals of Fortune

An account of the Sinclair Lewis episode and Cros's hazing by the Washington INS appeared in H. Allen Smith's *Low Man on a Totem Pole* (Philadelphia: Blakiston Company, 1945).

David Halberstam's *The Powers That Be* (New York: Knopf, 1975) describes the modus operandi of the Washington press corps during the time Cros was there, and recalls his confrontational style.

William G. Shepherd, in an article entitled "Our Ears in Washington" (*Everybody's Magazine*, October 1920: 68–73), provided further context on the Washington press corps at the time.

Timothy Messer-Cruse's *Banksters, Bosses, and Smart Money: A Social History of the Great Toledo Bank Crash of 1931* (Columbus: Ohio State University Press, 2004) brought to life the Toledo banking crisis that swallowed up the Bowen fortune.

For Mukden, I relied on Robert H Ferrell's "The Mukden Incident: September 18–19, 1931," published in *The Journal of Modern History* (University of Chicago Press) 27, no. 1 (March 1955): 66–72.

3. Greenwich Village Years

Carl Carmer's *Stars Fell on Alabama* (New York: Doubleday, 1934) demonstrates the style of documentary regionalism that influenced my father's reports to Carmer on his travels in the Hudson River Valley.

Three books by Malcolm Cowley, Cros's respected literary and political colleague and Sherman neighbor, were indispensible in understanding the cultural currents and crosscurrents of the 1920s and 1930s. They are *Exile's Return: A Literary Odyssey of the 1920s* (revised and expanded, New York: Viking Press, 1951), *The Dream of the Golden Mountains: Remembering the 1930s* (reprinted, New York: Viking Press, 1980), and *I Worked at the Writer's Trade: Chapters of Literary History, 1918–1978* (New York: Viking Press, 1978.)

Art in Theory 1900–1990: An Anthology of Changing Ideas by Charles Harrison and Paul J. Wood (Oxford: Blackwell, 2002) contains the John Reed Club of New York's "Draft Manifesto" on pages 401–4 and was very useful in understanding what Cros would have experienced at a John Reed Club meeting. I also relied on Virginia Hagelston Marquardt's "'New Masses' and John Reed Club Artists, 1926–1936: Evolution of Ideology, Subject Matter, and Style," in *The Journal of Decorative and Propaganda Arts* 12 (Spring 1989): 56–75.

Charles Norman's *Poets and People* (New York: Bobbs-Merrill, 1972), a memoir, contains reflections on Norman's life among many in the Carmer circle.

Ross Wetzsteon's *Republic of Dreams: The American Bohe-

mia, 1910–1960 (New York: Simon and Schuster, 2003) is a phenomenal compendium of Greenwich Village life.

4. Bowen's New Deal

The staff of the New York Public Library provided access to the Berenice Abbott papers, especially "Lecture Notes," which made clear what Cros would have learned from her at the New School.

"A Narrative for Nature's Nation: Constance Lindsay Skinner and the Making of *Rivers of America*" by Nicholaas Mink (*Environmental History*, October 2006, 751–74) helped me understand the concept of documentary realism that inspired Carmer and his researcher, Cros Bowen.

5. Bowen's Short War

This chapter is based on the manuscript of Cros's account of his war experience, since published as *Back From Tobruk* (Washington DC: Potomac, 2013).

George Rock's *The History of the American Field Service 1920–1955* (New York: Platen Press, 1956) is an official account of the activities of Middle East I, Bowen's unit, from June 1940 to December 1942.

6. Long War on the Home Front

Richard Goldstein's *Helluva Town: The Story of New York City During World War II* (New York: Simon and Schuster, 2010) provided useful detail on the war years in New York City.

The Manuscript Division of the Library of Congress provided copies of my father's correspondence with Supreme Court Justice Felix Frankfurter held in the Frankfurter Papers.

The Nieman Foundation for Journalism at Harvard holds the PM papers and graciously provided access to them.

Boston University holds the Ralph Ingersoll papers and several bound volumes of PM as well, all of which were very useful.

Margaret A. Blanchard's study "The Associated Press Antitrust Suit: A Philosophical Clash over Ownership of First Amendment Rights" in *The Business History Review* 61, no. 1 (Spring 1987), 43–85, helped me understand the legal issues at stake in the AP suit.

The Inside Story by Members of the Overseas Press Club of America (New York: Prentice-Hall, 1940) is a delicious anthology of stories international correspondents traded over the tables at the OPC.

7. Ahab in Seersucker

Patricial Bosworth's *Anything Your Little Heart Desires: An American Family Story* (New York: Simon and Schuster, 1998) provided an account of the closing days of PM, useful in constructing mine.

Steven Weisenburger's "The Columbians, Inc.: A Chapter of Racial Hatred from the Post-World War II South," *The Journal of Southern History* LXIX, no. 4 (November 2003) 831–60, tells the full story of the activities of Homer Loomis and their aftermath.

Paul Milkman's *PM: A New Deal in Journalism* (New Brunswick NJ: Rutgers University Press, 1997) is the only full account of the groundbreaking though ill-starred PM experiment, and the author's guidance helped me get straight conversations about the paper overheard when I was too young to understand what was said.

8. The Fifties and Its Discontents

William Keating's *The Man Who Rocked the Boat* (New York: Harper, 1956) contains the account of his encounter with Bowen as a reporter researching the Bob Brown story.

For supplying FBI records concerning my father (case file 94–49336), which I accessed under the Freedom of Information Act, I appreciate the cooperation of the staff of the

National Archives and Records Administration in College Park, Maryland.

The staff of the New York Public Library provided access to the *New Yorker* archives, which contained records of my father's time there.

9. A Darkness That Would Not Lift

Thomas E. Porter's "Jansenism and O'Neill's 'Black Mystery of the Soul'" in *The Eugene O'Neill Review* 26 (2004) explores the Jansenist strain in O'Neill's Irish Catholicism and was invaluable.